*To Dewar Brimhall
From Jarry # & Cheryl 1995 approx*

A TOUGH JOB IN A HARD LAND

COWBOYING

JAMES H. BECKSTEAD

WITH A FOREWORD BY
WILFORD BRIMLEY

*James H Beckstead
Enjoy!
11/29/91*

University of Utah Press
Salt Lake City, Utah
1991

University of Utah Publications in the American West, volume 27

6 5 4 3 2   *1991 1992 1993 1994 1995*

Jacket and interior design by Scott Engen/Booksmith, Salt Lake City, Utah.

Frontispiece: A Cowboy at Ogden, Utah, circa 1880. Photograph courtesy of the author's collection.

Photographs on page 179 of Charles Siringo and on page 189 of Siringo and O. W. Sayles from *A Cowboy Detective: A True Story of Twenty-two Years with a World-Famous Detective Agency*, by Charles A. Siringo. Reprinted 1988 by University of Nebraska Press with an Introduction by Frank Morn. Originally published in 1912 by the W. B. Conkey Co.

∞ The paper in this book meets the standards for permanence and durability established by the Committee on Production Guidelines for Book Longevity of the Council on Library Resources

Library of Congress Cataloging-in-Publication Data

Beckstead, James H.
    Cowboying : a tough job in a hard land / by James H. Beckstead ; foreword by A. Wilford Brimley.
       p.   cm. — (University of Utah publications in the American West ; v. 27)
    Includes bibliographical references and index.
    ISBN 0–87480–357–8 (alk. paper). — ISBN 0–87480–378–0 (pbk. : alk. paper)
    1. Cowboys—Utah—History.   2. Frontier and pioneer life—Utah.
3. Cattle drives—Utah—History.   4. Cattle trade—Utah—History.
5. Utah—Social life and customs.   I. Title.   II. Series.
F826.B428 1991
979.2—dc20   91–13181
                                           CIP

A TOUGH JOB IN A HARD LAND

COWBOYING

Contents

Foreword

I have been asked to write a foreword to this book. I have read it and I found it to be an accurate and very interesting history of the land and life-style that some of us are trying to hold on to with our fingernails.

The life of the cowboy on the western plains is all but gone. The freedom to ride a good horse through miles of open country is gone. Special interest groups have influenced our government to pass laws making it against the law to enjoy the freedom that this great land once afforded those of us that know firsthand what it's like to live on the land in harmony with the beasts and birds.

Though well meaning, most of these people are ignorant as to who the real protectors of the land really are. They drive through our land on the Interstate Highway and all of a sudden they know more about how we should live our lives and run our ranches than we do.

Well, my grandfather walked into this country in 1867 dragging a handcart, and by Hell I think I have the right to be here and should have the right to use and care for this land that means so much to me. I believe that I am a real environmentalist and I will fight to see that my grandchildren have as much of the same chance as I had if they choose to take it.

As you can tell by reading this I am no writer so I will borrow the words of a good one to tell how I feel about this book and the life-style of which I speak. Stephen Vincent Benét wrote,

> But I could not live when they fenced the land,
> For it broke my heart to see it.
>
> I saddled a red, unbroken colt
> And rode him into the day there;
> And he threw me down like a thunderbolt
> And rolled on me as I lay there.
>
> The hunter's whistle hummed in my ear
> As the city-men tried to move me,
> And I died in my boots like a pioneer
> With the whole wide sky above me.
>
> . . . .
>
> And my youth returns, like the rains of Spring,
> And my sons, like the wild-geese flying;
> And I lie and hear the meadow-lark sing
> And have much content in my dying.
>
> Go play with the towns you have built of blocks,
> The towns where you would have bound me!
> I sleep in my earth like a tired fox,
> And my buffalo have found me.

(The Ballad of William Sycamore)

Like the men in this book I am a cattle rancher. I am proud of my heritage and I apologize to no man or special interest group, be it the Sierra Club, Earth First or what have you for the way I have chosen to live my life. If what I do with my land and my animals doesn't suit you, come and see me and we'll talk about it. But not much. You see, I do the best I can to mind my own damn business.

A. Wilford Brimley

Wilford Brimley, noted motion picture and television actor, also owns and operates the B7 ranch in Lehi, Utah. Photograph courtesy of Tom Anastasion.

Cattle Trails of the West

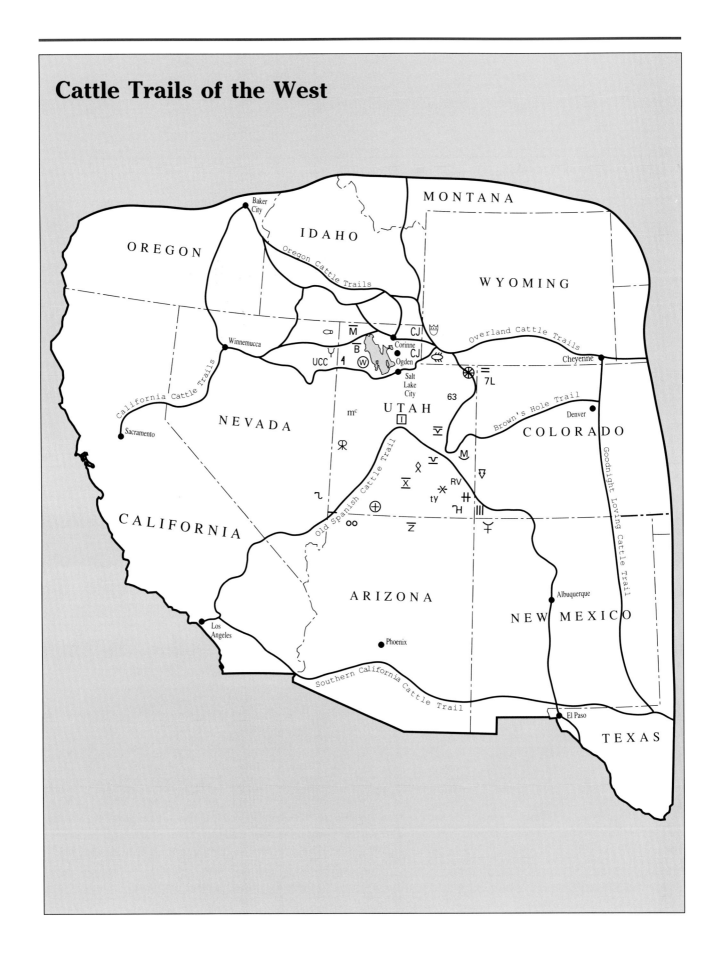

A Tough Job in a Hard Land

COWBOYING

1

The Legacy Begins

Years ago this region was noted for several things: chief among them was bunch grass, fat cattle and rattlesnakes . . . The grass was plentiful and the winters short . . . The country was covered with cattle: cattle everywhere."[1] This is how T. A. Davis remembered the land around Promontory in northern Utah from his cowboy days in the 1880s. This scene was not unique to Promontory. It was duplicated across the far-flung parts of what would become the State of Utah, from the Rincon region of San Juan County to Brown's Park in northeastern Utah and from Bear River Valley in Rich County to the Virgin River Valley in Utah's Dixie. The country was open range in those days, the grass was free, and it was the heyday of the American cowboy.

The story of the cowboy and the great cattle venture of the American West has captured the imagination of people for generations and has been documented in books, paintings, and plays. The cowboy has been depicted as both chivalrous and despicable, depending on who was telling the story. In reality, the average cowboy was neither chivalrous nor despicable. He was a common man doing a tough job in a hard land. However, as average as the individual cowboy may have been, he emerged as a genuine American hero. The color and drama as-

sociated with the cowboy has become a cherished part of Utah's legacy.

The cowboy history of Utah is entwined with small-time ranchers and powerful cattle barons who sought to control the grasslands. There were range wars between cowboys and sheepmen, and Indian raiders managed to keep parts of the Utah cattle range embroiled in warfare well into the twentieth century. Some of the most notorious outlaws in the West plied their trade on Utah cattle ranges, and some of the most famous lawmen on the western frontier made a gallant effort to stop them. The cowboys, the Indians, the outlaws, and the lawmen—good and bad—were part of the Utah scene.

The first longhorn cattle and horses were trailed into Utah by Spanish trading parties in the late 1700s, and it is generally believed that the first permanent cattle ranching operations in the area were established in the mid-1840s. As the trapper era of the region drew to a close when the demand for pelts and skins had diminished, several enterprising mountain men built trading posts to accommodate overland travelers journeying to the West Coast prior to the Mormon emigration. Along with other commodities, the emigrants were in need of good pulling oxen to replace their tired and footsore cattle. The entrepreneurs sold well-fed and strong cattle to the emigrants at a healthy profit or traded cattle at a ratio of two or three to one. In this manner sizable herds of cattle were established in a relatively short time.

Photograph from the 1890s of John Strang of Salina, Utah, roping a steer with a rope made of rawhide that appears to be at least sixty feet long. Photograph courtesy of Rell Francis.

3

Mormon frontiersmen who may have participated in a hunting expedition to rid the Salt Lake valley of predatory birds and animals that were taking a toll on the livestock industry. The photograph was probably taken in the late 1840s. Photograph courtesy of Beehive Collectors Gallery.

Jim Bridger was prominent in the cattle trade at this time. He used the grasslands along the streams flowing from the north slopes of the Uinta Mountains to feed his cattle. Jack Robinson also established a cattle ranch at the mouth of Henry's Fork River near present-day Manila, Utah. Captain Richard Grant wintered cattle in northern Utah and summered them in Montana, and Miles Goodyear established Fort Buenaventura on the banks of the Weber River near present-day Ogden, Utah, and traded cattle.

In July of 1847 Mormon pioneers entered the Great Salt Lake Valley and began to establish a permanent community. Captain James Brown, who had been a member of the Mormon Battalion during the Mexican War, was authorized by Mormon

Photograph taken in the 1880s in Scofield, Utah, of a man wearing buckskin clothing of the type that would have been worn by the mountain men who first established cattle ranches in the Utah area. Photograph courtesy of Rell Francis.

church leaders to negotiate with Miles Goodyear for the land he claimed along the Weber River. Brown bought the land and maintained Fort Buenaventura as a cattle operation.[2]

Within three years of the Mormons' arrival in Utah several settlements had developed between Ogden and the Salt Lake Valley. Small settlements had also been formed in Tooele Valley, Utah Valley, and Sanpete Valley. There were at least 12,000 cattle belonging to the Mormons in the area,[3] and more cattle came in with each arrival of Mormon wagon trains. Realizing that cattle would be of primary importance to the Mormon economy, Brigham Young encouraged Mormons coming to Utah to bring extra cattle with them—both pulling stock and breeding stock.[4] Cattle traveling across the plains to Utah were the shorthorn variety, primarily Devons and Durhams, but they were soon producing calves sired by the Mexican longhorn cattle which were first introduced to Utah during the Spanish era.[5]

The image of Utah as a barren wasteland has been

A cowboy working for the McPherson's Rocking M outfit on the East Tavaputs Plateau looks over some cows and calves. The photograph was taken in the early 1900s. Photograph courtesy of Don Wilcox.

highly exaggerated. Journals from early explorers and Mormon settlers extol the land, and it appears that highly nutritious grasses covered most of the land. Early Mormon leader Orson Hyde gives some insight into the appearance of the Salt Lake Valley when the Mormons arrived in 1847: "Between here and the mouth of Emigration Canyon, there was an abundance of grass over all those benches; they were covered with it like a meadow."[6] J. J. Watson, when interviewed about his cowboy days in the 1870s, indicated the following: "It is hard to describe it, the grass was everywhere as far as the eye could see."[7] World traveler Richard F. Burton visited Utah in 1860 and indicated that "the grass is rendered equal for pasturage to the far famed Salt Marshes of Essex and of the Atlantic Coast."[8]

To many, especially those accustomed to the lush green of the East, the land did appear weary, especially during late summer when the grasses in the valleys began turning yellow. Mormon cattlemen recognized early that the dried, cured grasses on the range were nutritious. During the winters the cattle would paw through the light snows of the valley floors to reach the grass below. As spring approached, cattle would follow the snow line up the side of the mountains and by mid-summer be grazing on the lush mountain meadows. The land may have had some drawbacks for farmers, but it had great potential for livestock grazing.

In an effort to bring more cattle into Utah, Brigham Young authorized a group of Mormon men to travel to California and purchase cattle. The men, led by Jefferson Hunt, a former captain in the Mormon Battalion, and the scout, Porter Rockwell, made it to the Santa Ana del Chino Rancho near San Bernardino, California, after a troubled journey when they nearly starved and were forced to eat some of their horses. After resting for several weeks, the men, with the exception of Porter Rockwell, began the return trip to Utah. The group started out with 200 cows, 40 bulls, and a number of mules and horses, but again encountered trouble crossing the

Cowboys of Jim McPherson's Rocking M outfit posing in the tall grass of the East Tavaputs Plateau north of Green River, Utah. The photograph was taken in the early 1900s. Photograph courtesy of Don Wilcox.

Mojave Desert. Many of the cattle and horses died,[9] and although the trip was only partially successful, it did serve as a learning experience for future Utah cowboys who would soon be driving cattle to the California gold fields.

When gold was discovered in California a year after the Mormons arrived, thousands of California gold seekers soon began passing through the settlements on their way to the bonanza. Mormon cattlemen, taking a tip from the old trappers who first established trading posts on the Oregon Trail, began trading strong, well-fed cattle for the trail-weary stock of the emigrants. Sometimes the trades were made at a two- or three-to-one ratio, which greatly increased the number of cattle in Utah.

With the influx of people to California, and especially the hard-working miners with an enormous appetite for beef, the supply of California cattle began to be depleted. For a time California cattlemen were unable to keep up with the demand; the Mormons, on the other hand, not only had cattle to meet their own needs, but enough to contribute to the needs of California.

By 1852 Mormon cattlemen were driving cattle to California on a regular basis. Pioneering the California trade was Howard Egan, one of the original pioneer settlers in the Salt Lake Valley. Egan contracted with the firm of Livingston and Kinkead (non-Mormon businessmen who had established a retail merchandise outlet and cattle-buying venture in the Salt Lake Valley) to drive cattle to the California market. One trail drive consisted of 1,500 head of cattle and 100 head of horses and mules.[10]

Another Mormon cattleman active in the California trade was Granville Huffaker. Huffaker eventually moved his base of operations to Ruby Valley in Nevada and became that state's first permanent cattleman.

The cattle moving out of Utah to California followed three primary trails. The northern trail hooked up with the Oregon Trail in Idaho, left that trail after some distance, and again traversed Utah

Billy Murray and Charles Stewart at the Pleasant Valley Ranch near Ibapah, Utah. Howard Egan pioneered a cattle trail to California that traversed this region in the early 1850s. The photograph was taken in the 1890s. Photograph courtesy of Ron Bateman.

near the Goose Creek Mountains, entered Nevada, and went westward to California. Egan established a trail west of Salt Lake City to the Deep Creek Mountains on the Nevada border and from there the trail went westward across Nevada to Sacramento, California. The other primary trail followed the Old Spanish Trail through southern Utah, across Nevada, and eventually into Los Angeles, California. The Old Spanish Trail, first established by Mexican traders in the 1830s, was the major cattle and horse trail leading from the New Mexico settlements to the ranchos of Southern California.

The Mormon church was also very active in the California cattle trade. Brigham Young encouraged Mormons to pay their tithes to the church with cattle. Tithing, an ancient biblical practice, was required by faithful Mormons to be in full compliance with church principles. A full tithe constituted 10 percent of the yearly increase, be it cattle, grain, or money earned. The cattle received by the church were placed on the church's grazing grounds on Antelope Island in the Great Salt Lake. Once the church had enough cattle for a drive, Mormon leaders requested volunteers to drive the herd to California. One drive in 1853 saw 2,300 head of tithing cattle driven to California.[11] The cattle were sold for gold, a needed commodity in the cash-poor Salt Lake Valley.

The boom in the California cattle market was a godsend to the people of Utah Territory, sorely in need of cash during the early years of settlement. Cattle were worth little in Utah, but were bringing $60 to $150 a head in California.[12] The gold returning to Utah from the sale of cattle brought new life to the struggling Mormon settlements.

The only visible export from Utah during much of

Photograph of a cowboy taken at the Daniels and Conkling studio, Provo City, Utah, in the 1880s. He is wearing clothing that has a distinct Spanish influence. Photograph courtesy of LDS Church Archives.

the 1850s was cattle, together with a few sheep. Brigham Young had said, "It is obvious to the most casual observer, that the natural wealth of this country consists in stock raising and grazing. This branch of business is occupying a large share of the attention of our citizens, and considerable investments have already been made. So long as the California markets remain dependent upon foreign supplies, we may naturally expect large accessions will be made to our flocks and herds."[13]

Although most of the cattle exported from Utah during the 1850s went to California, there were some exports to eastern cattle brokers. The early cattle trade with the East was created by the Mormon church's plan to bring converts to the church into Utah. In 1849 Brigham Young organized the Perpetual Emigrating Company (PEC) to provide wagons, cattle, and horses to members of the church too poor to make the journey across the plains. Companies of wagons were organized and made the journey east to pick up the converts. A cattle drover was assigned to each four wagons making the journey. The drover moved the cattle needed for the journey, plus extra cattle which were sold to cattle brokers at various eastern locations. The profit from the sale of these animals was placed into the PEC fund.[14]

The clothing worn by the Utah drovers was derived from the attire of Spanish vaqueros who worked on the ranchos of California. Leather pants called chaps protected legs from brush and thorns and the horns of the cattle. A wide-brimmed, low-crowned hat protected them from the scorching sun and kept the rain off their heads. A colorful kerchief worn around the neck could be placed over the mouth and nose as protection from dust raised by the cattle. Huge spurs with spiked rowels were worn over the high-topped leather boots. The jingle of the rowel helped prompt the horse on without a real application of the rowel. Many spurs were silver mounted, with two metal ball-like pendants hanging on each side of a star-shaped rowel. The balls, or jingle bobs, served to increase the jingling of the spur. A man who was not a good rider or who was riding a green horse could lock the jingle bobs together preventing the rowel from jingling and spooking the horse.[15] The rawhide reata, or lariat, first introduced by the vaqueros, remained basically the same for many years. In time, hemp lariats became more popular. The length of the lariat varied from 60 to more than 100 feet.[16] The saddle used by the drovers had a rawhide tree covered by a machila, two pieces of thick leather handsomely and fancifully worked or stamped, joined by a running thong in the center, and open to admit the pommel and cantle. The pommel was high, which allowed the lariat to be attached to it. The pommel could be dangerous if a rider was thrown against it. Richard Burton said that the pommel "is absolutely dangerous: during my short stay in the country I heard of two accidents, one fatal, caused by the rider being thrown forward on his fork."[17]

While working on the range with the cattle, and especially during the overland drives to California,

John Strang and a friend team-rope a steer at Salina, Utah, in the 1890s. A similar type of team-roping was used to throw down the horses on Antelope Island. Photograph courtesy of Rell Francis.

the drovers were subject to many hazards including wildfires, blizzards, choking dust, and long, hard days in the saddle. The one hazard most feared by the drovers was a stampede. When the cattle were bunched together at night, the crackle of a branch, a sneeze, or the sound of a nesting sage hen could spook them into stampeding. Thunder and lightning also spooked the cattle and caused the herd to stampede. During lightning storms, small levin-lights would often appear on the tips of the horns of the cattle, causing quite a fright for the animals and quite a spectacle for the drovers.[18]

Another source of danger for the drovers trailing cattle to California was the presence of hostile Indians and white desperadoes along the trail. When learning that the Richard F. Burton party was

Photograph of a cowboy taken at the Anderson studio in Springville, Utah, circa 1890. The leather stovepipe chaps and the spurs with large rowels were typical working clothes for cowboys. The clothing may have been provided by the studio since the coat does not quite fit in. Photograph courtesy of Rell Francis.

preparing to follow the Egan Trail to California, Porter Rockwell offered the following advice: "Carry a double barrelled gun loaded with buckshot . . . ever be ready for attack."[19]

The romance associated with the cowboy was in evidence very early on the Utah frontier. Brigham Young had personally supervised the development of the horse herd on Antelope Island, and on many occasions he delighted in taking visitors for a first-hand look at the horses and a display of horsemanship by the Mormon cowboys. Church leader Heber Kimball described one such gathering.

At 10 o'clock in the morning of the roundup, dust was seen toward the north end of the island. It had the appearance of a whirlwind moving southward at the rate of 25 miles an hour. Nothing could be seen but dust, until it had reached to within two miles of the house. Everybody was on tiptoe and the excitement was running high. Here they came—the speediest animals on the island, all of them white with foam, panting like chargers. There were about seventy-five of them in all; some of them as fine animals as could be found any-

Lunch break for a roundup crew in Cache Valley, Utah, in the 1880s. The first cattle herds taken to this high mountain valley were decimated by an early and very cold winter storm. Photograph courtesy of LDS Church Archives.

where. Those present from the old country who had never witnessed such a scene, stood almost paralyzed with excitement. Before they had recovered from the shock, another exhibition of horsemanship presented itself, which almost left the first in the shade.

Lot Smith and Judson Stoddard, with their partners, mounted four large and beautiful horses and entered the corral where the herd stood snorting like elk. Lot led the chase with his partner close behind him, followed by Judson Stoddard and his partner. While these wild animals were on the run around the large corral, Lot threw his lariat over the front foot of one of them, and at the same moment, his partner lassoed the same animal around the neck; and with their lariats around the horns of their saddles, and in less than a minute's time, had thrown the horse and dragged it over the smooth surface of the corral, a distance of several rods, to a place where the fire and branding irons were, and, in another half-minute, the horse was branded and turned loose. They had no more than gotten out of the way before Judson Stoddard and his partner had another horse ready for the finishing

Cowboy at Parley's Park east of Salt Lake City, Utah, in the 1870s. Cowboys in Utah in early days were "herders" who actually contracted out to stay with the cattle, move them to grazing grounds, and protect them from wild animals and rustlers. Photograph from author's collection.

touch. So it continued until the band had been disposed of and turned loose on the range to make room for the next one, which was expected at any moment.[20]

Although the dress and cowboying style of the western cattle culture was prominent in Utah from the very beginning, the manner of land distribution during the initial colonization of Utah was unique among western territories. Brigham Young advised settlers not to scatter out upon the land in the traditional ranching mode of other cattle states and later in areas of Utah. The major reason for this was to foster social interactions and religious bonds, which were better encouraged when people were living in close proximity. A second major reason was the protection proximity afforded from wild animals, unscrupulous whites, and hostile Indians. Consequently, most Mormon settlers, including cattlemen, lived in the town district of the community.

The Mormon settlements were laid out in rectangular blocks with adjoining land to the settlement divided into five-, ten-, twenty-, and forty-acre plots for farming. Land was distributed to the settlers based on their needs and their ability to work the land. Although the federal government did not ac-

Stacking alfalfa hay at the Blue Creek Ranch at Howell, Utah, circa 1880. The winter of 1855 was so devastating to the livestock of northern Utah that it resulted in the development of supplemental feeding of livestock. Photograph courtesy of LDS Church Archives.

cept land ownership claims in the territory until land policies were enacted in 1869, most of the Mormon homesteaders were allowed to claim the land they had homesteaded after that time.

Early territorial laws required that farmers fence their land and the burden of responsibility to keep livestock away from the cultivated fields fell directly upon the farmers rather than the cattlemen. These laws came about because of the need for cattle to range for grazing and because the cattle business itself was the major economic endeavor in the territory. All land not so fenced was expressly declared common range. However, the common range in the Mormon land system did not automatically imply open range in the traditional sense. Cattle and horses were not allowed to spread out over the open range. That would have been an open invitation for rustling by the Indians and white desperadoes. Rather, the early Mormons pulled their herds

A young boy in Moab, Utah, in the 1880s. Most young Mormon boys were very good riders and in many instances took care of the town's livestock herds. Photograph courtesy of Blaine Yorgason.

together and put them on what was known as the "big range." The big range was an area near each settlement set aside for grazing animals. Brigham Young suggested that the big range should be a fenced tract of land fifty thousand acres in size.[21] Because fencing materials were scarce, very little fencing was done. Instead, professional herders were employed to watch over horses and cattle. The herders moved the animals to new bedding grounds every three or four days and protected them against attacks by wild animals and rustlers. The herders were required to be bonded and were held responsible for any animals lost due to neglect.[22]

It was not uncommon for professional herders to advertise for cattle. Philander Bell advertised the following in the *Deseret News*, "HERDING—The Subscriber wishes to give notice to the citizens generally, that he is prepared to keep a herd of cattle, on the west side of Utah Lake, and on the finest range in the country. He will be responsible for all cattle placed in his charge, should they be lost or stolen. Terms, 2 cents per head per day."[23]

Because the animals were grazed in more confined areas, overgrazing became a problem near the

settlements. Many of the lush grasslands first encountered by the Mormons soon gave way to sage, rabbit brush, and desert weeds. This problem was aggravated by the town's livestock, which were grazed in a common area. Each morning the herd boys would blow a horn signaling the farmers to release their animals from the corrals. They were then gathered by the herd boys and driven to the river bottoms or onto the mountain foothills. After the day's grazing the herd boys would gather the animals and return them to the individual owners.

Again because fencing materials were not readily available, livestock often strayed onto unfenced fields, ruining the crops and causing many problems between farmers and cattlemen. Mormon leader George A. Smith declared that "I do know that there has been more quarrelling, fault-finding, and complaining in consequence of bad fences, in consequence of men neglecting to fence their fields and secure their crops, than from almost any other source of annoyance."[24] In another society these feuds might have ended in bloodshed; however, because of the religious bonds and the ability of Mormon leaders to intercede, problems between farmers and cattlemen were usually worked out peaceably.

There were problems of a more serious nature on the Mormon frontier. In an effort to colonize the Utah wilderness Brigham Young organized groups of pioneers to move to the outlying valleys removed from Salt Lake City. As these small settlements developed there was a need to expand cattle grazing areas. The herds continued to grow, and it became necessary to move them farther from the settlements. The summer of 1855 had been very dry and overgrazed lands around the Salt Lake settlements were in sorry condition. Hordes of grasshoppers invaded the central Utah valleys during the summer and fall, further deteriorating the range. To secure better grazing for the church herd, Brigham Young decided to move a portion of it to the as yet unsettled Cache Valley in northern Utah. Three thousand cattle, some of which were privately owned by

Young man in Springville, Utah, in the 1890s. He is probably typical of a town youth who worked with livestock. Photograph courtesy of Rell Francis.

George Cotterell participated with the Lot Smith Company of volunteers to guard the Overland Mail routes east of Salt Lake City during the early years of the Civil War. Photograph from author's collection.

Brigham Young, Heber Kimball, and other church leaders, were driven to a new location in the northern mountains, where they were allowed to range free.

Although the Mormons had experienced heavy winters since their arrival in Utah, usually the cattle had been able to obtain enough feed by pawing through the snow to the grasses beneath. The ranch hands in Cache Valley knew supplemental feed would be essential because of the higher elevation, and they began harvesting wild hay. They still were not prepared for the severe winter which was coming.

An early fall snowstorm caught the cattle in the high meadows. A freezing wind followed, dropping temperatures below zero and creating a sheet of

A Ute warrior and young woman on the eastern slope of the Wasatch Mountains. Photograph by John K. Hillers of the Powell Expedition, 1873 or 1874. Photograph courtesy of Smithsonian Office of Anthropology.

hard, crusted snow that made it impossible for the cattle to reach the grass below. More snow came, falling day after day. The herders tried to drive the cattle into the lower valleys, but many were too weak to make it. When the drovers reached the lower valleys with the remnants of the herd, they found the snowpack too deep there. The wild hay was gone in a matter of days and the herders decided to move the remaining cattle over Sardine Pass into lower Box Elder Valley. Of the original 3,000 cattle, only 400 made it across the divide to Box Elder Valley, which was also snowbound.

The winter of 1855 affected the entire cattle industry in northern Utah. It is estimated that at least 50 percent of the cattle in the northern half of the territory perished that year. For the first time cattlemen realized that supplementary feed must be used dur-

ing the winter months, and this influenced the development of the alfalfa industry in the territory.[25]

Despite the winter kill of 1855 there were enough cattle in the territory to justify several drives to California in 1856 and 1857.[26] However, the California market was beginning to wane by the late 1850s. The original market for cattle in California resulted from an influx of miners and diminishing cattle herds following termination of the Padre Missions. As well, Californians were developing herds large enough to meet their own market demands.

The loss of the California beef market was accelerated when word reached Utah that President Buchanan had ordered the removal of Brigham Young as territorial governor. Buchanan also was sending several thousand federal troops to Utah to quell a perceived rebellion by the Mormons. To counter the advancing army Brigham Young mobilized the Utah Militia, which was prepared to place more than 5,000 men on the field of battle. Young wanted to avoid bloodshed if at all possible, but was determined not to let the army invade Utah. A plan was

Photograph thought to be of Levi Kendall of Springville, Utah, who was a rancher and who participated with Mormon guerrilla forces against the federal army as it made its way to Utah in 1857. Photograph courtesy of Rell Francis.

A Shoshone warrior photographed at the Savage studio in Salt Lake City in the 1860s. Photograph courtesy of LDS Church Archives.

Chief Black Hawk led a large force of renegade Utes, Shoshones, and Navajos against the settlers of central Utah. Photograph courtesy of Utah State Historical Society.

developed to disrupt the flow of supplies for the federal army as it crossed the plains. To accomplish this, cavalry units were sent out to intercept the supply trains. Going without provisions and under instructions to board at Uncle Sam's expense, these cavalry units captured several government supply trains and set fire to the wagons. They also rustled thousands of government horses and cattle, which were driven to the Salt Lake Valley.

The army became bogged down on the Wyoming plains, and with winter approaching, military officers decided to wait for better weather before continuing the invasion of Utah. In the interim, an amicable agreement was worked out between the Mormons and the federal government. The troops would be allowed to enter Utah, but had to build their fort away from the Mormon settlements.

Under the command of General Albert Sidney Johnston, the federal troops established Camp Floyd forty miles southwest of Salt Lake City. Known later

as Fort Crittenden, the post became the largest military post west of the Mississippi River for a time. Approximately 4,000 troops were stationed there. Another 3,000 non-Mormon suppliers, employees, and camp followers located at a place called "Dobietown" or "Frogtown," now called Fairfield.

The occupation of Utah was a windfall. Mormons were able to supply the camp and town with agricultural goods including cattle.[27] There were also negative aspects of the occupation. The Mormons, who had theretofore lived in a society virtually vice-free, were inundated by persons of poor reputation. Gamblers, saloon keepers, "soiled doves," and criminals of every type congregated at Frogtown. In time this element drifted northward into the very heart of Salt Lake City. By 1859 gambling houses, saloons, and houses of ill repute were firmly entrenched and Salt Lake City took on the appearance of a wide-open frontier town.

The occupation also affected the common-range

Utah territorial militia at Camp Wasatch circa 1866. The militia took the offensive during the Black Hawk War. Photograph courtesy of Utah State Historical Society.

concept shared by Mormon cattlemen. Competion for the range soon erupted into violence. Typical of this violence was an episode between Sergeant Ralph Pike and a Mormon herder, Howard Spencer. Spencer was herding cattle several miles from Camp Floyd in Rush Valley when Sgt. Pike and a detachment of soldiers drove a herd of army horses onto the range and demanded that Spencer gather his herd and leave immediately. Spencer argued the point and Sgt. Pike hit him over the head with his revolver. The soldiers then drove the cattle off the range.

Several months later Spencer saw Sgt. Pike in Salt Lake City with several other soldiers. Spencer drew his pistol and delivered a fatal shot to Pike. Several of the soldiers chased Spencer, but were unable to apprehend him.[28]

A more serious situation existed between the settlers and Indians within the territory. As early as 1849 Mormon militiamen had fought with Indian cattle rustlers at Battle Creek in Utah Valley. Several other Indian/white conflicts led to the Walker War during 1853–54. During this year-long war several settlements were abandoned, casualties were incurred, and thousands of dollars' worth of livestock were stolen or killed. The war impeded the ability of the Mormons to develop new settlements and expand the livestock industry. Even after the war had ended there was a hesitancy to venture into the wilderness in search of new grazing areas. This hesitancy was well founded, since time and time again settlers moving out of established settlements were subject to hostilities.[29]

After federal troops were established in the territory at Camp Floyd and later Fort Douglas, a series of Indian campaigns against the Gosiutes of Western Utah, the Shoshones of Northern Utah and to some extent the Utes of central Utah made the northern half of the territory safer for expansion. Venturing out to establish cattle ranches at this time were Howard Egan at Ibapah, Porter Rockwell at Government Creek, and Henry J. Faust at Rush Valley.

Although Utah had exported cattle to California during much of the 1850s, by 1859 there were not enough beef cattle in Utah to supply the influx of people coming into the territory. In that year Howard Egan drove a large herd of cattle and some mules from California to Salt Lake City. The herd numbered over 1,000 head.[30] People flowing into the territory were Mormon converts and miners. Fort Douglas commander Colonel Patrick E. Connor had encouraged his soldiers to seek for precious

Boots and Spurs

Left: Cowboy boots circa 1880. The stitching provided support to the stovepipe leg. Courtesy of Bumbleberry Inn.

Right: Cowboy boots circa 1870. Initially, cowboy boots were patterned after military boots. From author's collection.

Left: Mule Ear Cowboy boots circa 1890. The mule ears were used to pull on the boots. Courtesy of Vernal Daughters of the Utah Pioneers.

Below left: Silver inlaid spurs made by C. D. Stone, San Francisco, circa 1860. Courtesy of Bob Fehr.

Below: Double sided overlay spurs by Crockett, circa 1930. Courtesy of Southwest Indian Traders, Park City, Utah.

Below: Spurs with jingle bobs circa 1880. Courtesy of Bob Fehr.

A miner at Sunnyside, Utah, in the 1890s. Photograph courtesy of Rell Francis.

metals during their off-hours and consequently several rich veins of gold and silver were discovered in the Oquirrh and Wasatch mountains. Wild mining towns—Bingham, Alta, and Park City—sprang up and miners from around the world came to these new glory holes bringing visions of instant wealth and appetites for liquor and beefsteak.

The Utah cattlemen should have been ready for this influx of beef eaters into the territory and in probability would have been had it not been for a series of Indian wars that flared up in the mid-1860s. Beginning in 1865 a Ute chief named Black Hawk took to the warpath. During this war seventy Mormons were killed and over a million dollars in property and livestock was lost. All of the Mormon settlements in Piute County and Sevier County were abandoned, as were several other communities in Kane, Washington, and Iron counties. Raids took place from Utah County south to the Arizona border. Although Black Hawk left the warpath in 1867, other Indians committed depredations until 1872, including a Navajo warrior known as the White Horse Chief.

Although isolated incidents of Indian warfare broke out from time to time in the territory, by 1872 most of the tribes had settled on reservations that had been set aside for them. Freed from the Indian wars, the Mormons were able to begin colonizing the far reaches of the territory. However, they had competition for the new lands. Thousands of non-Mormons were streaming into the territory. Utah was having its very own gold rush.

With the influx of people into the territory came a great demand for beef cattle. Like Californians during the Gold Rush of 1849 the Mormon cattlemen were not prepared to meet the demand. Years of federal interference and Indian warfare had taken its toll on the Utah cattle industry. Millions of acres of virgin grasslands went unused while the burgeoning cities of Utah cried for beef. The territory was not unlike the eastern half of the United States which had had a shortage of beef during the Civil War. The vast herds of Texas were called upon to fill the need.

2

The Texas Trail Drivers

A great bawling herd, a mile long straggling down the river through Bluff—yellow cattle, white, black, brindle—all of them starving and hollow from the long trail—all of them coyote-like in form, little better in size. And horns! Such a river of horns as you might see in a nightmare—horns reaching out and up, out and up again in fantastic corkscrews."[1]

This colorful description of Texas cattle coming onto the ranges of Utah was provided by Bluff City pioneer Albert Lyman, who in the year of 1886 was a witness to a typical trail-weary herd of longhorn cattle that had come up from Texas. This was only one of many Texas-originated herds that came to Utah during the cattle boom years between 1865 and 1890.

The Texas cowboys coming into Utah were trail-tough fellows, ready and willing to partake of the carnal pleasures that had crept into Utah during the Utah War years. A Mormon cowboy, William Jones Bowen, rode with some Texas cowboys for a time on the Nutter range (Nine Mile Canyon, north of Price, Utah) and offered the following: "Very fine fellows to work with, but they were all card and whiskey men. They all wore guns, they were the first things they put on in the morning."[2] Many of

them were just young men looking for adventure. Others were hardened gunslingers, especially the Texas cowboys who came to southern Utah during the 1890s. Chances were they were running from the law at the time.

Between 1866 and 1880 very few of the Texas trail drivers opted to remain in Utah. There was little need for them on the Mormon-controlled cattle ranges. This changed during the 1880s when many large non-Mormon cattle companies moved into Utah. The big outfits liked hiring Texans who were willing to protect range rights with a loaded gun. Texans who remained in Utah added a colorful legacy to the cattle range.

The Texas style of cowboying was not entirely new to the Utah country prior to the Civil War. Many early converts to the Mormon church were from Texas. Many of the converts owned cattle and drove them to Utah when they decided to settle in Zion. One such drive in 1857 was organized by a Mormon missionary from Utah named Homer Duncan. Duncan had gone to Texas in 1855 on a proselyting mission to convert people to the Mormon church. Upon his release from the mission in 1857, he organized a wagon train comprised of newly converted Mormons who wanted to come to Utah. Homer had purchased 500 head of cattle before leaving Texas. These cattle, together with an additional 800 head, accompanied the Duncan wagon train to Utah.[3]

Non-Mormon Texans also came through Utah during the 1850s, driving herds of longhorns to Califor-

A well-armed cowboy poses for his photograph at what is thought to be Thompson, Utah, in the 1880s. Most of the Texas cowboys coming to Utah wore guns and were card and whiskey men. Photograph courtesy of Howell Photography.

Driving cattle along the Green River near Jensen, Utah, in the early 1900s. A similar event took place along the San Juan River near Bluff, Utah, in the 1880s. Photograph courtesy of Ila Cowans.

nia. Like the early Utah cattlemen, the Texans capitalized on the beef bonanza in California, delivering thousands of longhorns to that state until the late 1850s. Two of the main cattle trails from the Lone Star state to the Golden state passed through Utah. Some Texans chose the southern route over the Old Spanish Trail. Others utilized the more northerly route that entered Utah in the Grand River Valley, proceeded northward through the Book Cliff Mountains into the Uinta Basin, over Diamond Mountain, and into Brown's Hole. Many of the herds wintered in Brown's Hole and in the spring were moved out on the Oregon Trail. In Idaho the herds swung south along the California Trail, reentered Utah near the Raft River, crossed through the Goose Creek Valley, and proceeded to California across Nevada. Once the trail-weary herds reached their destination they grazed on the lush meadows for several weeks, allowing them to fatten before being sold.

A cowboy poses for his photograph in a Price, Utah, studio in the 1890s. Typical of the earlier Texas cowboys who came into Utah, this fellow is quite young and enjoys the security of a side arm. Photograph courtesy of Brigham Young University, Photo Archives.

Texans making the drives to California were usually on the trail for the better part of a year. Trail herds coming from Utah could make the trip in less than half the time. There was no way, however, that Utah could supply all the beef needed by California during the initial gold rush. Texans had more than enough beef cattle, and prices for cattle in California made the Texas drives possible, regardless of time spent and miles traveled.

Texas, with her thousands of miles of grasslands, was destined to be our country's motherland of the cattle industry. It is estimated that by the 1860s there were more than 3,500,000 wild cattle roaming over the open ranges of Texas.[4] As early as the 1840s the Texans began driving a few cattle as far north as Ohio, and by 1846 they were making regular drives to New Orleans. By the mid-1850s thousands of the longhorns were driven through Utah on their way to California until that market closed down shortly before the beginning of the Civil War.

Texas seceded from the Union and joined the Confederate States of America in 1861. During the Civil War more than 50,000 Texans fought on the side of the South. The last battle of the Civil War was fought at Palmito Hill near the mouth of the Rio Grande

A horse sunfishes at Nine Mile Canyon, Utah, circa 1900. Photograph courtesy of University of Utah Libraries, Special Collections Department.

River a full month after General Lee had surrendered to the North on April 9, 1865.

When the ranchers returned to their lands they found millions of wild, unbranded longhorn cattle roaming over the plains. Northeastern regions of the country, as well as many of the western territories, had had a shortage of beef cattle during the war years and were willing to pay good prices for the animals. In a bold move the ranchers organized great cattle roundups to gather the longhorns, brand them and prepare them for drives to the northern markets. Men from all walks of life came to the Texas cow country, where jobs were plentiful if a fellow didn't mind working from the back of a horse. Ex-soldiers, former slaves, men running from the law or an irate woman, and boys barely tall enough to reach the stirrups found themselves working as cowboys. The name "cowboy" with reference to these men and boys became common vernacular. Prior to that time, men working with cattle were referred to as vaqueros, drovers, or herders. The

A cowboy and his dog at Price, Utah, in the 1890s. Dogs were a help in working with the cattle on the trail. Photograph courtesy of Brigham Young University, Photo Archives.

post–Civil War cowboys, hardened by the war, were a carefree, wild, and the devil-be-damned sort who were not opposed to using a gun to settle any dispute.

By March of 1866 Texans were prepared to send 260,000 head of cattle to the railhead at Sedalia, Missouri, moving herds of up to 2,500 head along different routes, hoping to cash in on the lucrative eastern market. As the herds reached the Missouri border, they were met with resistance by border guards who feared the longhorns carried and would spread "Texas Fever" to their domestic cattle. The longhorns did, in fact, carry the disease transmitted by ticks, but they were immune to it. These border guards turned back the Texas herds, using a Missouri law that prohibited the entry of diseased cattle into the state. Other Missouri ruffians, citing the Texas Fever as an excuse, attacked the herds, killed a number of cowboys, and stole thousands of cattle which they intended to sell on the black market. Few of the cattle starting out from Texas that first year made it to Sedalia.[5]

Some of the herders were fortunate to meet an agent of Joe McCoy, a cattle buyer, before reaching the Missouri border. The agent informed the trail

Texas trail drivers at lunch in the 1880s. Photograph courtesy of Brigham Young University, Photo Archives.

bosses that McCoy was building cattle pens in the small railhead town of Abilene, Kansas, and further that he had made arrangements with the railroad to ship Texas cattle to the East. Many of the trail bosses elected to turn their herds back to Texas and to make the drive to Kansas the following year.[6]

The Texas herds made it to Abilene in the spring of 1867, and the cowboys were met with jubilation by the town citizenry. The cowboys, their pockets filled with trail wages, were more than willing to spend that money for the worldly pleasures to be found in the saloons and whorehouses of Abilene. Other Kansas towns—Dodge City and Hays—rolled out the red carpet as the Texas trail herds continued to make the long trek from Texas to Kansas. By 1871 more than 700,000 head of longhorns had been moved north from Texas to the cow towns of Kansas.[7]

Most of the cattle from Texas were four-year-old steers. The best-size herd consisted of approximately 2,500 head, which could be managed by twelve cowboys, including the trail boss.[8] A herd this size could move along the trail at the rate of 450 to 500 miles a month. Younger steers and cows were also on the trails to Kansas, but they moved much

slower and were more difficult to handle. Even though 2,500 head was considered to be the best size, it was not uncommon for some trail herds to contain as many as seven to eight thousand animals. Some ranchers might have as many as three herds moving on various trails at the same time. Other trail herds consisted of cattle belonging to several small ranchers.

The cowboys on these drives were usually assigned six horses that they would ride in rotation a half day each.[9] The horses were range broncs, known as mustangs, usually only partially rider broken. On the Texas ranges they were nearly as numerous as the wild longhorns. It was not at all uncommon for these horses to "buck and sunfish" for a short spell each time the cowboy mounted up. This challenge, several times a day, helped relieve some of the boredom during the long cattle drives.

Once the cattle arrived at the Kansas railhead they were held on the range outside of town, grazing and fattening up while a buyer was sought. When sold, most of the cattle were shipped by rail to the stockyards of Chicago. However, thousands of head were purchased by buyers from the western territories, including Utah.

Many of the Texas cowboys hired to drive cattle to Abilene were surprised to be asked to continue on with the drive farther west. One can imagine the disappointment in trailing a herd of longhorn cattle a thousand miles to Kansas and then having to face

A cowboy at Manti, Utah, in the 1890s. The long hair on the horse and the cowboy's clothing indicate winter was coming on—a particularly hard time for cowboys. Photograph courtesy of Rell Francis.

A herd of cattle on the Great Plains in the 1870s—perhaps heading for Utah. Photograph courtesy of LDS Church Archives.

another thousand-mile drive to Salt Lake City. Although the railroad continued west across the country by 1869, it was still cheaper to drive the cattle overland.

The post–Civil War longhorn drives to Utah began as early as 1866. Although the Texans had a difficult time pushing their herds through to Sedalia, Missouri, during that year, enough made it through to warrant buyers for the cattle. One such buyer was Williams Jennings, the owner of a large slaughter yard and butcher shop in Salt Lake City. Jennings contracted with an ex–Union Army officer, John Morgan, and his friend to drive a herd of longhorns from Sedalia to Salt Lake City. The first post–Civil War Texas longhorn herd arrived on December 23, 1866.[10] John Morgan stayed in Salt Lake City and was soon converted to the Mormon religion. In time he became a respected leader in the church.

Between 1866 and 1876 thousands of Texas longhorns were trailed to Utah. It would be impossible to determine just how many of the cattle were driven to the territory during this decade, but it must have been a goodly number. The Salt Lake *Daily Herald* editorialized on September 11, 1878, "Many thou-

John David Boyd at Pima, Arizona, in the 1880s. He came to Utah on several occasions with trail herds. Photograph courtesy of Ida Boyd Reid.

sands of Texas cattle were brought to Utah, at one time our ranges being almost exclusively stocked by them."

Some of the Texas cowboys coming to Utah left brief descriptions of life on the trail. H. D. Gruene, age nineteen, hired on to drive cattle from Texas to Abilene in 1870 for a wage of $30 per month. When the herd reached Abilene they were held on the grasslands for several weeks until they were purchased by a buyer from Cheyenne. Gruene and several other cowboys agreed to stay on for the drive to Cheyenne and, after a hard drive, reached their destination. Once in Cheyenne, the cowboys were informed that the cattle had been sold to another party who wanted the cattle delivered to the Bear River in Utah. Gruene agreed to stay on the drive to Utah only after the trail boss raised his wages to $60 a month.

After another hard month the longhorns were delivered to the Bear River site. Gruene collected his pay in twenty-dollar gold pieces and took the train to Salt Lake City, where he and his comrades purchased new clothes and had a general "clean up" because "we were pretty much inhabited with body lice, the greatest pest encountered on the trail".[11]

At age sixteen E. A. Robuck began the trail life from his home in Texas.

Jim Owens on a mule and Amon Davis to his right look over the range that at one time was part of the huge Kanarra Cattle Company circa 1900. Amon was the grandson of John Davis who managed the company. Photograph courtesy of Brent Baldwin.

I made my first trip up the trail to Utah Territory in 1873 with old man Coleman Jones, who was boss for a herd belonging to Colonel Jack Meyers. This herd was put up at the Smith and Wimberly ranch in Gillespie County. I gained wonderful experience on this trip in the stampedes, high water, hailstorms, thunder and lightning which played on the horns of the cattle and on my horse's ears. We suffered from cold and hunger and often slept on wet blankets and wore wet clothing for several days and nights at a time, but it was all in the game, and we were compensated for the unpleasant things by the sport of roping buffalo and seeing sights we had never seen before.[12]

George Mohle started up the trail to Abilene in 1869 with 4,500 head of cattle. When his outfit reached Abilene they camped for about a month until the cattle were finally sold to a Mr. Evans of California with the understanding that Black Bill Montgomery, Bill Henderson, Mohle himself, and "Gov," the black cook, would continue with the trail drive west. In Wyoming George encountered a little problem.

Jim McPherson, who circa 1900 drove several thousand cattle to the East Tavaputs Plateau and established the Rocking M Ranch. Photograph courtesy of Don Wilcox.

I drank from a spring on the side of the mountain, thinking the water was good, and in a short time I thought I was going to die. An Irishman came along and I told him I was sick from drinking the water, and he informed me that it was very poisonous. He carried me to a store and bought me some whiskey and pretty soon I was able to travel. We went up Green River and crossed it at the mouth of Hamsford, and then crossed the divide between Wyoming and Utah. The temperature was down to zero, and when we reached the little town of Clarksville, Utah, we remained there two weeks. Mr. Evans sent the cattle up into the mountains and we took stage for Corrine, just north of Salt Lake City, where we boarded the train for home.[13]

In 1871 Sam Garner and Wash Murray gathered together enough of their own cattle to make a herd and went along with another herd to Kansas.

We sold this herd to Colonel Myers and delivered them on the Solomon River in Kansas, from where I took them to Salt Lake City for him. On this trip we had a great many hardships. Snow fell so deep that it covered the grass and our cattle and horses froze to death right in camp, and many of the cattle died. The old wild beeves became as gentle as work oxen, and we could handle them easily enough, but the extreme cold caused us much suffering. Our cattle would bog down

George Baldwin and Earl "Cowboy" Baldwin pull a cow out of a bog on the Paria River circa 1900. The Baldwin's range south of Cannonville, Utah, was at one time a part of the Kanarra outfit. Photograph courtesy of Brent Baldwin.

in the snow just the same as if it was mud, and we frequently were compelled to ram snow in their nostrils to make them get up and move. We had to walk about three hundred miles through the snow, for we could make no headway on horseback. We could not night herd because we were afoot, and it took us many weeks to make the trip, and when we arrived at the place of delivery the parties who had contracted for the cattle refused to receive them until the weather moderated because they wanted to wait and see how many of them would die from the effects of the weather. It may have been good business on their part, but it gave us boys the devil to hold the herd still longer after all we had gone through to get them there."[14]

The following year Sam took another herd to Salt Lake City but he left earlier in the year and had a much more pleasant trip.

Colonel J. J. Meyers, one of the first cowboys to reach Abilene, contracted with some of the best cowboys in the business to drive cattle to Utah. Among them were Dick Head, Billy Campbell, Noah Ellis, and J. J. Roberts. The Colonel's herds came to Utah in 1871, 1872, 1873, and 1874. Joe McCoy considered the Colonel to be one of the all-time great trail drivers. According to McCoy, the Colonel's customers were

genuine Mormons of the true polygamist faith . . . little disposed to trade with, or buy anything, of a Gentile. Therefore, to avoid this religious prejudice, and in order to get into and through the Territory without trouble, or having to pay exorbitant damage bills to the Latter Day Saints, it was his practice to instruct his men to tell every resident of Utah they met that the cattle belonged to Heber Kimball, one of the elders or high priests in Mormondom. No matter whose farm the cattle run over, nor how much damage they done to crops, it was all settled amicable by telling the residents that the cattle were Elder Kimball's. No charge or complaint was ever made, after that statement was heard, and it did appear that if Heber Kimball's cattle should run over the Saints bodily and tread them into the earth, it would have been all right, and not a murmur would have been heard to escape their lips . . . the Mormons appeared to consider it a great privilege to buy of the Sainted Elder, although they were paying from one to three dollars in gold more per head for the cattle than they would have had to pay to the Gentile drover."[15]

Taylor Button and Edward Lamb at Cane Beds, Arizona, circa 1892. Lamb was manager for the Canaan Cattle Company. Photograph courtesy of LDS Church Archives.

There was more truth than fiction to McCoy's description of Colonel Meyers's instructions to his cowboys. Ever since Johnston's Army came to Utah in 1857, there was a general tendency among Mormons to distrust Gentiles (non-Mormons). This distrust ultimately developed into the cooperative movement, which prompted Mormons to form co-op companies in virtually every Mormon settlement. The cooperatives were made up of retail stores and factories owned and operated by the brethren. Each adult in the settlements was encouraged to invest in the companies and was requested to trade strictly with those companies. Each stockholder was entitled to dividends, according to the number of shares held. These co-ops developed during the 1860s, reached their peak in the 1870s, and began to die out by 1884. They were designed to prevent Gentiles from profiteering at the Mormons' expense and to prevent outsiders from assimilating the means and property of the Mormons, thereby eventually controlling Utah Territory.[16]

The cooperative movement also involved Mormon cattlemen. Almost every settlement had co-op cattle companies, who laid claim to the grazing lands surrounding the settlement. Unlike the common grazing philosophy where numerous cattle wearing different brands ranged together, the co-ops were actually stock companies in which the cattlemen invested. Stock was issued to the individuals according to the number of animals contributed to the company. All cattle and horses owned by the cooperative wore the same brand. The companies not only offered an economic base for the cattlemen, but by virtue of strength in numbers, the cattlemen were, for the most part, able to keep outsiders off the range surrounding the settlements. This continued after 1869 when the land was technically open range.

One of the cooperative bylaws indicated the Mormons should not trade with outsiders.[17] Because of this philosophy, Gentile cowboys entering the territory, including Colonel Meyers's men, were better off to tell a lie. At least that way they were assured of finding buyers for the cattle. Even Mormons dealing with Gentiles could find themselves on the outside looking in. A case in point was Homer Duncan,

The Thomas brothers at Scofield, Utah, in the 1890s. The family set up a ranching operation in the area after the Indian wars abated. Photograph courtesy of Rell Francis.

the man who originally brought Texas longhorns to the Cedar City area. During 1879 Homer had his cattle in with the Cedar City Cattle Co-op, better known as the CCC. When a Texas trail herd containing 2,500 head passed through the area, it was purchased by a Gentile trader who went by the name of Spanish George. Duncan, in turn, bought 1,200 head of these cattle and put them out to graze with the co-op herd. He immediately came under fire from other members of the church, who claimed that the range was already overcrowded. The matter was brought before the local Mormon bishop (ecclesiastical leader), and for a time it appeared that Duncan would be disfellowshipped from the church. Apparently the transgression was a very serious one, and it was resolved only when Duncan agreed to move

Photograph taken in Millard County, Utah, in the 1870s of John King, who moved some of the first herds of cattle to the Boulder Mountain area of eastern Utah. Photograph courtesy of Don D. Walker.

the cattle off the range.[18] The degree of hostility that Duncan encountered from his fellow Mormons most likely came about because he bought cattle from a Gentile and moved them onto the range without consulting other co-op members.

Although the distrust between Mormons and Gentiles continued for a number of years, the idea of not trading with the Gentiles proved to be impractical. It was simply not in the best interests of the Mormons. They needed many of the commodities which the Gentiles offered. Consequently, many thousands of head of cattle coming into the territory from Texas were eventually purchased by the settlements' co-op companies. By the mid-1870s the rangeland controlled by the co-ops was bulging with cattle.

Two co-op companies started in the early 1870s were the Kanarra Cattle Company and the Canaan Cattle Company. Of all the settlement cooperatives, these two were the largest and most impressive. The Kanarra Cattle Company ranged cattle over a remote and far-flung empire that included the Kolob

Bill Chynoweth and Roy Twitchell at Cannonville, Utah, circa 1900. Photograph from author's collection.

Terrace, Ash Creek Valley, Kanab Valley, Paria Valley, and much of the southern high plateaus. The main ranch, located northwest of Bryce Canyon, was known as the Blue Fly. At peak operation the company ran 23,000 head of cattle.[19]

The Canaan Cattle Company ranged cattle from St. George to the Colorado River in Arizona. The main ranch was located at Canaan Springs, just north of the Arizona border. Thirty miles west of Canaan Springs was Pipe Springs, lying just inside the Arizona border on land known as "the Strip." The Arizona Strip was that region of land from the Utah border to the Grand Canyon which, in historical times, was more geographically and socially connected to Utah because of the natural barrier of the Grand Canyon. Pipe Springs was also an important ranch and it was operated by the Mormon church. The Pipe Springs Cattle Company was later incorpo-

rated into the Canaan Company and, together, it is possible that they ran as many as 6,000 head of cattle.[20]

Many Mormon cattlemen elected not to join the cooperative movement and operated by themselves instead. They, together with the many Gentile cattlemen, began moving herds to the remote regions of the territory. Although some early Mormons, such as Howard Egan and Porter Rockwell, had established ranches away from the core of Mormon settlements prior to the end of the Indian wars, the general tendency was to operate fairly close to the settlements. Once the cattlemen broke out of the settlement culture, Utah took on the more traditional ranching culture of the West.

Cattle being driven to the unoccupied ranges of Utah came from three different sources. Many were purchased from the settlement herds between

Harry Ballard in the mountains north of Thompson, Utah, in the 1890s. Photograph courtesy of G. Ballard.

Logan to St. George. Others were from Texas trail herds, and a third source was Oregon cattle. The Oregon herds were Durham cattle which had not been as infiltrated by the Texas longhorn movement and therefore had maintained purer bloodlines. Many of these cattle had been driven to California during the gold rush. By the mid-1870s Oregon cattlemen had driven several thousand head of cattle to the markets in Wyoming and Utah.[21] With the reintroduction of purebred Durham cattle in Utah, a slow process of upgrading the cattle on the Utah ranges began.

Many of the cattlemen who located in the far reaches of the territory were genuine cowboys at one time. They owned little more than a horse and saddle and had worked the Texas trail drives at a small wage and found. Usually they finally saved enough to put a herd together. With a couple of

hired hands and the cattle, they were then ready to build a cattle kingdom. One such cowboy was Joshua B. "Spud" Hudson. He worked for the Picket Wire Outfit in southern Colorado. While working for this outfit he had had occasion to enter Utah near the Blue Mountains in San Juan County. He was impressed by the miles and miles of virgin grasses which reached the belly of his horse. Spud made his way to the Wasatch settlements, where he purchased 2,000 head of cattle. He drove them to the base of the Blue Mountains and established his headquarters at the Double Cabins, just a few miles north of present-day Monticello. A year later another Colorado cowboy by the name of Peters drove 2,000 head of cattle to the Blue Mountains and established his headquarters at Peter's Spring.[22]

Other cattlemen streamed to the southeast corner of Utah during the 1870s. Two brothers named Tay-

Cowboys driving Hereford or white-faced cattle to market near Salt Lake City circa 1920. Herefords eventually became the most prominent breed of cattle in Utah and the West. Photograph courtesy of Utah State Historical Society.

lor drove 3,000 head of cattle from Nevada to the region. Philander Maxwell and Billie McCarty brought in a herd of 2,000. Al Nunn brought in 1,200 head of cattle, and the Wilson family brought in several hundred head of cattle.[23]

The Whitmore brothers established ranches along the Price River at the base of the Book Cliff Mountains. Lord Elliot, an English aristocrat, founded the Big Spring Ranch at present-day Sunnyside. The Miller brothers located southeast of the Price River near Huntington. Justus Wellington Seely also moved his herds into the Huntington area. The Bennion family, who customarily ran cattle in the Skull and Rush valleys of west-central Utah, moved 2,000 head of cattle into Castle Valley. Preston Nutter moved thousands of cattle into the region around present-day Thompson Springs in the early 1880s. He was followed into the region by the Ballard brothers and the McPherson family.

A family named Tidwell located in Fremont Valley on the south slopes of Fish Lake Mountain. Hugh J. McClellan and Beason Lewis also came to the Fremont Valley. John King and Philo Allen drove some of the first herds of cattle into Boulder Valley on the south slopes of the Aquarius Plateau. The Dodd brothers from Pioche, Nevada, moved several thousand head of cattle to Pine Valley in western Utah. The Murdock family drove their cattle to the area around present-day Milford, and the Deardon family moved herds to the Snake Valley on the Utah-Nevada border. Ebenezer Bryce moved his cattle to the now-famous Bryce Canyon region in 1875. He soon declared that the colorful canyon was a hell of a place to lose a cow.

For years Brown's Hole, now known as Brown's Park, in northeastern Utah was used as a winter range for the Texas trail herds. One of the Texas cowboys who kept his longhorns in the Park was Dr.

Keiser. During the spring of 1873 he moved his 1,300 head of cattle to a permanent location south of the Park on the Utah-Colorado border. Also locating in the area was Abram Hatch, who operated on Blue Mountain, just north of present-day Jensen. Lige Driscoll, moved his herd of cattle and horses to the Green River near present-day Manila. Crawford and Thompson bought a herd of longhorns that had come up the trail from New Mexico and placed them on the Crawford Mountains near present-day Randolph. This herd was driven to Brown's Park by Jesse Hoy during the winter of 1872 and was returned to the Crawford Mountains in the spring. The pattern continued, and this became the first permanent cattle herd to use the Park.[24]

William White established cattle in the Bear River Mountains and John Tinnin brought Texas cattle to the Goose Creek Mountains along the Utah-Idaho border. The Rose family moved 2,000 head of cattle to the southern slopes of the Raft River Mountains in what is now known as Park Valley. J. W. Taylor had several thousand head of cattle grazing beside the Raft River along the Utah-Idaho border, and the McIntyre brothers established themselves in the Tintic Valley.

Judge William Carter came to Fort Bridger with Johnston's Army in 1857. He began bringing cattle from Oregon to the ranges around Fort Bridger as early as the mid-1860s. The five Goodwin brothers moved cattle to the grasslands northwest of Logan, and Alexander Toponce began moving cattle to the range north of Corinne.

The men mentioned were just a few of the cattlemen who established herds in the far reaches of the territory in the 1870s and early 1880s. Some were Mormons and some were Gentiles. Some were tied into the California cattle culture and some came from the Texas cattle culture. The two cultures merged on the grasslands of Utah. As the cultures merged, the cowboys took the best from both systems.

With the establishment of large cattle interests in the territory, the movement of Texas cattle to Utah began to wane. In 1873, Joseph McCoy wrote, "Utah, notwithstanding her great city and her immense mining operations, has now more than a supply of cattle for her own consumption, and is beginning to export cattle to Chicago and the east." McCoy also noted that in 1873 "several thousand head of fat beeves were driven from Utah over the mountains to Cheyenne and there shipped to Chicago."[25]

Colonel Meyers brought his last large herd of Texas longhorns to the territory in 1874, but by then Utah was on the verge of reaching success as a cattle exporting territory. On September 14, 1878, the Cheyenne *Daily Leader* ran the following story:

Texas is fast losing its leadership as the cattle raising state of the Union. One who has resided a few years in any of the Western states or territories can recall the time when the Lone Star State enjoyed the cattle trade monopoly, not only supplying the beef for the eastern markets, but furnishing large herds with which to stock the regions east and west of the Rocky Mountains.

Many thousands of Texas cattle, says the Salt Lake Herald, were brought to Utah, at one time our ranges being almost exclusively stocked by them. The same was the case with Wyoming, Nevada, Idaho, Montana and even Washington territory and Oregon. Within the past few years this has all been changed. Cattle are no longer seen coming west, but on the contrary, the territories mentioned are driving large herds to the east, and competing for the trade of Chicago, New York, Philadelphia and other large markets. Montana is preparing to ship largely direct to Chicago. This change is not due to diminished herds or failing pastures in Texas, but to the facts that the western ranges and grazing grounds are being utilized, and the quality of stock is being improved.

The Texas cattle brought into the west have been crossed with better breeds, and the quality of their progeny so improved by the introduction of fine-blooded stock as to bring a higher price in the eastern market.

Last year and this season many thousands of head of cattle were shipped and driven east from Utah and other territories, and a late estimate of the herds remaining, places the total at 3,000,000 head. It may be a long time before the West can become the leading producers of beef, but the fact that in so short a time we have acquired so fair a share of the trade, and are acknowledged competitors with the favored region of Texas, is encouraging. Our western graziers, however, should not forget that their success is due almost exclusively to the improvement and better care of

Chaps

Batwing chaps made by J. G. Read, Ogden, Utah, circa 1915. Courtesy of Wayne Schoenfeld.

Unmarked batwing chaps worn by Joe Hickman of Grover, Utah, circa 1920. From author's collection.

Batwing chaps made by Newton Brothers, Vernal, Utah, circa 1920. Courtesy of Roslyn Grose.

Left: Shotgun chaps made by Cross Brothers, Ogden, Utah, circa 1900. From author's collection.

Right: Angora goatskin or woolly chaps made by Salt Lake Hardware Co., circa 1912. From author's collection.

their stock. If they would continue to hold the custom already obtained and acquire more, they must go on improving the breeds of cattle, working out the scrubs and replacing them with fine bloods.

As mentioned earlier, the improvement of the herds began with the reintroduction of Durham cattle that had been driven to the Rocky Mountain territories from Oregon. During the latter part of the 1870s the movement of these cattle from Oregon almost rivaled the trail drives from Texas. Although most of these cattle were driven directly to the ranges of Montana, Idaho, and Wyoming, a goodly number came down into northern Utah. The Cheyenne *Daily Leader*, dated September 29, 1878, indicated that "more than a hundred thousand head of cattle will be driven into Utah and Wyoming from Oregon before the season closes."

Interestingly, the men who made the drives from Oregon to the Rocky Mountains were, for the most part, Texans who were well schooled in the art of trail driving. The Cheyenne *Sun*, dated March 4, 1879, ran a story about these hardened trail drivers:

> The expedition which left Cheyenne today was composed almost exclusively of Texans—young men who have spent years on the trail between Texas and Kansas . . . they go over the Union Pacific to Ogden, Utah, where they fit up their teams and start northward. They will pass through northern Utah, the entire length of Idaho and enter Oregon near Baker City, where their herds will be organized for the return trip.

At the same time these Oregon cattle were moving to the Rocky Mountains, Utah cowboys were driving cattle out of the territory in increasing numbers. In 1877 an estimated 23,500 head of cattle were driven to Wyoming, Colorado, and Nebraska. In 1878, 35,000 head were driven eastward and another 2,000 were shipped by rail to Chicago. In 1879 an estimated 47,000 head were driven east, and in 1880 at least 53,000 head were driven to

Wyoming, Nebraska, South Dakota, Arizona, and the eastern markets. In all, an estimated 180,000 head of cattle were driven from Utah during that four-year period.[26] The actual number of cattle leaving the territory may have been much higher, for in the 1870s an accurate count was almost nonexistent.

The Utah cattlemen did their share to upgrade the cattle during the latter part of the 1870s and early 1880s. The Durham cattle coming from Oregon improved the bloodlines of the longhorn cattle. William Jennings of Salt Lake City had imported twenty-five pure-blooded shorthorns from Canada and by 1880 had produced a number of quality cattle, including a model steer called "Perfection."[27]

Henry J. Faust was instrumental in bringing the first Hereford cattle into the territory in the early 1880s.[28] These men were the pioneers of cattle improvement in the territory. However, the upgrading of beef cattle on the western ranges was a constant but slow process which did not immediately doom the longhorn breed. The demand for beef throughout the eastern and western markets insured a need for the longhorns through the turn of the century.

The constant flow of cattle leaving the territory during the late 1870s and early 1880s included longhorns and other upgraded beef. The cattle moving to the eastern markets were usually four-year-old steers. Cattle moving to other western territories for the most part were heifers, bulls, and cows, which would provide foundation stock. The men who owned these cattle were a colorful lot. Some of them never managed to make more than a meager livelihood from the cow business. Some could lay claim to 3,000 head of cattle, which was no small accomplishment in the territory. A few others managed to claw their way to the top of the hill and become legitimate cattle barons. A cattle baron, at least for the purpose of this book, was a cattleman who could lay claim to at least 7,000 head of cattle.

3

The Cattle Barons

While delivering mail between Kanab and Rockville in the 1880s Nephi Johnson was impressed with the number of cattle in the area. He claimed there were "3,000 cattle at one ranch, 4,000 at another ranch, and even more at a ranch in Johnson Canyon."[1] In northeastern Utah along the Wyoming border it was claimed Judge Carter had cattle on a thousand hills. In southeastern Utah, many old-timers claimed Preston Nutter never actually knew just how many cattle he had.

During this period of eminent cattle activity, records gathered by the Bureau of Statistics for tax purposes in regard to number of cattle on the open range were unusually conservative. In 1880 the United States Bureau of Statistics reported there were 132,655 head of cattle in Utah, yet in 1878 the Cheyenne *Daily* reported there were an estimated 300,000 cattle in Utah, while Wyoming had 350,000, and Colorado had 400,000. In 1887 the Denver and Rio Grande Western Railway published a pamphlet stating Utah had no less than 500,000 cattle and 300,000 horses on the range. Yet in 1890 the Bureau of Statistics reported there were only 278,313 head of cattle in Utah. An early historian of the cattle trade found this count so incomplete that it must have "caused a smile to some of the big cattlemen of that portion of the country."[2]

The fundamental reason for the discrepancy in the number of cattle reported and the actual numbers on the range was that tax collectors had to depend on range managers and ranch owners when it came to counting cows. There was no way a tax collector could physically count the cattle, since cattle on the open range had different brands and mixed continuously. Most of the big cattlemen didn't even know the exact number of cattle they owned. Many itinerant herds also moved in and out of the territory, making an accurate count difficult.

It was quite fashionable for cattlemen to downplay the number of animals they owned. During an interview with Governor West in Salt Lake City in 1894, a cattleman in San Juan County stated that the Carlisle Cattle Company owned 20,000 cattle, the Pittsburgh Cattle Company owned 12,000 head, and the LC Cattle Company had 10,000 cows.[3] However, in 1896 when the Carlisle Company left Utah it was reported they drove 30,000 cattle out of San Juan County. The same report indicated that the LC Cattle Company sold a number of cattle locally and drove out of Utah an estimated 22,000 head of cattle during the same year.[4]

Likewise, it is not an easy task to determine the size of some cattle operations in Utah during the last twenty years of the nineteenth century. Records are incomplete or nonexistent, and sometimes a short article in the local newspaper is the only indication a pretty big outfit was even in the area. Still, enough information has filtered down to document some of

The Crandall brothers at the Anderson studio, Salt Lake City, in the 1870s. The Crandall family owned several ranches throughout the Utah area. Photograph from author's collection.

A cowboy poses in front of what would appear to be a very wealthy and prominent ranch in central Utah circa 1900. Photograph courtesy of Brigham Young University, Photo Archives.

the large outfits and the colorful cattle barons who controlled them.

One of the first cattle barons on the Utah scene was French-born Alexander Toponce. Toponce immigrated to America with his parents in 1846, and they settled down on a small southeastern cattle ranch. Boredom soon set in, and, while still a teenager, Toponce decided to run away from home. He found a number of jobs as he worked his way west—the most substantial of which were as a stage driver for Ben Holladay out of Fort Kearney and as an assistant wagon boss for Albert Sidney Johnston's Army, which was moving toward Utah in 1857. During his trip to Utah he was an eyewitness to Mormon raids on government wagon trains. His first encounter with the Mormons left a lasting impression on the young man and later in life he wrote in his memoirs, "What Lot Smith and his Mormon cowboys did to the wagon trains on the Sandy put a crimp in our trip to Utah."[5]

After arriving in Utah, Toponce spent some time in and around Camp Floyd and Salt Lake City before moving on to California. While in California he made substantial money moving freight to the California gold diggings. He soon expanded this business to the mining fields of Montana.

In 1867 Toponce returned to Utah and went on a cattle-buying venture. By September of that year he had gathered 6,000 cattle, which he kept in one herd around Garfield Beach along the Great Salt Lake. He hired several hands and, in one big trail herd, he moved all of the cattle to California. By the time the trail drive reached Walker Lake, Nevada, the snows were so deep in the Sierra Nevada range that Toponce decided to winter the herd in Nevada. Toponce later managed to sell all of the cattle to buyers in Virginia City and Carson City at a substantial profit.[6] He then returned to Utah and bought more cattle, which he sold to the railroad camps building the tracks that would link the nation together on Promontory summit in 1869.

Shortly after the rails of the Central Pacific and the

A cowboy takes a moment to reflect the day's activities in his southern Idaho cabin circa 1900. Photograph courtesy of Brigham Young University, Photo Archives.

Union Pacific railroads were linked and the last spike was driven, Toponce decided to go into the cattle and freight business in an even bigger way. He operated a freighting service between the railroad town of Corinne in northern Utah and the mine diggings of Montana. With the profits from his freighting business he purchased thousands of head of cattle and ranged them along the Bear River from Corinne to Garland—approximately forty miles north of Corinne. The exact number of cattle he had on the range is not known, but it was somewhere between 10,000 to 15,000 head. He indicated in his memoirs that for a time he was the major cattle supplier to the beef markets in Salt Lake City.[7]

In 1871 Toponce purchased a herd of 9,000 head of Texas longhorn cattle and had them driven to the Fort Hall Indian Reservation in Idaho, where he rented pasture. Apparently at this time his range in Utah was full to capacity. He maintained a herd of 10,000 head on the Idaho range until 1879, at which time he sold the herd to the Sparks outfit, whose main headquarters was located in Nevada.[8]

By 1883 the vast rangeland along the Bear River claimed by Toponce had shrunk as homesteaders came into the area. During that year he decided to purchase land from the railroad and, with a partner by the name of John W. Kerr, was able to claim deeds to 90,000 acres. They formed the Corinne Mill, Canal and Stock Company, stocking the land with 5,000 head of cattle, 1,000 horses, and 26,000 sheep (which belonged to John Kerr). Through a double-cross, Kerr ended up with all of the shares in the company. Toponce fought the take-over, but because of the legal process, court costs, lawyer's fees, etc., both men lost their shirts. It was a bitter defeat for one of Utah's first cattle barons.[9]

Another cattleman who arrived on the Utah scene with Johnston's Army was Judge William Carter. He was sutler to the military expedition that reached Fort Bridger in 1857. He later secured a job as post sutler at Fort Bridger and procured appointments as postmaster and probate judge.

A cowboy in northwestern Utah circa 1910. Woolie or angora-goatskin chaps were popular on the northern ranges during the winter months. Photograph from author's collection.

Judge Carter began ranging cattle along the rivers running out of the Uinta Mountains in the early 1860s. By the late 1860s he had established himself as the largest cattle baron in Green River County, Utah. Judge Carter, however, did not like being a resident of Mormon-dominated Utah and used his influence to persuade Congress to establish Wyoming. In 1868 Green River County, Utah, was officially deeded to the Territory of Wyoming.[10]

Judge Carter brought some longhorn cattle in from Texas, but he was bent on upgrading the range cattle. He brought in a railcar of purebred shorthorn

Worth Cook displays a pearl-handled revolver and white woolies at his ranch in Ibapah, Utah, circa 1910. Photograph courtesy of Ron Bateman.

bulls from the East and stocked his range with shorthorn cattle from Oregon. These cattle grazed on the lush meadows of the Uinta Mountains during the summer and utilized the flatlands around Fort Bridger during the winter.

In 1881 the military established Fort Thornburgh near Vernal, Utah, to keep an eye on the Utes who had been moved to the Uintah Reservation. Judge Carter won a government contract to build a supply road from Fort Bridger across the Uinta Mountains to Fort Thornburgh. In the process of managing the construction of this road, Judge Carter contracted pneumonia and died in November of 1881. His widow and son, Willie Carter, took charge of the Judge's interests and finished the road.

In 1883 Willie Carter organized the Carter Cattle

Tom Casto and Cecil Davis in the Uinta Mountains south of Evanston, Wyoming, in the 1880s. Photograph courtesy of Wyoming State Archives, Museums and Historical Department.

Company, which ranged cattle in Wyoming, Utah, Idaho, and Montana. The company used a very unusual brand called the "Bug." Carter Cattle Company operated until the turn of the century, when company holdings were sold off to several investors.

Unlike Judge Carter, the McIntyre brothers, William and Samuel, wanted to be in Mormon country. They had been converted to the church in Texas and came to Utah in the late 1860s. When their father, who had remained in Texas, passed away, the brothers went back to Texas to settle his estate. With their inheritances they bought about 7,000 head of longhorn cattle and started them up the Chisholm Trail in 1871. Several months later the herd arrived in Utah, and the brothers found virgin range for them on the west side of the Tintic Mountains. The cattle wintered very well and in the spring the brothers were able to sell them for $24.00 per

head. They had bought the cattle in Texas at $3.75 a head, which gave the brothers a tremendous profit, considering that the grass the cattle ate during the winter was free.[11]

With their pockets bulging with money, the brothers went to Omaha, where they purchased another large herd of longhorns and drove them back to the Tintic range. The next spring these cattle, too, were sold at a tremendous profit. It was during this time the brothers decided to establish a permanent cattle ranch and, by 1873, 10,000 head were wearing the MC brand.[12]

During 1873 the brothers traded some of the cattle for a mining stake known as the Mammoth Mine. The mine was a bonanza, propelling the young brothers into the world of high finance. They became heavily involved in the stock market and soon built a mansion in Salt Lake City. At the same time

Carter Cattle Company roundup crew south of Evanston, Wyoming, in the 1880s. Photograph courtesy of Wyoming State Archives, Museums and Historical Department.

they continued to improve the ranch at Tintic and established another ranch in Leamington thirty miles south of the Tintic headquarters.

During peak times of the McIntyre Cattle Company operation, it is possible that they ran 15,000 head of cattle over the open range from the Tintic Mountains to the Nevada border.[13] The range could be mighty good at times and mighty hard at others. Overgrazing was a problem and there was contention with other cattlemen and sheepmen using the same range. By 1890 William McIntyre decided he had had enough of the conditions in Utah and moved his portion of horses and cattle to new territory in Canada.

Samuel continued to operate the Utah ranch and began buying up homesteads in Nevada. Soon he had 15,000 cattle wearing the running MC brand in Elko County, Nevada.[14] When Samuel was killed in

an automobile accident in Salt Lake City in 1931, his sons and widow took over the ranching operations. But by 1950 all of the Nevada operation was liquidated. The Utah ranch continues to operate to the present time but on a much smaller scale.

Antelope Island in the Great Salt Lake had been used for grazing purposes from the very beginning of Mormon colonization. Over the past 139 years, many men and companies have owned or leased all or part of the 50,000-acre island. One of the men casting a shadow upon the island was William White. William was an Englishman who came to the Salt Lake Valley during the early Mormon migration. He and his son John began raising cattle along the bench areas in Davis County and had built up a sizable herd by 1876. In that year the church officials contracted with the Whites to round up the horses on Antelope Island and take them to Salt

Ranch hands and their families at the McIntyre Ranch, Leamington, Utah, circa 1900. Photograph courtesy of Leo Olson.

Lake City where they were sold to individual buyers. The horses on the island had run free from the time the church herdsman on the island, Briant Stringham, died in 1871. By 1876 the horse herd had grown to approximately 3,000 head and, although the horses were purebred and some of the finest horses in the country, they were as wild as any mustang in the territory. Getting the horses off the island was no easy task.[15]

By the early 1880s the White and Sons Cattle Company had expanded to the point where they required additional range. During this time they were able to buy a part of Antelope Island and they began

Burt Johnson, Del Bradfield, and Cal Brimley in front of the huge McIntyre barn circa 1910. Photograph courtesy of Lawrence Bradfield.

moving some cattle onto that range. They also acquired land in Cache County and developed a home ranch at present-day Avon. The ranch at Avon became the headquarters for a vast cattle operation which saw White's cattle grazing on the open ranges of the Bear River Mountains from the Huntsville road to the Wyoming border.[16] They probably had another 1,000 to 2,000 head of cattle on their range in Davis County and Antelope Island, and, for a time, they ran an additional 2,000 head of cattle on range purchased in Carbon County.

The Whites were active in upgrading the herds and purchased the prize steer "Perfection" from William Jennings. The Whites took the steer to various county fairs and offered a reward of $400 to anyone who could produce a better steer. They also operated a meat shop in Salt Lake City and, in 1883,

McIntyre cowboy Jack Usses at the Leamington ranch circa 1910. Photograph courtesy of Lawrence Bradfield.

began advertising their company as "the leading butchers of Utah."[17]

Some sources indicate that William White was the first person to put buffalo on Antelope Island. The small herd was purchased from "Buffalo" Jones, who raised the animals on his ranch south of Kanab. The buffalo on the island today are the descendants of this herd.[18]

The White and Sons Cattle Company broke up upon the death of John White in 1914. At the time of his death the ranch holdings were heavily mortgaged and had to be sold to satisfy the debts. John's widow and sons were left practically penniless, a condition not uncommon in the open-range cattle business.[19]

One family which eventually fared more favorably was the Whitmores. Dr. James Whitmore, a

Texan, drove 500 longhorns to Utah in the 1850s. He settled in St. George and while seeking rangeland for his cattle came upon Pipe Springs. While his family remained in St. George, Dr. Whitmore moved his cattle to the new range. In 1866 Navajos began raiding Kanab and St. George. During this time of conflict, Dr. Whitmore and his hired hand were killed by the renegades.[20] His widow moved with her family to central Utah shortly thereafter.

Thirteen years after the death of their father, James, Jr., and George made their way to the Price area and began their own cattle operation. They soon had close to 15,000 head of cattle ranging over an immense range, which included all the land north of the Price River from Colton on the west to Green River on the east. The range also included the upper reaches of the Book Cliff Mountains.[21]

Del Bradfield, circa 1910, was foreman for the McIntyre Ranch at Leamington, Utah. Photograph courtesy of Floyd Bradfield.

The Whitmores had two ranch headquarters. One was situated on the bottomlands along the Price River where the town of Price is presently located. The other headquarters was in Whitmore Canyon near present-day Sunnyside. At one time the Whitmores hired thirty full-time cowboys and ranch hands.

The company was plagued by cattle rustlers, and violence was not uncommon on their range. Railroad and mining interests besieged them and eventually broke up the cattle empire. However, by this time most of the Whitmores were financially set. James Whitmore, Jr., opened a bank following his ranching days.

In 1879 an English gentleman named Lord Elliot found himself in the Price River country occupied by the Whitmore family. It is said that his relatives, who

were royalty, wanted him out of Britain because of his reputation as a black sheep. Purportedly they gave him a substantial amount of money to leave the country.[22]

Lord Elliot established a cattle ranch at some natural springs just a few miles south of present-day Sunnyside, Utah. He built a beautiful home that looked like a mansion, particularly in the wilds of eastern Utah. During the next ten years the ranch became very profitable and Lord Elliot was caught up in the western mystique. He was a tall, quiet man who fancied wearing a pearl-handled Colt revolver on each hip.[23]

During the 1890s Lord Elliot brought thousands of head of sheep onto his range. Naturally, this did not please the Whitmores. During this same time a drought had depleted the water and grass on the

Roscoe Whitmore at Sunnyside, Utah, circa 1899. Whitmore was a son of the founders of the Whitmore Cattle Company. Photograph courtesy of Brigham Young University, Photo Archives.

range, which deepened the chasm between the two outfits. During one altercation at a watering hole, thirty Whitmore cowboys and a like number of Elliot's men stood toe-to-toe, ready to begin shooting at each other. Cool heads apparently won out when the men began using their fists instead. The result was one whale of a donnybrook.[24]

At the turn of the century Lord Elliot had withstood drought, range wars, and takeover attempts by the Rio Grande Railroad. However, when his beloved wife died suddenly, he was never the same. Soon after he sold his sheep and cattle, some of which were purchased by White and Sons of northern Utah. After the sale Lord Elliot simply walked out, leaving his possessions, mounted his horse, and rode off, never to be heard from again.[25]

One of the best-known cattle barons on the Utah scene was the indomitable Preston Nutter. Nutter was the son of a successful cattle grower in Virginia, but was orphaned at the age of nine. At eleven he ran away from relatives who were attempting to raise him. He worked on a Mississippi riverboat as a cabin boy for two years and then went to work with a government wagon train headed west. When he purchased his first horse in 1863, he branded it with a "63" to commemorate the year. The "63" brand would continue to mark Nutter horses and mules for the next 120 years.[26]

Nutter eventually made his way to California, where he became active in the freighting business. This occupation enabled him to see much of the West, and he eventually settled down to ranching in

A cowboy at Thompson, Utah, in the 1890s. Thompson was a major supply point for cowboys working in the Grand River valley.
Photograph courtesy of Baker and Lacy copyright 1979.

Colorado. Nutter stocked his ranch near Montrose, Colorado, with cattle he purchased from the Wasatch settlements. On the drives from Utah to Colorado, Nutter took note of the largely unoccupied land along the southern slopes of the Book Cliff Mountains. After a short stay in Colorado as a rancher and a politician, Nutter decided he wanted to go into the cattle ranching business in a big way and began looking for a range where he could run 20,000 head of cattle. He decided Utah would be the best place to go looking.[27]

In 1886 Nutter drove a herd of cattle out of Colorado to his new range in the vicinity of Thompson Springs. Right from the start Nutter was interested in upgrading the cattle on his range and entered into a mutual agreement with the Cleveland Cattle Com-

pany of Fairplay, Colorado, to exchange 1,000 head of mixed-breed Utah cattle for an equal number of the Cleveland Company's cows and bulls. The Cleveland Company was experimenting with Hereford cattle, but wanted the more marketable Utah cattle to take to market. Nutter wanted the Herefords because he believed that in time the breed would be the dominant type in the West.[28]

In 1888 Nutter entered into a partnership with Ed Sands and Tom Wheeler to form the Grand Cattle Company. The company operated in a triangle between Thompson Springs, Cisco, and Moab. A year later Nutter bought Sands and Wheeler out and expanded the company's range farther into the Book Cliffs. He was able to secure a contract with the federal government to supply beef to the army and In-

Corrals at the Big Springs Ranch in the 1890s. The cowboy on the horse could be the colorful Lord Elliot. Photograph courtesy of Rell Francis.

dian agencies at Fort Duchesne. At this time in Nutter's career, he could lay claim to at least 5,000 head of cattle, but the quality and quantity of the cattle were constantly increasing.[29]

The Uintah Indian Reservation in eastern Utah included the high, wide, and lonesome Strawberry Valley, containing some 665,000 acres of lush virgin grasslands with plenty of water. Nutter was able to secure a government contract to lease this valley for his cattle operation; however, to do so, the government required Nutter to sell all of his holdings in the territory. Nutter sold out lock, stock, and barrel, including 5,000 head of cattle, to the Webster City Cattle Company. After the sale Nutter, with the help of Sands and Wheeler, who were now New York businessmen, formed the Strawberry Cattle Company. They secured the lease on the Strawberry Valley from the government for a five-year period.[30]

The Strawberry Valley was snowbound during the winter months, requiring Nutter to find breeding and winter grazing ground for his cattle. Because he could not own Utah property, he went to the Arizona Strip where he tried to arrange land deals with the cattlemen who were already there. Most of them refused water rights to Nutter but, undaunted, he began digging his own wells.

For the next several years Nutter and his cowboys moved cattle from the Strip to the Strawberry Valley at least twice each year. During this time he was also able to buy out most of the cattlemen on the Arizona Strip. The range, itself, was open, but any wells and improvements on the land could be legally owned by individuals, and by 1898 Nutter owned most of them. His cattle during this time had increased to 25,000 head.[31]

Nutter was able to secure a one-year extension on the Strawberry lease, but the writing was on the wall. Utah sheepmen had been petitioning Washington to allow them to use the Strawberry Valley. Realizing that Washington would not hold the

Preston Nutter at Nine Mile Canyon in the early 1900s. Even though it was said that he preferred to ride a mule, note that he is riding a horse. Photograph courtesy of University of Utah Libraries, Special Collections Department.

sheepmen back, Nutter decided to find a new summer range. The Strip was excellent breeding ground, but the high country was desirable to put the steers in shape for market.

In 1901 Nutter bought out his New York partners and began buying up ranches along Nine Mile Canyon, which crossed the Book Cliff Mountains. Actually, the name "Nine Mile Canyon" is a misnomer since the canyon extends for more than a hundred miles. Nutter's new holdings in Nine Mile became known as "The Nutter Corporation," which claimed 300,000 acres from Nine Mile east to the Green River. Nutter began branding his cattle with the Circle Brand at this time, but he continued to use the "63" brand on his horses and mules.

Nutter was in the saddle for days on end traveling the vast distances between Arizona and Utah. He rode both horses and mules, but preferred the mules. He said, "A horse will go beyond his endurance. A mule knows his limitations and when to

stop." Nutter also indicated that a mule had a different gait than a horse, "a gait which permits the rider to more easily sleep in the saddle."[32]

A year after Nutter's death in 1936, the Arizona portion of the ranch was sold. Until 1986 the ranch was still being operated by the Nutter family and was continuing to run approximately 10,000 head of cattle. The ranch has since been sold to the Sabine Corporation of Dallas, Texas, and they have continued the ranching operations while also exploring for oil and gas.

One of the cattlemen who opposed Preston Nutter's move to the Arizona Strip was B. F. Saunders. For years Saunders had been the largest cattle buyer in southern Utah and northern Arizona. He traveled through the area buying local cattle and driving them to the Arizona Strip. Once on the Strip the cattle would feed while Saunders was out purchasing more cattle. In this manner Saunders would accumulate great herds of cattle, which were then

A ranch house in Cache Valley circa 1880. Photograph courtesy of LDS Church Archives.

driven to the railhead at Lund, Utah. The cattle were loaded on trains and sold in California. There were times when as many as 5,000 head would be trailed to Lund in one huge drive.[33]

During the late 1880s Saunders was able to purchase portions of the Canaan Cattle Company from the Mormon church.[34] The church was having financial difficulties because the federal government was confiscating its properties and livestock in an effort to force the abolishment of the practice of polygamy. With the land claims Saunders hoped to force off all newcomers to the Strip, including Nutter. Nutter stuck to his guns and forged out his own empire on the Strip.

A cowboy at the Nutter Ranch in Nine Mile Canyon circa 1910. Photograph courtesy of University of Utah Libraries, Special Collections Department.

Saunders maintained his holdings on the Strip for several years and then sold portions of his land claims to Preston Nutter and other cattlemen operating in the region. Around 1920 he went into partnership with Ora Haley, who was a wealthy cattleman in Wyoming. Headquartered at Salt Lake City, the Saunders-Haley enterprise bought and sold cattle and sheep throughout the West. In 1922 they bought, trailed, and sold 500,000 sheep and 80,000 cattle. Frank Paxton was the foreman and trail boss for the company.[35] The company broke up at the time of Saunders's death in the mid-1920s.

Joseph Yates and Joseph Frodsham were counterparts to B. F. Saunders in the northern portion of Utah. During the 1880s they traveled as far north as Jackson Hole, Wyoming, and as far west as Ruby Valley, Nevada, buying up cattle from small ranchers. Cowboys working for the company drove the

Evan Kimber near Grouse Creek, Utah, in the 1890s. Photograph courtesy of Rhea Toyn.

ever-increasing herds to a bedding ground near present-day Tremonton. Yates and Frodsham never actually owned any ranch or land holdings, but they still supplied Ogden and Salt Lake City with thousands of pounds of beef. Some of the herds belonging to these men could reach as many as 7,000 head by the time they arrived at their destination.[36]

A cattleman in northeastern Utah, James W. Taylor, could lay claim to 12,000 head of cattle. The *Ogden Pilot* reported on May 1, 1881, that "James Taylor came in this morning from his cattle ranch on Raft River and went to Salt Lake. He reports stock as doing well, and one of his herds is now moving

Ute Indian cowboys in the 1890s at Fort Duchesne, Utah. Indians, blacks, and Mexicans were well represented on the cattle ranges of Utah. Photograph courtesy of Thorne Studio.

toward Cheyenne. He will start two more herds as soon as he can secure men for that purpose." On May 20, 1881, the *Ogden Pilot* reported the following: "James W. Taylor has now three herds of cattle on the road from his ranch on Raft River to either Laramie or Cheyenne. These herds aggregate nearly 6,000 animals, which will reach their destination in the fall in good condition for shipping east. He has about the same number of animals on his ranch, which are doing well."

Little is actually known about James Taylor. Exactly when he arrived on the Raft River is a mystery. He apparently sold his ranch holdings in 1886 to become the foreman of a corporate cattle empire that will be discussed in the next chapter.

Elijah "Lige" Driscoll came to Utah with Johnston's Army in 1857. After being mustered out of the

Branding a horse, Little Dry Valley, circa 1900. George Baldwin (standing), Amon Davis (at right). Photograph courtesy of Rita Baldwin.

army in 1863, he began trading cattle with the emigrants along the Oregon Trail. He soon had thousands of cattle and horses that ranged around the Flaming Gorge country. His main ranch headquarters was located at the mouth of Henry's Fork near present-day Manila, Utah.

Driscoll originated the "Wagon Wheel" brand, which was placed on the left side of his cattle and horses. During the 1880s his herds became so numerous that old-timers claimed he shipped cattle to the eastern markets by the trainload.[37] If this is true, considering that twenty-five animals were placed in each car, and a train had a hundred cars, this would have amounted to 2,500 head of cattle per trainload. At any rate, "Lige" Driscoll was a colorful character who married a Shoshone Indian woman. It appears that his cattle kingdom broke up after his death, near the turn of the century.

The largest individually owned cattle operation in the entire west was the Sparks Tinnin Cattle Com-

Will James, noted western writer and author, was once arrested for cattle rustling. Photograph courtesy of Vern Jeffers.

pany. Although this was primarily a Nevada ranch, its cattle range spilled over the borders of Utah, Idaho, and Oregon. At its peak the company ran upward of 175,000 head of cattle and several thousand horses. In 1885 the company branded 38,000 calves.[38] Utah portions of the ranch included the Goose Creek and Raft River Mountains, plus the arid Bonneville Salt Flats, which were used as a winter range.

The Sparks Tinnin outfit was an outcrop of four good-sized cattle companies which, through a process of purchase and combining of partnerships, came together in one giant cattle empire. First on the scene was Jasper Harrell, a wealthy Californian. He established a herd of 25,000 longhorns along Goose Creek in southern Idaho and northern Utah. Harrell's outfit was known as the Shoesole. Shortly after Harrell had founded the Shoesole, a man by the name of Armstrong established a large cattle herd at Thousand Springs in northeastern Nevada. His range extended east and north to the Winecup Field on Goose Creek. This outfit would become known as the Winecup.

Brands and Branding Irons

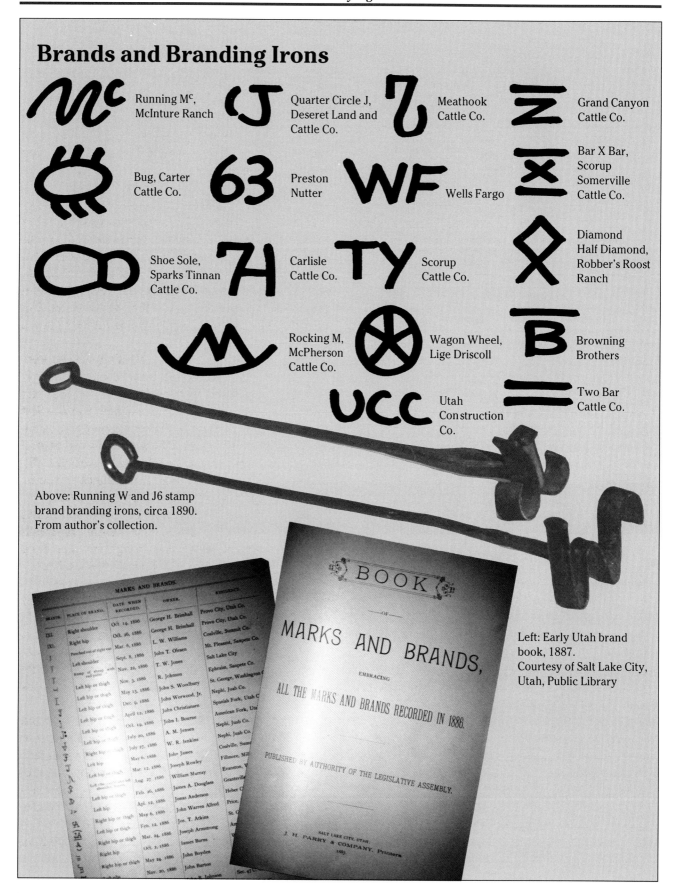

Running M^c, McInture Ranch

Quarter Circle J, Deseret Land and Cattle Co.

Meathook Cattle Co.

Grand Canyon Cattle Co.

Bug, Carter Cattle Co.

Preston Nutter

Wells Fargo

Bar X Bar, Scorup Somerville Cattle Co.

Shoe Sole, Sparks Tinnan Cattle Co.

Carlisle Cattle Co.

Scorup Cattle Co.

Diamond Half Diamond, Robber's Roost Ranch

Rocking M, McPherson Cattle Co.

Wagon Wheel, Lige Driscoll

Browning Brothers

Utah Construction Co.

Two Bar Cattle Co.

Above: Running W and J6 stamp brand branding irons, circa 1890. From author's collection.

Left: Early Utah brand book, 1887. Courtesy of Salt Lake City, Utah, Public Library

Colonel John Tinnin had come to the Utah territory in the early 1860s and worked as a cattle buyer for the Salt Lake City–based Ingram and Company. The Ingram and Company held its cattle in the vicinity of Goose Creek in northwestern Utah, and consequently John Tinnan became very familiar with the wide-open cattle range in the area. John bought out the Winecup outfit and a smaller outfit known as the HD from a Mr. Downing in the late 1870s. A short time later he persuaded his long-time friend and Texas cattleman John Sparks to relocate at Thousand Springs.[39]

In 1882 John Tinnin and John Sparks bought out Mr. Harrell's Shoesole outfit, and in 1883 the Sparks-Tinnin outfit was being hailed in the country newspapers as the largest individually owned cattle operation in the entire West.[40] Their cattle ranged on lush mountain meadows during the spring and summer, and then were drifted down to the low-lying sage and grass valleys during the winter. Thousands of the older and hardier cattle were driven onto the sparsely vegetated Bonneville Salt Flats to eke out a living during the winter.

Severe droughts during the years of 1886 through 1891 depleted up to 65 percent of the herds, a loss which John Tinnin was unable to absorb. John sold his interest in the company to A. J. Harrell, the son of the original owner of the Shoesole, Jasper Harrell. Sparks and Harrell ran the ranch until 1908. They sold out at that time to a group of Ogden businessmen, who changed the name of the company to the Vineyard Land and Stock Company.[41] John Sparks went on to become governor of the State of Nevada.

The Crandall family of Springville, Utah, was involved in both railroad building and cattle ranching. The father, Martin P. Crandall, contracted to grade roads for the Union Pacific Railroad in Weber Canyon and for the Denver and Rio Grande Western Railroad near Colton, Utah. Martin and his sons, Edward Mix (Brig), Myron, and Milan, invested the capital from railroad building into land and cattle. The family owned ranches near Clear Lake, Springville, Colton, and Thompson Springs. The Clear Lake Ranch was purchased in 1884 from the Ketchum family, who would later become infamous outlaws.[42]

The last cattle baron discussed in this chapter may, in fact, have been Utah's first cattle baron.

English-born William Jennings came to America in the 1850s with little more than his burning desire to seek his fortune. He met a Mormon girl and married her, consequently finding himself in Utah amongst the Mormons. He soon established a butcher shop and tannery in Salt Lake City and was instrumental in bringing the first post–Civil War Texas longhorn cattle to Utah Territory.

In a sense, Williams Jennings was more a cattle broker than a cattle rancher. He preferred to purchase cattle and slaughter them, or have them driven to the mining towns of Nevada, rather than to raise the cattle on the range. He did, however, maintain a herd of 3,000 cattle at all times to insure that he would be able to fulfill any orders on a moment's notice.

William Jennings did not limit his business ventures to cattle, branching out into the railroad, banking, and merchandising businesses. In 1864 he established the Eagle Emporium, which was the first department store in Utah. This company was eventually absorbed by the Mormon church–owned Zion's Cooperative Mercantile Institution (ZCMI). Jennings was successful in all his business ventures, and is considered to be Utah's first millionaire.[43]

Most of the men who became cattle barons during the 1870s and early 1880s began humbly and built their empires through sound judgment and hard work. Many of them—John White, Preston Nutter, and the McIntyres—were working cowboys who made it big. Judge William Carter, Alexander Toponce and William Jennings were able to build their cattle empires with the help of and in conjunction with freighting and mining ventures. Lord Elliot had money to start with and bought himself a cattle empire. He did, however, have the tenacity to work on the land and to develop his kingdom.

During the mid-1880s a new kind of cattle baron came into being. Instead of forging out a kingdom with sweat, tears and blood, they simply invested their money. These investors rarely visited their empires and were satisfied merely knowing their financial resources were creating the greatest cattle venture known to man. It was the time of the corporate cattle kings, and they created the heyday of the American cowboy.

4

The Corporate Cattle Companies

When the Sioux Indian wars abated in the late 1870s, millions of acres of virgin grasslands in Wyoming, Montana, and the Dakotas were thrown open for settlement. Unlike the 1860s and 1870s when small-time cattlemen came to the virgin ranges of the West in hopes of becoming cattle barons, this newly opened range became the playground of capitalists with money to spend and a desire to cash in on the cattle business. While western promoters were extolling the virtues of the land and promoting the cattle business with tales of quick profits and rich rewards, mining and railroad tycoons, together with bankers and serious investors from as far away as England and Scotland, were lining up to get in on the action. As one eastern investor aptly put it, "You couldn't keep me out."[1]

Almost overnight great cattle kingdoms were formed in the elaborate board rooms of the East and Europe. Ranch managers were secured, thousands of animals purchased, and some of the greatest livestock companies of all time were formed. By the mid-1880s the move to establish corporate cattle empires had spread throughout much of the West with such names as the Swan Land and Cattle Company, the Prairie Cattle Company, Ten in Texas, Anglo-American, Aztec, Bay State, and the great Matador Cattle Company. Many of these companies

Walter Eugene "Latigo" Gordon circa 1883. He was foreman for the Carlisle Cattle Company. Photograph courtesy of Elaine Turner.

were soon running in excess of 125,000 head of cattle.

The cattle being used to stock these great ranches were coming primarily from Texas, Oregon, and Utah. According to Edgar Beecher Bronson, annual drives from these states were ". . . doubling, increasing at a rate that made it sure that ranges would soon become so badly overcrowded that profitable breeding and beef-fattening would no longer be possible."[2] It would be impossible to determine just how many cattle were driven out of Utah to stock these ranches, but it must have been impressive. Hi Bernard, who at one time worked for the Swan outfit and later was employed as a cattle buyer for some of the larger outfits in Wyoming, led a group of cowboys to Kelton, Utah, where they gathered 16,000 head of cattle to be driven to Wyoming.[3] Perhaps that was the greatest single cattle drive ever to originate from Utah.

The giant corporations bought out small cattle operators and tried legally to obtain large amounts of rangeland. At times, though, the cattle companies were not opposed to moving onto the range by force. This was best accomplished by placing thousands of cattle on the range and allowing them to literally absorb any small cattle herds. The small-time operator could look for his cattle, but this was a long-drawn-out process, especially when many of the large cattle companies employed cowboys of the carefree, gunslinging type.

Although Utah was well stocked with cattle by

Joe Farrer at the Jim McPherson's Rocking M Ranch in the 1900's. Farrer was a prominent Provo, Utah, banker who invested in the cattle business. Photograph courtesy of Don Wilcox.

mid-1880, a number of large corporate cattle companies chose to move cattle onto Utah ranges. These companies prospered for a number of years and made a profit. But when droughts, low cattle prices, and general hard times took their toll on the open-range cattle business, these companies were the first to pull up stakes and leave. Still, some of the most exciting and colorful cowboy history in the territory was created during the two decades of their existence.

The greatest concentration of corporate cattle companies in Utah Territory developed along the Utah-Colorado border. In 1884 the *Wyoming Livestock Journal* observed that "the entire range country is full of stock except in very few localities." "There is room," it added, "for a few cattle west of the main ridge of the Rockies in Colorado and Utah."[4] Included in this region were the verdant grasslands along the slopes of the La Sal and Blue mountains in the San Juan country of southeastern Utah. Some cattlemen claimed this area to be the finest grazing land in the entire southwest.

The first large cattle company to come into this area was the Lacy Cattle Company, better known as "The LC outfit." Because the company made little effort to obtain legal right to the lands it claimed, information concerning the company and its capitalization is not available. In any case, the company had sufficient assets to accumulate a herd of between 20,000 and 25,000 head of cattle during the sixteen years it operated in Utah.[5]

The LC outfit located along Montezuma Creek, a tributary to the San Juan River. Almost from the beginning of its stay in Utah, the LC outfit was violence prone. Shortly after arriving on Montezuma Creek, the owner, I. W. Lacy, was killed in a brawl at Fort Lewis, Colorado. During 1884 and 1887 several cowboys working for the LC were either wounded or killed by hostile Indians. Later the foreman of the outfit, Bill Ball, was killed while attempting to apprehend two horse thieves. There was trouble as well between the LC outfit and the Mormons who had settled Bluff City in 1880. The trouble involved range rights, and although no violence erupted be-

Breaking a horse circa 1900. The big outfits hired full-time wranglers to break and train horses for working range cattle. Photograph from author's collection.

tween the two groups, there were periods of time when it might have flared up.

The Bluff settlers had come to San Juan at the request of Brigham Young in an effort to extend Mormon influence into the southeastern corner of Utah. At first the Mormons sought to establish a farming economy, but soon they realized the area was more suited for livestock grazing. The Mormons' decision to enter the cattle business was hastened when the LC cowboys began bringing cattle to the summer ranges on Elk Mountain west of Bluff. At the same time the Mormons formed the Bluff Cattle Pool and advertised for fellow Mormons to bring their cattle to the ranges west of Bluff.

The LC outfit allowed at least 4,000 head of its cattle to spill over into the Bluff Cattle Pool's range, and the Mormons went to the county courts to get the cattle removed. Apparently the LC Company did not want to test the Mormon-influenced court and backed off the grazing lands claimed by the Bluff Cattle Pool. The victory was short-lived, however, for in the winter of 1887–88 a Texas cattle outfit, led

by a Mr. Gahleger, drove 2,000 head of longhorn cattle to Comb Wash in the very heart of the Bluff Cattle Pool's winter range. The company settled on the Rincon west of Bluff and totally ignored the Mormons' claim to prior rights of the range. In the spring the Texans moved their cattle to the Elk Mountains and belligerently began calling their outfit "The Elk Mountain Cattle Company."[6]

Mr. Gahleger offered to sell the poor-quality cattle to the Mormons at an inflated price, which the Mormons refused. Instead, the Mormons began to influence local Indians to establish permanent camps along the drift avenues to the Elk Mountains, thus creating an obstacle for the cattle that naturally drifted from the winter range to summer pastures. The Mormons also established permanent ranches at key meadows and passes of the mountains to discourage the Texans.[7]

The Texas cowboys retaliated by riding into Bluff shooting their six-guns into the air and threatening the settlers. In a rare show of force, the Mormons told the cowboys that the next time they came into

Branding calves near La Sal, Utah, circa 1900. Photograph courtesy of Carol Hines.

Bluff with drawn guns they would be met by the Mormons' drawn guns.[8] The threat must have worked because in 1888 the Texans were willing to sell their cattle to the Bluff Pool at a much better price.

Once the offensive started, the Mormons, who were then being referred to as "The Bluff Tigers,"[9] turned their attention to the prime rangeland spreading out from the Blue Mountains. This country was claimed by the L C outfit and the Carlisle outfit, the latter one of the most colorful of all Utah cattle companies. The official name of the Carlisle company was the Kansas and New Mexico Land and Cattle Company. The company came to Utah in 1883 and began buying up all the small cattle operators around the Blue Mountains with $720,000 of British capital. Primary stockholders in the company were two English brothers, Harold and Edmund Carlisle.[10] Unlike many of the other foreign investors who never came west, the Carlisles were active cattle buyers and lived on their ranch holdings.

"Latigo" Gordon at Moab, Utah, circa 1915. Photograph courtesy of Elaine Turner.

The main headquarters of the Carlisle company was at the Double Cabins, seven miles north of present-day Monticello. Although the company had cattle in both Kansas and New Mexico—hence the name—the Utah operation was, by far, the biggest. At its peak the company had eleven different brands registered in Utah, the most famous of which was the "Three-Bar," which consisted of a bar on the hip, side, and shoulder of the cattle. Because of the brand, the company has also been known as the "Hip-side and Shoulder Cattle Company." In its heyday the Carlisle cattle company had at least 30,000 head of cattle on the Utah range, and there is some indication this figure could have gone much higher.[11]

Long-time foreman for the Carlisle outfit was Eugene "Latigo" Gordon. Born in North Carolina in 1865, Gordon worked on ranches in Kansas and Texas before drifting into Utah in the 1880s. He was a typical Texas cowboy, tough minded, fearless and gun toting. He was not only a top-notch cowboy, but he also had a good mind for business. In an effort to keep the eighty-odd cowboys working the Carlisle range happy, he built a saloon called "The Blue Goose." This establishment became the most famous

Cowboys at Bluff, Utah, circa 1900. The "Bluff Tigers" were a force to be reckoned with during the 1880s. Photograph courtesy of University of Utah Libraries, Special Collections Department.

watering hole in the southeast corner of Utah.[12]

In 1887 a party of Mormons from Bluff moved into the heart of the Carlisle cattle range for the purpose of establishing a settlement, thus gaining more control of the San Juan region. The party of settlers were met by a group of Carlisle cowboys who gave them an ultimatum—leave the area or suffer the consequences. The Mormons had no reason to believe the cowboys would not keep their word. The year before Carlisle cowboys had killed a sheepherder near Farmington, New Mexico. At the time of this incident the governor of New Mexico made the following statement: "I have, officially and otherwise, sufficient information to satisfy me that the Carlisle Cattle Company is what is known in common parlance as a 'hurrah outfit,' reckless, and to a degree, irresponsible."[13]

Rather than heed the warning of the Carlisle cowboys, the Mormons chose to stay and hold their ground. During the summer of 1887 the Navajos and Paiutes had initiated hostile actions. The cowboys and Mormons alike had requested protection from the military post at Fort Lewis, Colorado. Two detachments of troops were sent to Utah, one stationed at the mouth of Recapture Wash on the San Juan River and the other at Soldier Spring one and one-half miles south of Monticello.[14]

The army had sent troops into the area on a number of occasions. In 1881 Utes had killed three cowboys near the La Sal Mountains. A posse of cowboys

Photograph of an unknown cowboy near Monticello, Utah, in the 1880s. He is typical of the Texas cowboys that came to the cattle ranges of southeastern Utah in the 1880s. Photograph from author's collection.

from Colorado chased the Indians to the Pinhook Valley northeast of Moab, and, in a major battle, eight of the cowboys were killed. Two more men from Moab were later killed by the fleeing Indians. The army arrived several hours late during this conflict. Again in 1884 the army came when two prospectors were killed in Monument Valley. The army and a posse of cowboys chased the Indians to White Canyon, northwest of Bluff, where a short battle took place. A cowboy and a government scout were killed at that time. The trouble in 1887 began with the killing of a Mormon settler by Navajo Indians at Rincon on the San Juan River, and other hostile Indians killed an LC cowboy on the slopes of the Blue Mountains.

The presence of federal troops in southeastern Utah prevented the Carlisle cowboys from carrying out their threats. The Mormons established the town of Monticello on the northeast edge of the Blue Mountains not more than seven miles from the Carlisle headquarters. By the time the army returned to Colorado, Monticello was well established, much to the consternation of both the Carlisle cattle company and the LC outfit.

Trouble between the Mormons and the Gentile cattle companies continued for a number of years. The Mormons laid claim to the water running off the Blue Mountains and dug a canal into Monticello. Armed cowboys dammed the canal and threatened to shoot any Mormon who tried to remove the dam.

Pink Trout, who worked for the cattle outfits around Monticello, Utah, later operated his own outfit. Photograph courtesy of Carol Hines.

The Mormons, holding political clout in the county, were able to get legal rights to at least half of the water.[15]

During this range war, cowboys rode into Monticello and shot up the town on numerous occasions. They weren't looking to kill anyone, they just wanted to scare the Mormons. On many occasions, though, they did kill Mormon cattle. One young cowboy who had gone to work for the Carlisle outfit after most of the violence had occurred claimed that an old Carlisle cowboy "took me to a swale and pointed to a pile of bones bleaching in the sun. 'See what happens to Mormon cattle when they come on our range,' he said with an oath, 'there was 300 head in that bunch.' "[16]

The Mormons tried to placate the cowboys and invited them to their social dances. On one occasion

A cowboy in the slickrock country of southeastern Utah circa 1900. Photograph from author's collection.

there were just too many cowboys to fit into the dance hall at once. In an effort to be fair, the Mormons gave out numbers and allowed a few cowboys in at a time. A cowboy by the name of Tom Roach didn't like that idea and barged into the dance. When some Mormons asked him to leave, Roach pulled out his revolver and demanded that the band strike up the music. A fellow cowboy tried to reason with Roach and was shot dead for his efforts. Once the shooting began, all hell broke loose and a Mormon lady, Mrs. Jane Walton, was killed by a stray bullet.[17]

The shootings at the dance are the only known Mormon deaths at the hands of area cowboys, but on another occasion several cowboys who had been drinking at the Blue Goose came into town and began shooting at the school bell. When the children started to scream, the cowboys shot out the schoolhouse windows. Another time two cowboys in a drunken stupor, Kid Jackson and Bill Johnson, went to Bishop Frederic Jones's house to shoot him. While walking down the road Kid Jackson fell into a ditch, but Johnson continued on to the house. Bishop Jones had decided in his mind that he would shoot the cowboy if he appeared and said a quiet prayer as the staggering cowboy approached. "O Lord, if You don't want me to kill that man, stop him before he gets here. I'll kill him if he comes."[18]

Just as Bill Johnson approached the bishop's house a shot rang out. Bill turned around and saw Kid Jackson take playful aim at him to get off another shot. At that, Bill forgot his original errand, walked back to the ditch where he and Kid Jackson wrestled for a moment and then collapsed.

Relations between the Mormons and the Gentile cowboys in and around Monticello and Bluff continued to be strained for the next several years. There were many other killings in the area, but, in most instances, they occurred between cowboys who were feeling the effects of too much red-eye whiskey. One took place when two cowboys under the influence came riding into Monticello. They had been quarreling as they rode and suddenly one pulled his gun and fired two shots, each of which passed precariously close to the other fellow's ears. The recipient of the two shots threw his hat at the other cowboy and swore, "You son of a bitch, you

The Carlisle ranch house near Monticello, Utah. The house burned down in 1915. Photograph courtesy of Elaine Turner.

ain't killed me yet."[19] A third shot rang out and hit the poor fellow right between the eyes.

Unlike the LC outfit, it appears that the Carlisle company made an effort to obtain their land legally. This company, like many of the corporate outfits, used what was known as a "rubber forty" technique, which allowed them to control vast amounts of land because they controlled the strategic water holes and streams. They accomplished this by having company cowboys file homesteading claims with the county courts. Homesteaders were allowed up to 160 acres of land if they could prove they could bring water to the land. It was then possible for the companies to own or control key portions of land, which virtually locked-up hundreds of thousands of acres of open range.[20]

In an effort to keep out pesky homesteaders and sheepmen, the corporate companies began fencing

Many cowboys like this one courted and married local women. Photograph taken at Orangeville, Utah, in the 1890s. Photograph courtesy of Rell Francis.

the land with barbed wire. This was a reversal from when the wire was first invented to keep cattle off of the Kansas farmlands. By the late 1880s the cattle companies were using millions of feet of the wire to keep out the farmers. The Carlisles began using barbed wire on the lands they claimed in the late 1880s.[21] One of the fences cut off the main road leading into the town of Monticello. The Mormons went to court over this issue, but the Carlisles won out and the road course was changed.

Although the Carlisle and LC outfits made a gallant effort to control their cattle kingdoms, the forces of change were too great. Farmers and sheepmen were unrelenting in their bids to occupy the land. Cattle rustlers in the country were also taking a toll on corporate coffers. As cattle prices began dropping in the 1890s, together with drought and poor range conditions, it was time for the corporate cattle companies to move on. In 1896 both the Carlisle and LC outfits moved out of Utah. The Carlisle company sold several thousand head of cattle locally and drove an estimated 30,000 head

A young man preparing to break a horse near La Sal, Utah, circa 1910. Photograph courtesy of Carol Hines.

out of the territory to Albuquerque, New Mexico. The LC Company sold several thousand head locally and drove an estimated 22,000 head of cattle to Dolores, Colorado.[22]

Some of the cowboys on these big outfits ended up marrying Mormon girls and decided to remain in Utah. The colorful "Latigo" Gordon was one who opted to stay. Gordon bought the ranch buildings and several thousand deeded acres from the Carlisles, including the white house on the main ranch a few miles north of Monticello. Even though many of the Mormons accepted Gordon and even came to his defense when he was arrested in a shooting incident with a local official, the wounds of the range war ran deep. It was rumored that some of the locals wanted him out of the area and, in fact, Gordon was ambushed and severely wounded. The two men who shot Gordon were never apprehended. Some time later the beautiful white house burnt to the ground, and arson was not ruled out. In 1915 Gordon decided to sell his holdings and he moved his family to Moab. He died in Ogden, Utah, in 1937.[23]

Robert Allen worked the cattle ranges near Moab, Utah. Photograph taken at the Savage Studio in Salt Lake City in the 1880s. Photograph courtesy of Blaine M. Yorgason.

Another corporate cattle company which came to the southeast cattle ranges of Utah in the 1880s and eventually sold out to local interests was the Pittsburgh Land and Cattle Company. Unlike the Carlisle company, the PCC seemed to work at getting along with the Mormons, and the management became involved with political and social issues which took into account the needs of both the cattlemen and the local farmers. Cowboys riding for the company, however, were typical range riders who drank too heavily during their trips to the Moab saloons. Consequently, Moab citizens were treated, from time to time, to horse racing and gunplay on the main street running through the town.

The PCC was organized in 1884 by a group of Pennsylvania businessmen who sent Charles H. Ogden and James Blood to southeastern Utah for the purpose of buying cattle and land. Within a year Ogden and Blood had bought out the interests of several cattlemen, including the Rays, the Maxwells, the McCartys, and Green Robinson. The company adopted the "Cross H" brand which had belonged to Green Robinson, and by the latter 1880s between 15,000 and 20,000 head of cattle were wearing the Cross H. Main headquarters for the cattle company was located at La Sal, which lies on the southern slopes of the La Sal Mountains.[24]

Ballard cowboys in camp on the East Tavaputs Plateau in the 1890s. Photograph courtesy of G. Ballard.

J. M. Cunningham was the PCC manager and Thomas B. Carpenter was the company foreman. These two men operated the company in a superb manner and were able to provide the Pennsylvania businessmen with a tidy profit for several years. However, during the 1890s, as cattle prices dropped and competition for the range became more acute, the eastern businessmen opted to sell out. Cunningham and Carpenter, along with a fellow named Fred N. Prewer, bought the PCC and changed the name to the La Sal Cattle Company. The company continued to use the Cross H brand.

In 1898 Cunningham and Carpenter bought out Fred Prewer and changed the name to the Cunningham and Carpenter Cattle Company. Still known as the Cross H outfit, the company expanded into the

Ephraim Moore, David Perkins, and Felix Murphy at Moab, Utah, circa 1896. Photograph courtesy of Verona Stocks.

Book Cliff Mountains and brought in a herd of sheep, which were beginning to dominate some of the cattle ranges by the late 1890s. The company continued to operate under Cunningham and Carpenter until they sold out to a group of local businessmen led by Lemuel H. Redd and J. A. Scorup in 1914.[25]

The area between the La Sal Mountains and the Book Cliff Mountains, known as the Grand River Valley, was dominated for a time by a family from England. The Ballard brothers, Harry and Arthur, established a cattle herd in the vicinity of present-day Thompson, which was originally known as Thompson Springs. It was founded by the Ballards, who owned several businesses in the town. The Rio Grande Railroad came through Thompson in 1883, which furthered the importance of the town as a livestock center.

Although Harry Ballard's interest centered on cattle and several businesses in Thompson, he was

Rocking M cowboys at the Jim McPherson Ranch north of Green River, Utah, circa 1900. Photograph courtesy of Don Wilcox.

also active in prospecting. He discovered coal in the Book Cliff Mountains and made quite a bit of money with his mining interests. Having a great deal of wealth, Harry was able to build his cattle kingdom to a considerable size. This included much of the land around Thompson, land in the Book Cliff Mountains, and several thousand acres near the railroad town of Cisco.

The Ballard Cattle Company was sold to the Turner brothers in 1911. The Turners operated the Lazy Y Cross Ranch with its main headquarters at Cisco for many years until it was broken up in the 1950s.[26]

The vast East and West Tavaputs plateaus in eastern Utah, called collectively the Book Cliff Mountains, were used by several cattle companies over the years. Already mentioned in an earlier chapter were the Whitmore Cattle Company, Big Springs Ranch, and Nutter Corporation. Several other cattle companies were significant to this region.

In the late 1880s Jim McPherson drove several thousand cattle to Florence Creek on the East Tavaputs. He soon realized that this area was utilized by various outlaw gangs, including the Wild Bunch, to graze their horses and stolen cattle. In order to survive, Jim had to tolerate the outlaw element that frequented his ranch, and although he maintained his integrity and honest dealings, he was known to have good friends amongst the outlaw element.[27]

Jim left Florence Creek for a spell, married, and made his home in Heber, Utah. When the outlaw element had finally been cleared from the area he returned to his ranch and raised his family. In 1927 he sold the ranch to his son-in-law, Ray (Budge) Wilcox. It was bought in 1942 by the government when the Uintah Ute Reservation boundaries were extended.[28]

The most mysterious of all big corporate cattle companies in Utah was the Webster City Cattle Company. Founded in the 1880s by a group of Webster

Cowboys from the Ballard outfit pose in front of the water tower at Thompson Springs, Utah, in the 1890s. Photograph courtesy of Pearl Baker.

City, Iowa, businessmen, the company became the biggest cattle operation on the Book Cliff Mountains. The home ranch was located at the head of Hill Creek high in the Book Cliffs, approximately twenty miles north of Thompson. The outfit was run by Clarence Knight, who managed the building of a small town to accommodate the large number of cowboys working for the company. The main bunkhouse was so elaborate that the cowboys took to calling it "The Webster City Hotel." Cabins were also built to accommodate the cowboys who were married. The general store and saloon known as the "Commissary" ofttimes doubled as a school for the employees' children.[29]

The main cattle brand used by Webster City was the "Bar Flying V Bar." Just how many cattle the outfit ran has not been recorded, but it must have been a considerable amount. In 1884 Stephen Washburn Chipman moved his cattle from Emery County to Grand County just outside of Thompson Springs. Keeping in mind that Harry Ballard was running several thousand head of cattle, the comments made by Chipman are significant regarding the Webster City outfit. Chipman wrote in his diary the following: "Herefords were first introduced into Castle Valley by William Jennings, a prominent merchant of Salt Lake City and the outstanding cattleman and leading horse and hog man in Utah at that time. His best Herefords were bought by the Webster City Cattle Company, the only cattle outfit of any size at that time."[30]

When Preston Nutter had to sell his Utah holdings in 1893, the Webster City Company bought his cattle for a sum of $58,740. Five thousand cattle changed hands. The cattle were tally branded at the time with a bar placed over Nutter's "63" brand. Correspondence between Nutter and his lawyer in the late 1890s indicates that the Webster City Cattle Company continued to use the Bar 63 brand on some of its stock and actually registered the brand. This action caused quite a problem between Webster City and Preston Nutter.[31]

Rocking M roundup crew circa 1900. Photograph courtesy of Don Wilcox.

The Webster City headquarters was located on the outlaw trail that ran from Brown's Park to the Robber's Roost in Wayne County. Although Clarence Knight never intended it to be so, the town became a stopover for many famous outlaws. The cattle company was also plagued by cattle rustling. Mr. Fullerton, foreman, indicated that the rustlers were not just satisfied to run off a steer or two, but were running whole herds off the range. In an effort to stem the rustling activity, Fullerton began hiring known rustlers and outlaws in hopes they would not rob the company that fed them. It was rumored that Butch Cassidy, Elzy Lay, and the Sundance Kid worked for Webster City for a spell. These outlaws were not rustlers at the time of employment but had moved on to robbing banks and trains. Old-timers claim that while Cassidy and his fellow outlaws were working for Webster City, the rustling activity appeared to be nonexistent.[32]

At least three well-known shoot-outs took place on the Webster City Cattle Company range. On May 13, 1898, a posse under Sheriff C. W. Allred of Price gunned down Joe Walker and John Herring between Horsecorn Canyon and Wolf Flat. On April 17, 1900, a combined posse from Vernal and Moab killed Flat Nose George Curry on the banks of the Green River. The fatal shot to Curry's head was delivered by either Clarence King, manager of Webster City, or Sheriff Jesse M. "Jack" Tyler, sheriff of Moab. Both men claimed they fired the fatal shot. On May 26, 1900, Sheriff Tyler and his deputy, Sam Jenkins, were gunned down on the banks of Hill Creek between Death Point and Wolf Flat. The two lawmen were killed by the outlaw Kid Curry and it may have been in retaliation for the killing of Flat Nose George Curry.[33]

Numerous authors mention the Webster City Cattle Company, as do local newspapers during the 1890s. Strangely, other than brand record books, county records are nonexistent concerning the company. No recorded history of it has been found and yet it must have been one of the biggest cattle companies in eastern Utah. Conservative estimates of the number of cattle Webster City ran would be from 25,000 to 35,000 head. Webster City began selling off its holdings in the late 1890s. Carpenter and Cunningham purchased land from it as did the Taylors from Moab. Webster City registered its brand in Utah as late as 1912, but there are no subsequent entries in the brand books.

Rocking M cowboy with a dead coyote circa 1900. Photograph courtesy of Don Wilcox.

At least three other large cattle companies operated in the Book Cliff Mountains prior to the turn of the century. Unfortunately, little history has been recorded about them. The Range Valley Cattle Company registered a brand at Woodside, Utah, in 1884. This company was also started by a group of businessmen from Iowa. The company ran its cattle on the West Tavaputs Plateau in Range Valley. Preston Nutter moved onto the summer pastures used by Range Valley in 1901. A small range war occurred between the two outfits before Range Valley decided to pull up stakes and leave.[34]

The Dolores Cattle Company registered a brand at Moab (then in Emery County) in 1884. This company operated along the Utah-Colorado border north of the La Sal Mountains and into the Book Cliff Mountains. The Kramer and Marble Cattle Company was established by two Englishmen in the extreme western edge of the Book Cliffs. These two men helped establish the town of Colton, which became an important shipping point along the Rio Grande Railroad.[35]

The Utah-Colorado border north of the Book Cliff Mountains had several corporate cattle companies with much better histories. The K Ranch, located east of Jensen, Utah, was established in 1873 by Dr. Keiser. A Texan, Dr. Keiser and his partner, whose name was Gilson, drove 1,300 longhorns from Texas to Brown's Park during the fall of 1872. They wintered the cattle in the Park and the following spring moved them to the Jensen area.

In 1880 Dr. Keiser and Gilson sold their ranch holdings and cattle to a Jewish businessman, Charles Popper, who lived in New York City but who had several businesses in Salt Lake City, including a butcher shop. Popper bought several thousand more cattle and had them driven to the K Ranch. Popper never lived on the ranch, but came out from time to time to inspect his holdings.

Hyrum Meeks, general foreman of the K Ranch, worked with the company until it was sold in 1908. Meeks then went to live in Vernal where he spent some time as city marshal. At the time of the sale approximately 2,000 head of cattle were wearing the K brand. This was a small fraction of the several thousand cattle owned by Charles Popper during the 1880s and 1890s. The ranch changed hands several times over the years, and continues to operate at the present time.[36]

The Red Butte Cattle Company operated seven

Roping a big steer, Springville, Utah, circa 1910. Photograph courtesy of Brigham Young University, Photo Archives.

miles east of Jensen and was established by a group of New York businessmen in the 1880s. The company summered their cattle on Blue Mountain, which straddles the Utah-Colorado border north of Jensen. Their winter range reached as far south as Ouray, at the confluence of the Green and Duchesne rivers.

There are some indications that the Red Butte Ranch and the K Ranch were the settings for a book written by Julie Opp Fabersham and Edwin Royal, entitled *Squaw Man*. Aaron Daniels, a local cowman, and his Indian wife were supposedly the inspiration for this novel.

In the 1890s Frank Bourdette bought the home ranch of Red Butte and changed its name to the Dugout Ranch. Bourdette always smoked a pipe and kept the tobacco for the pipe in his vest pocket. One day Bourdette and some fellow cowboys were sitting around in a line cabin when the pipe he was smoking exploded. Bourdette had thought one of the other cowboys had shot the pipe out of his mouth until he realized that one of the .22 bullets he

Photograph of Hyrum Meeks taken in the 1880s. Photograph courtesy of Doris Burton.

kept in his other vest pocket had somehow gotten mixed in with the tobacco he had tamped down inside the pipe. It was a good smoke until the heat caused the .22 bullet to go off.[37]

The Bar A H Cattle Company also summered cattle on Blue Mountain and wintered them in the vicinity of the junction of the White and Green rivers in east-central Utah. Established around 1875 by Abram Hatch, the company was described as a "three thousand cow outfit."[38] Pardon Dodds was the first foreman of the company.

The Bar A H was sold to the Lazy Y Cattle Company of Rangely, Colorado, around 1913. In 1915 the company was sold to three bankers from Vernal, Utah. The Lazy Y probably ran in excess of 20,000 head of cattle. One year 10,000 calves were branded. After the Bar A H and Lazy Y merged there were too many cattle to trail together off of Blue Mountain so the herd was split.[39] Operating on a much smaller scale today, the Lazy Y and the K Ranch are owned by the Carl Kent family of Dinosaur, Colorado.

Another ranch straddling the Utah-Colorado line was the Luxen and Brown Cattle Company. Joe Luxen and Sam Brown had come to Ashley Valley

Cowboys camped near Jensen, Utah, in the 1880s. Photograph courtesy of Ila Cowans.

with the military in 1881. Both men were civilian mule skinners and soon quit the army after arriving in Utah. In 1882 the two men opened a saloon near Fort Thornburgh and a few months later moved the saloon to Ashley Town, which was near the present town of Vernal, Utah. The saloon business was good and brought in a lot of money for the two business-men. With their new-found wealth, Luxen and Brown bought several thousand cattle and formed a cattle company that ranged cattle in Ashley Valley and on Blue Mountain. The company also estab-lished a ranch on the White River near Rangely, Colorado. It prospered for many years until portions were sold off at the turn of the century.

Joe Luxen and Sam Brown also expanded their merchandising business in Vernal when they built the Big Elephant store. This general merchandise store occupied a two-story brick building and for some time was known as one of the finest stores in eastern Utah and western Colorado.[40]

A 10,000-head cattle outfit, which operated south of Jensen along the Utah-Colorado border, was the U C Cattle Company. The company branded both

horses and cattle with an iron in the shape of a keystone and became locally known as the Keystone Outfit. The company also used its initials—"UCC"—on the left shoulder, side, and hip of the cattle.

In 1900 Teddy Roosevelt used the headquarters of the UCC as a base for a mountain lion hunting expe-dition. During the time Roosevelt spent in the moun-tains in all probability he pondered the beauty and isolation of the western wilderness as an area which needed to be preserved for future generations.[41] During his first term as president of the United States, he took steps to preserve the forest lands of America by signing the Forest Reserve Act.

There were three large ranches that operated on the east end of Blue Mountain in Colorado during the latter part of the nineteenth century. The Two-Bar, operated by Ora Haley; the Two-Circle Bar, operated by Sam Cary; and the Sevens, operated by the Pierce brothers, were primarily Colorado outfits, but their ranges did extend across the Utah border. Each of these outfits were running between 15,000 and 25,000 head of cattle. These companies and

Cowboys Alfred Hall and Net Blackburn at Dry Forks, Utah, circa 1900. Photograph courtesy of Dan Hall.

cattle companies across the Utah border joined forces during roundups and many of the cowboys working for the Colorado companies came from Utah. Two cowboys in particular who made their names known on both sides of the border were Jim Robinson and Marcus Jensen. Jim rode for the Two-Bar for a number of years and finally settled down on his own ranch in Jensen, Utah. Marcus Jensen rode for the A. H. Ranch, UCC outfit, Brown's Park Cattle Company, and the Nutter Ranch before settling down in Jensen.[42]

The next largest concentration of corporate cattle companies in Utah was in Box Elder, Weber, Cache, and Rich counties. Much of the land in this area was awarded to the railroads, and consequently large tracts of land were available for purchase by the corporate cattle giants.

The largest of these cattle empires and the largest cattle kingdom ever to exist within the confines of Utah Territory was the Golden State Land and Livestock Company, better known locally as the Bar M outfit. The owner was an indomitable railroad tycoon by the name of Charles Crocker. He was one of the principal owners of the Central Pacific Railroad and as such acquired vast amounts of railroad land grants. He owned 400,000 acres of land outright and probably controlled three times that amount because he controlled most of the water in Box Elder County. For a time in the 1880s, the Bar M outfit was running 75,000 head of cattle on rangelands that extended from Promontory west to the Nevada border and north across the Idaho border.[43]

Crocker built an eight-bedroom mansion on the home ranch, just one mile north of the famous driving of the Golden Spike, and brought in a bevy of Chinese cooks to cater to the numerous cowboys working on the ranch. The mansion itself was reserved for Crocker when he ventured into Utah for short stays. Usually on these visits he would bring several upper-crust friends and business associates who were desirous of getting a firsthand look at the Wild West.[44]

J. W. Taylor was the first manager of the Bar M outfit. He had previously owned his own cattle spread on the north slopes of the Raft River Mountains. Many of the early settlers in Box Elder County

Plateau cowboys on the Colorado-Utah border circa 1880. Photograph courtesy of Utah State Historical Society.

warned Taylor that the Bar M was running too many cattle and they doubted that the range could support them.[45]

The winter of 1886–87 was one of the worst on record in the West and affected cattlemen throughout the northern states and territories. Utah was not an exception to the severe weather, which saw thousands of cattle die of starvation because they could not paw down to grass under the deep snow. The Bar M lost an estimated 30,000 cattle during the winter.[46] Perhaps many of the settlers of northern Utah who had resented the monopoly of the rangeland by corporate barons found the Bar M losses sweet revenge.

After the severe winter the Bar M kept cattle numbers down into the 45,000-head level. Upon the death of Crocker in the 1890s, the ranch was divided into two companies to better handle the vast stock ranches operating on the property. They became known as the Promontory Ranch Company and the Curlew Ranch Company. The two ranches controlled most of the wells and waterways in Box Elder County, and there was a great push by local citizens

Photograph of Jim Robinson taken in the 1880s. Photograph courtesy of Hoyle Robinson.

to break up the ranches. The Crocker interests refused to sell any portion of the land in small parcels, which caused many problems for the locals. Finally, in 1909, a group of businessmen led by the banking tycoon, David Eccles, bought out the Crocker holdings.[47]

The new owners of the Bar M property formed the Promontory-Curlew Land Company and began advertising parcels of rangeland, dry-farm wheat land, and irrigated land for sale by the acre. In this manner the original Bar M outfit was broken up.[48]

Another cattle company operating in northern Utah was owned by one of the most famous banking and freight businesses in the West. Henry Wells and William G. Fargo had been operating an express business for a number of years prior to buying out Ben Holladay's Overland Stage and Mail Line. With the purchase, Wells Fargo and Company developed a virtual monopoly on express and freight lines between the Missouri River and California. The company also established a vast banking empire with branches in San Francisco, New York, Carson City, Virginia City, Portland, and Salt Lake City.

Manager of the Salt Lake operations of Wells Fargo Bank was John Dooly, who had a keen interest in the cattle business. During his tenure with

The Corporate Cattle Companies

A cowboy and his camp near the Utah-Idaho border circa 1890. Photograph from author's collection.

the bank, John began investing company assets into cattle and land in the vicinity of Avon in Cache Valley. At one time, during the 1890s, the company had several thousand deeded acres of land and was running several thousand head of cattle on this land and the surrounding open range.[49] The Wells Fargo Bank and land acquisitions were sold to the Walker Brothers Banking Company in 1905. Incidentally, some time after the purchase, John Dooly opened his own bank in Ogden.

Several large corporate cattle companies operated in the Bear River Valley along the Utah-Wyoming border near present-day Woodruff during the last century. The Beckwith and Quinn Cattle Company, owned by Chicago businessmen, ran upwards of 20,000 cattle over rangelands that extended from Randolph, Utah, to Cokeville, Wyoming, across the border into Idaho and back into Utah at the southern end of Bear Lake. This outfit broke up in the early nineteen hundreds.[50]

An Evanston, Wyoming, firm, Crawford and Thompson, ranged 12,000 head of cattle along the Bear River near Woodruff, Utah, during much of the

A cowboy at Springville, Utah, in the 1890s. Photograph courtesy of Rell Francis.

latter nineteenth century. This is the company that first used Brown's Park as a permanent winter range in the 1870s. The main ranch headquarters was located just west of Woodruff and was known locally as the Two Bar Outfit. The outfit broke up around the turn of the century when quarreling amongst the officers of the corporation resulted in some untimely deaths.[51]

There were several more companies registering brands in the northeast corner of Utah during the 1800s but little information exists on these companies. Included in this group was the Indiana Land and Livestock Company, the Bear River Land and Livestock Company, and the Echo Land and Livestock Company.

There were a few large corporate cattle operations in southwestern Utah during the 1880s and 1890s, but, as in other parts of the territory, few records of these companies exist. Newspaper accounts mention a company by the name of Bell and Hake operating in Juab County, but county records do not list it. It must have been fairly big because on at least one occasion the company purchased 5,000 head of cattle from the Sparks Cattle Company and drove them to its range in Juab County.[52] Another company which registered a brand in 1884 was the

Ereckson roundup crew at Skull Valley, Utah, circa 1900. Photograph courtesy of Quentin Ereckson.

Utah Nevada Cattle Company, but no records can be found pertaining to this company.

More information is available concerning the ranching enterprise started by the Ereckson Brothers, Henry and Jonas. The brothers went to the California gold fields shortly after their arrival in the Salt Lake Valley in the late 1840s. Finding success in the gold fields, the brothers returned to Salt Lake City and began buying land along the foothills of the Wasatch Mountains.

During the 1870s the Ereckson family, including the son of Jonas, Jonas T., drove a herd of longhorns from Texas to land they owned in Juab County. The cattle operation grew from that point, although the exact number of cattle they owned has not been recorded.

The property of the Ereckson enterprises was divided up at the death of Jonas Ereckson. The

A cowboy at Woodruff, Utah, circa 1910. Note the letter in his shirt pocket. Photograph courtesy of Wallace Schulthess.

property at that time included the ranch in Juab County, a ranch at the mouth of Big Cottonwood Canyon in the Salt Lake Valley, several farms, and a number of businesses in the Murray area near Salt Lake City.[53]

A giant cattle corporation in Beaver County was the Ryan Ream Cattle Company, which first registered the "RR" Brand in Frisco, Utah, in 1884. Several members of the Ryan family formed the company with other investors from Frisco. James Ryan along with Samuel Hawkes discovered the Horn Silver mine, which was the richest silver producer in Utah.[54]

Beginning in 1885 the RR outfit began buying out ranches. They purchased the holdings on Beaver Bottoms from Murdock and Farnsworth, two Beaver, Utah, cattlemen. The transaction included at least 2,500 head of cattle.[55] They then bought out the Pine Grove Ranch southeast of Garrison, Utah, and stocked this ranch with 5,000 head of cattle.[56]

Robert Leroy Parker, who would later become fa-

Cowboys at Salina, Utah, in the 1890s. Photograph courtesy of Rell Francis.

mous as the notorious Butch Cassidy, worked as a cowboy for the RR outfit for a time. Pat Ryan claimed that Parker was a good cowboy but was hard on horses.[57]

At its peak the RR outfit ran 10,000 to 15,000 cattle on open range extending from the Mineral Mountains east of Milford to the Nevada border. Typical of the large corporate cattle companies operating in the West, the outfit ran roughshod over the little ranchers operating in the area.[58] The company broke up sometime around the turn of the century.

Of all the land in Utah, the mountains running down the middle of the territory from Salt Lake City to the Arizona border produced the fewest number of corporate cattle companies. This was the core of the Mormon colonization in Utah and outsiders were not welcome upon the lands which were claimed by individual Mormons and church co-op livestock companies. In their own right, the Canaan

A cowboy in the Bear River Mountains near Woodruff, Utah, in the 1880s. Photograph from author's collection.

Cattle Company and some of the larger co-op companies were utilizing the rangelands to the maximum. There was no free grass for outsiders. A few Gentiles did, however, make some inroads into these vast rangelands.

In 1878 a mining engineer by the name of Ireland came to Salina Canyon to do some surveying. While there, Ireland noticed the lush grasslands on the high mountain slopes. He returned to Park City and persuaded a number of influential businessmen to look at the area for a cattle venture. These men liked what they saw and decided to purchase three existing ranches in the area. The Mountain Ranch, the Oak Springs Ranch, and the Christianson Ranch, comprising some 45,000 deeded acres, were purchased and the Ireland Cattle Company was born.

By using the "rubber forty" method of ranching—allowing employees to claim homesteader rights—the businessmen were able to lock up several hundred thousand acres of open range between the three ranches, and they stocked the range with ten thousand head of cattle.[59] The company registered

Livestock Market

As the corporate cattle companies came into prominence, the business of raising, transporting, and selling livestock became more organized and efficient. Shown are correspondence, advertising, and records. Courtesy of Steve Lacy.

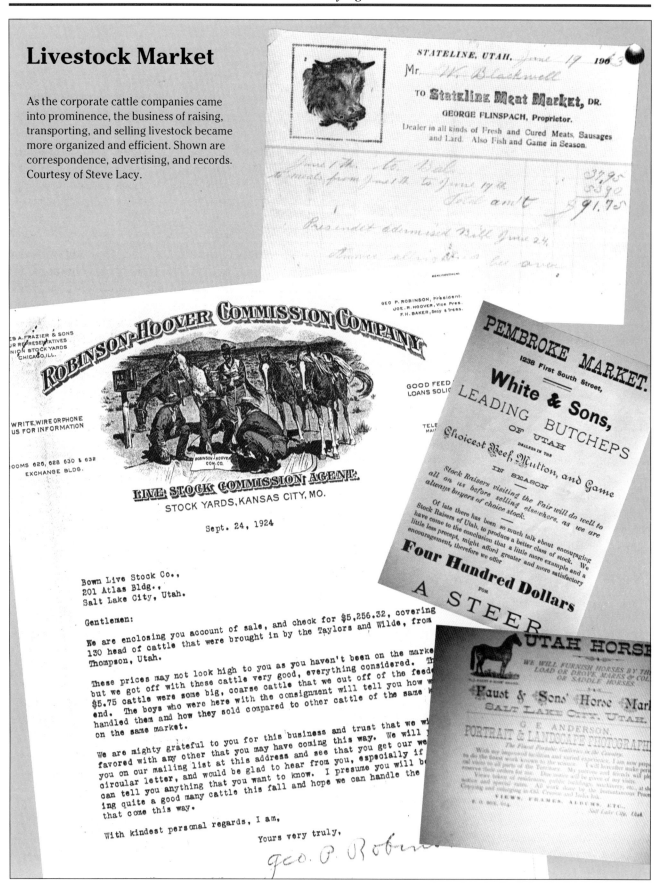

Joe Wagoner at Garrison, Utah, circa 1910. He worked for the Ryan Ream outfit. Photograph courtesy of Daisey Rowley.

several brands in the territory, including the "Three Bar," "I," and "Open Box."

In 1884 a British syndicate bought out the Park City businessmen and began importing purebred shorthorn cattle to the range. The new owners also brought in several hundred head of purebred horses. In the late 1880s the United States government contracted with the company to range 6,000 head of cattle that had been confiscated from the Mormon church. Ironically, when the government requested the return of the cattle several years later, only 400 of the original herd remained. The rest of the cattle were allegedly taken by rustlers.[60]

The British syndicate sold the Ireland Cattle Company to a group of Denver businessmen in 1892. Retaining the name and the brands, the Denver people began fencing in large portions of public land. In 1902 Albert F. Potter made a several-month sojourn through the Utah mountains in what was to be the beginning of an effort at public management of natural resources in Utah. He indicates in his diary that the Ireland Cattle Company was the largest cattle outfit in central Utah, and he noted that the company had fenced off several different areas of public domain totaling some 40,000 acres of lush mountain meadows.[61]

The Ireland Cattle Company broke up in 1905 when a group of businessmen from Manti and Salina bought out the Denver men. The new company was called the Manti Livestock Company. This company was sold to the Anderson family in the 1930s and they, in turn, sold the ranch a few years later to the

Johnson family. The Johnson family currently operates the ranch under the name of the M and 0 Ranches, referring to the original Mountain Ranch and the original Oak Springs Ranch. The ranch is currently one of the finest purebred beef cattle companies in the United States.

Another corporate cattle company established by Park City businessmen was the Hazen outfit located in Castle Valley. Established about the same time as the Ireland Cattle Company, the Hazen outfit grew to about three thousand head of cattle. It was sold to an English syndication in the 1880s and continued to operate under foreign direction until it was sold off in 1905.[62]

There were several more corporate cattle companies operating in Utah during the latter part of the nineteenth century, but unless some dusty pages of history spring forth—perhaps from a corner of some old attic—the histories of these companies may be lost in time. The Denver and Rio Grande Railroad registered a brand in Utah in 1884, and the company probably ran a considerable number of cattle and horses on lands granted to it by the United States government. As with other railroad land grants, the Rio Grande profited with the land deals that were given as an incentive for building the railroads. A group of businessmen from Denver formed the Garfield County Cattle and Land Company in 1884. There was also the Arizona Cattle and Wool Company that registered a brand at St. George in 1884. Perhaps more information on these cattle companies will be forthcoming.

The railroad elite—the bankers, the merchandisers, and the mining tycoons—provided the capital for the cattle boom of the 1880s and 1890s. By so doing, they also created jobs for the riders of the range. During this time those hell-bent-for-leather fellows reached their greatest pinnacle. It was the heyday of the American cowboy.

The movement of cattle along the cattle trails to the railheads or markets must have been phenomenal during the last two decades of the nineteenth century. Virtually every town along the trail became a cow town, at least for a time. Some of these cow towns and eldorados of Utah saw their most colorful history when the cowboys dropped by to wash down a hundred miles or so of trail dust.

5

The Cow Towns and Eldorados

We were not disappointed at the news that we would have to spend the night at Kelton, for our legs needed stretching, and our interest in the sights of the new town kept us well entertained. There was music to be heard in many places, the tinkle of the piano, and the sound of the little ivory ball as it dropped into its metal stall on the roulette wheel, a sound that meant good luck to the fortunate one, and bad luck to others; and while some girls danced with the men of the party I listened to two girls singing a song I liked. It ran, "Oh, my darling, oh, my darling, oh, my darling Clementine—you are lost and gone forever—dreadful sorry, Clementine."

As the town was full of people going to the new country, it was hard to find a place to sleep, so those of us who slept at all packed our beds to the stage barn and rolled them out in the harness room. But some of our boys made a night of it, and we did not see them until morning. They all told what a rip-roaring place Kelton was, and we had no reason to doubt them.[1]

This colorful description of Kelton, Utah, was provided by a young Texas trail driver named Jack Porter, who, along with a number of other young Texas cowboys, had an opportunity to sample the night life there in 1879. Kelton was one of numerous Gentile towns that sprang up in Utah Territory during the second half of the nineteenth century. Unlike the serene Mormon settlements, the Gentile towns

seemed bent on riotous living. They were railroad towns, mining towns, and towns created by military camp followers. They all boasted several things in common—mainly saloons, gambling dens, and whorehouses. Much to the Mormons' dismay, at times some of the sinful pleasures offered by these towns crept into and became a part of the Mormon settlements.

Many of the earliest cattle drives in the territory were made directly to the military and mining camps and the end-of-the-rail towns. The cowboys, by nature, were not city dwellers and preferred the wide open spaces, but the solitude and lack of feminine company could be tolerated only so long. Once the cowboys reached town, they usually overindulged themselves in an effort to make up for lost time. In many instances, the end result would be a donnybrook, gunplay, and a night in jail—if they were lucky. If they weren't lucky, they could easily wind up dead.

Life in the Gentile towns was tough at best. John F. Everett, when interviewed in 1938, claimed that "in mining towns like Bingham, men were shot every day. No time was wasted on trials. I carried a six-shooter and a Bowie knife all the time; everyone did. We had to in order to be safe."[2] Many of the men and women who came to these towns were criminals or fugitives who had fled from the East. Violence was a way of life with many of the town dwellers. There were, of course, good citizens in these communities who made a great effort to stem

Two "soiled doves" photographed in their parlor on Commercial Street in Salt Lake City, Utah, in the 1880s. Photograph courtesy of Nelson Wadsworth.

Cowboys working for the Meathook Cattle Company liked spending time at State Line, Utah, circa 1900. Photograph courtesy of Mike Flinspach.

the violence. Nevertheless, some of the frontier towns in Utah were as wild as any towns in the entire West.

The town of Alta, high in the Wasatch Mountains east of Salt Lake City, was a pretty tough town. On one Fourth of July the townspeople awoke to the sight of a man hanging by his neck from the new flagpole which had been erected to celebrate the holiday. Whoever did the hanging added insult to injury by greasing the flagpole. In order to retrieve the dead man, the townspeople had to chop the pole down. During the day's festivities at least one man was killed in one of the town's twenty-six saloons. To make the day complete, someone carelessly dropped a lighted cigar next to a fireworks display. All the fireworks went off prematurely, causing bystanders to run screaming for cover.[3]

History related that 110 men were killed inside the swinging doors of just two of Alta's saloons—the Bucket of Blood and the Gold Miner's Daughter.[4] Undoubtedly, a few cowboys were included in that

A wild night on the town could result in a stay at the local jail. Photograph courtesy of Hal Cannon.

bunch of men who were carted off to Boot Hill.

Frisco, a gold mining town west of Milford, was so wild the townspeople hired a gunslinging sheriff by the name of Pearson to clean up the town. He is reported to have killed as many as six men in one night. That may sound like an exaggeration, but when one considers how violent these men of the West were, the prospect does not seem unreasonable. Stories coming out of Frisco were legend. Bill Thomas, a cowboy, and a gambler named Curby drew on each other in the Pat Malloy saloon one day. Thomas was wounded and Curby was killed. One night a gambler called Brannon killed five men over an argument which started during a Faro game. Friends of the five overpowered Brannon and tarred and feathered him—then they hung him.[5]

Park City, a silver mining town on the eastern slopes of the Wasatch Mountains, had its share of violence. Henry Nugent and Peter Clark drew on each other during a poker game in one of the many saloons in town. Clark was wounded and Nugent was killed in the fight. Neil Mullow killed A. Hughes in another saloon brawl. Black Jack Murphy got the worst treatment, however. He killed a fellow during

Gamblers at a Bingham, Utah, saloon enjoy a game of faro circa 1900. Photograph courtesy of Utah State Historical Society.

a barroom brawl and was placed in the Park City dungeon. The sheriff transferred him to the jail in Coalville, some twenty miles away, because of rumors of a lynching. Some Park City miners commandeered a train engine and took it to Coalville, where they broke Murphy out of jail. They brought him back to Park City and hung him on a telegraph pole.[6]

In Eureka, a mining town in the West Tintic Mountains, Joe Fisher shot and killed a fellow named Conners in what appeared to be a fair fight. Regardless, vigilantes broke Fisher out of jail and lynched him.[7]

The several mining towns mentioned were just a few of the approximately one hundred mining

A typical resident of the wild mining towns was usually well armed as is this fellow. Photograph from author's collection.

towns and camps which sprang up in the territory. Some of the towns lasted long enough to play out the mines and then became ghosts. Others, like Eureka and Park City, are alive and well to the present day. Similar in violence to those mining camps were the railroad towns which began to dot Utah in the late 1860s. Some of these towns were permanent in nature, but most died out, leaving only memories of song, dance, and violence.

At Uintah, a Hell-on-wheels town at the mouth of Weber Canyon, a man was shot and hung because he was a "damned nigger."[8] Three men were lynched at Wahsatch, a rail camp, located in Echo Canyon.[9] Similar violence occurred at Promontory, Kelton, Terrace, and Watercress—towns along the Union Pacific and Central Pacific rails in northern Utah.

These gamblers at Price, Utah, in the 1890s, portray the act of cheating, which could mean a premature death for the perpetrator. Photograph courtesy of Nelson Wadsworth.

Corinne, known as "the Gentile capital of Utah" or "The Burg on the Bear" by many of the Mormon faithful, was the major railroad town in northern Utah for a number of years. Any sensual gratification known to man could be had in Corinne, including a slot machine which would give out a legal and binding divorce decree for one silver dollar. Shootings were common in the town and at least one fellow, a Chinese named Ah Sing, was lynched.[10]

Towns and camps created in conjunction with the establishment of military reservations in the territory, fewer in number than the mining camps and rail towns, did not lack for violence. Fairfield, next to Camp Floyd, boasted seventeen saloons and an assortment of gamblers, harlots, slickers, and thieves who were more than willing to take the hard-earned money away from the soldiers, freighters, and cowboys who ventured into town.

The toughest camp situated next to a military reservation was known simply as "The Strip." The Strip was a triangle-shaped piece of land between the Uncompahgre and Uintah Indian reservations.

Federal, territorial, and county law officers were undecided as to which agency had jurisdiction over the area and consequently none of the agencies bothered to police The Strip. Indians from the reservation, soldiers from the fort, including a company of black "Buffalo Soldiers," freighters, cowboys, and outlaws kept the saloons, gaming tables, and prostitutes on The Strip busy twenty-four hours a day.

Sixteen known deaths by shooting occurred on The Strip during its short life. A few of note included the killing of a white rancher, Jack Thomas, by a black soldier named William Carter. George Hughes was killed in a gunfight by a tinhorn gambler who, with the help of a dance-hall girl, had earlier swiped George's gun long enough to file down the firing pin. George outdrew the gambler, but his gun did not fire. Tabby Weep White, an Indian who was known as the fastest gun in the area, killed three men during a shootout on The Strip. Later Tabby killed Bob Reynolds in a gunfight. Tabby claimed self-defense, but the jury did not see it that way and gave him a life sentence at the Utah Penitentiary.[11]

Cowboys at Jensen, Utah, in the 1890s take time out for a little gambling. Cowboys liked to come to town to try their luck at cards. Photograph courtesy of Doris Burton.

Myton was a tough town twenty miles west of The Strip. The town was located at the head of Nine Mile Canyon, the main road leading into the Uinta Basin. For many years the town played host to freighters, soldiers, cowboys, and outlaws moving in and out of the Basin. At the other end of Nine Mile Canyon sat the town of Price. Originally a Mormon settlement, Price began losing its initial cultural identity when mining activities developed on the Book Cliff Mountains. As hundreds of Gentile miners poured into the surrounding region, Price took on the appearance of a typical Wild West town. The area around it was also cattle country, and the town became an outfitting point for the cowboys working the nearby ranges.

Several other Mormon settlements in the territory began to develop wild natures as they catered to the pleasures of miners, soldiers, freighters, and cowboys. Vernal played host to hundreds of outlaws who moved up and down the Outlaw Trail. Green River was also a supply point for them. Elizabeth Farrer Leman wrote about her early days in Green

River and indicated it was "nothing to hear shooting night and day in town."[12] She also recalled the time when Big George Heck killed a fellow named Ferry in 1883. A group of vigilantes chased George down and shot him.

Moab, Monticello, Blanding, and Bluff all became cow towns as they were forced to accommodate numerous cowboys working on the southeast ranges. One eyewitness claimed she saw seventy-five cowboys riding up and down the street firing their six-guns one night in Monticello. She counted them "by the lights of their own guns."[13]

The Mormon settlement of Logan in northern Utah was a supply center for cowboys working in the Bear River Mountains. Miners from the silver camp of La Plata also frequented the town. The serenity of Logan was broken one day when a cowboy by the name of Charley Benson killed a man called David Crockett. A group of vigilantes decided to take the law into their own hands and lynched Benson.[14]

In the extreme southwestern corner of Utah, the

The back of this picture postcard sent to Vernal, Utah, read, "Hellow girls, this is fer Florence and Rosie." Perhaps these cowpokes had made some interesting alliances while visiting the town in the early 1900s. Photograph from author's collection.

These cowboys working for the Seaman Ranch near Glendale, Utah, circa 1900 appear to have their going-to-town clothes on. Photograph courtesy of Utah State Historical Society.

Wayne County cowboy Enoch Sorenson in his working clothes circa 1890. Photograph from author's collection.

Mormon settlement of St. George catered to the miners of several camps in Utah and Nevada, including the famous Silver Reef just north of St. George. St. George was also a supply point for the numerous cowboys working on the Arizona Strip. The peace in St. George was disrupted on the night of October 5, 1880, when a group of miners from Silver Reef caught up with the fugitive Thomas Forrest. They promptly lynched him.[15]

Other settlements taking on a flair of toughness because of their proximity to the cattle ranges and mining operations were Spanish Fork, Salina, Nephi, Heber, Cedar City, Kanab, and Milford. Each of these towns were major supply points and end-of-trail towns for the numerous herds of cattle and later sheep being trailed in the territory.

Gentile cowboys, miners, and soldiers coming into Salt Lake City could drink and gamble in the many saloons which dotted Main Street. The city did, however, limit, as far as possible, the whorehouses, bath houses, and Chinese opium dens to Commercial Street which ran between Main and State streets and First and Second South. Every worldly appetite of man could be satisfied on Commercial Street.

The paradox of Salt Lake City was that it was the home of the Mormon religion, which taught Christianity, high morals, and brotherly love, yet because of its proximity to mining camps, military forts, and railroad towns, sections of the city became wide-open frontier towns. In addition to the numerous killings which took place in the city, two events solidified its wild reputation. The first was the celebrated gunfight on Christmas Day in 1859 between Bill Hickman and his gang and a rival gang led by Lot Huntington. Although no one was killed during the fight, at least forty shots were fired, making that particular Christmas Day more like a typical Fourth of July.[16]

The second major Wild West event occurred on August 25, 1883. William H. "Sam Joe" Harvey, an unemployed black, had an altercation with another black man and threatened him. He later purchased a rifle with what was apparently stolen money. Popular Chief of Police Andrew Burt became aware of the situation and tried to arrest Harvey. Burt was mortally wounded in the attempt. Harvey was captured a short time later and placed in the Salt Lake City jail. After being beaten by the jailers, he was

A saloon in Randolph, Utah, circa 1890. Photograph courtesy of Pearl Rex.

turned over to a mob estimated at two thousand and hanged in a nearby stable.[17]

The "Queen of Cow Towns" in the Utah Territory was the city of Ogden. It started out as a typically serene Mormon settlement. When the railroad came to the territory in 1869, Corinne was the major terminal city, but within a few years, as more railroad spurs branched out into the territory, Ogden took over the role of junction city. As such, all of the wild element which resided in Corinne eventually made their way to Ogden and set up business on the notorious Twenty-fifth Street, known in some circles as "Two Bit Street." Lined with whorehouses, saloons, and gambling and opium dens, the area was as tough as any place in the entire Wild West. It was almost worth a man's life to walk down the street alone.

Ogden was the major supply center for cowboys working the outlying cattle country. Together with Kelton, Utah, it was also the major supply point for hundreds of Texas cowboys who made their way to

Enoch Sorenson dressed up for his trip to Loa, Utah, circa 1890. Photograph courtesy of Barbara Pace.

the Oregon country during the 1880s. A good portion of these cowboys spent some of their hard-earned money at Fanny Porter's and Belle London's houses, two of Ogden's higher class brothels.

Violence was a way of life on "Two Bit Street" and included the lynching of George Segal, a Japanese laborer, who had shot his lady boss. He was apprehended by two Ogden policemen and placed in the city jail. An angry mob soon took him from the jail at gunpoint and lynched him from the courtyard bell tower.[18] Perhaps a few in this lynch mob were cowboys showing their final respects to the lady.

The drinking, fighting, and wild escapades of the cow towns and eldorados of Utah were perpetrated by numerous frontier types, including cowboys. The cowboys, however, spent far more time on the range than they did in the wild towns. Town life was only a sometime thing for the cowboys of the 1880s and 1890s. The sound of bawling cattle was far more familiar than the sound of the roulette wheel. The smell of burning cowhide filled a cowboy's nostrils much more often than the sweet smell of French perfume.

There were numerous cattle trails crisscrossing

Most of the men in front of this Myton, Utah, real estate office are carrying guns, which attests to the wild nature of the town. Photograph courtesy of Utah State Historical Society.

The saloon at Fort Duchesne, Utah, circa 1888. Photograph courtesy of Vernal Daughters of the Utah Pioneers.

Saloon at Ibapah, Utah, circa 1900. Photograph courtesy of La Dawn Farr.

Utah during the open-range period. These included major routes leading into and out of Utah as well as to mining camps, railheads, and from the winter to summer ranges. All of these trails were more like home to the cowboys than were the towns. Some of the trails can still be documented, while others have been completely plowed over.

Major trails leading into Utah included the Oregon Trail, with its several California branches, the Mormon Trail, the Brown's Park Trail, and the Old Spanish Trail. Cattle coming into Utah from Oregon established a path leading directly to the railhead at Kelton and another which entered Utah on the western shores of Bear Lake. From Bear Lake, it followed the Bear River Valley to the railhead at Evanston.

Trails leading out of Utah during the California Gold Rush were the Old Spanish Trail and the more northerly Overland Trail, which was first used by the cattle herds belonging to Howard Egan. As Utah began to export cattle following the Civil War, the major overland trails were utilized and a few new ones were developed. Large herds of cattle from the Wasatch settlements were driven through the Strawberry Valley to Vernal. (One drive, in 1878, began in Levan, went through Salt Canyon to India-

nola, up Spanish Fork Canyon to Strawberry Valley, then on to Vernal.) From Vernal the route went up and over Diamond Mountain, then dropped into Brown's Park. From there it met up with the Oregon Trail in Wyoming and terminated at either Laramie or Cheyenne. Herds belonging to the Whitmores and Lord Elliot were driven overland through the Grand River Valley and all the way to Denver. Cattle on the San Juan ranges were driven to the mining camps of southern Colorado and northern New Mexico.

As the railroads penetrated into the heartland of Utah there was less need to trail herds for long distances. Some cattlemen, however, chose to continue the long cattle drives up until the turn of the century. One such trail drive, numbering nearly 7,000 head, originated in Utah and passed through Colorado on its way to the Sweetwater Range of Wyoming.[19]

Major cattle trails within the territory led to several key railroad towns and sidings where stockyards and corrals were built to accommodate the herds. Stockyards along the Union Pacific and Central Pacific railroads in northern Utah were located at Wasatch, Ogden, Corinne, Kelton, and a little-known siding called Bovine in extreme western

Alton Allred, Will Crosland, and Bart Smithson, Ryan Ream cowboys, depict the wild side of Milford, Utah, in the 1890s. Photograph courtesy of Daisy Rowley.

Utah, so named because of the large herds of wild cattle which roamed the area, lost by pioneer stockmen. Once the rails reached this area, the railroad provided an outlet to market for the cattle.[20]

Herds from the eastern portion of the Book Cliffs were driven to Woodside, Thompson Springs, and Cisco. These three sidings were also utilized by thousands of head of cattle coming up from the La Sal and San Juan ranges. Of special interest were the

Palace Saloon at Provo, Utah, circa 1900. Photograph courtesy of Palace Drugs.

drives coming north from these ranges, since they had to go directly through the town of Moab. The canyons of the Colorado River are so narrow at the point the river reaches Moab, the cattlemen had no choice but to push through town. These cattle drives continued well into the 1960s.

Cattle from the Kanab region and north to Wayne County were trailed to the siding at Marysvale. Farther north in central Utah, they were sent to Salina, Ephraim, Spanish Fork, and Heber. Cattle coming off the vast west-central ranges, which ran from the Wasatch Mountains to the Nevada border,

A saloon in Moab, Utah, circa 1890. Photograph courtesy of Moab Daughters of the Utah Pioneers.

Happy hour in Castle Gate, Utah, in the 1890s. Photograph courtesy of Rell Francis.

CHESAPEAKE BAR

CHESAPEAKE BAR, 23 WEST 2ND SOUTH, SALT LAKE CITY.
"THIS IS WHERE THEY STAMPEDE."

Cowboys in front of the Chesapeake Bar in Salt Lake City, circa 1910. Photograph courtesy of Ken Fee.

were driven to Delta, Leamington, and Nephi.

Cattle coming from the Snake River Range, Pine Valley, and other stock ranges in southwestern Utah were destined for Milford, Lund, and Modena. Numerous herds coming in from the Arizona Strip were also driven to these stockyards for shipment. One early-day author described the character of Milford when the town played host to the annual cattle drives as follows: "Then for days, and sometimes weeks, Milford was a cowboy's town in every sense of the word. A stranger, in town for the first time, might be led to believe he was on the great plains, witnessing one of the roundups."[21]

In addition to the major routes leading in and out of the territory to and from the stockyards, hundreds of trails dotted the countryside between the summer and winter ranges. Commencing in April, the cattle on the winter ranges were rounded up and driven to high mountain summer ranges. They were then again rounded up in the fall and driven back down to lower country.

Cattle from several different outfits were run together because of local open-range conditions. Cowboys representing the different outfits would join together for the roundups. A calf was branded with the brand of the cow nursing it. Some of the larger outfits in outlying areas sent representatives to local roundups, just in case some of their cattle had wandered too far.

Cattle buyers such as B. F. Saunders, Joseph Yates, and Joseph Frodsham attended these roundups and would buy any stock offered for sale, including bulls and old cows. Many of the smaller ranchers opted to sell their cattle to these buyers, saving the

Two cowboys at Rockville, Utah, enjoy a little "red eye" in the 1890s. Photograph courtesy of Lynne Clark Photography.

Selecting a horse at the Jensen Cash Store, Jensen, Utah, circa 1900. Photograph courtesy of Doris Burton.

Three Beckstead brothers at Spanish Fork, Utah, in the 1890s. Photograph courtesy of Robert M. Beckstead.

expense of driving the cattle to market. Large cattle outfits also sometimes bought cattle from the small outfits. The cattle buyers and large outfits then either drove the herds to market or placed them on the range for further fattening.[22] In earlier days cattle were not sent to market until they had reached the age of four or five years, and many of the cattle moved to market were much older. These old steers and cows would not be considered prime, tender beef today.

The big cattle outfits usually provided several horses to the cowboys for use on the cattle drives and range work. They also provided food and living quarters for their cowboys. All the rest of the gear was supplied by the cowboys themselves, including clothing, chaps, spurs, lariats, and a good saddle. Weapons were generally optional, but many cowboys wore revolvers and had access to rifles.

The primary weapon used by cowboys was a single-action Colt revolver, usually a .44–.40 calibre or a .45 calibre. Remington revolvers were also common on the frontier. Winchester repeating rifles were by far the most common of the long guns used by cowboys. These weapons could be purchased throughout the territory in gun shops and dry goods stores. There were also several gunsmiths scattered throughout the territory where fine-quality custom-made guns could be purchased. Two of the most notable gunsmiths in the territory were Johnathan Browning and his son, John Moses Browning. Under the tutelage of his father, and then by his own experimentation, John Browning eventually emerged as one of the finest gun makers in the world.

Leather goods could be purchased at saddle shops in many of the towns in the territory. Most of these saddleries were small businesses known in the trade as "buckeye shops." They rarely used a hallmark or "cartouche" stamping in the leather to indicate who the maker was. There were, however, several shops in the territory that found a widespread market for their saddles and leather goods. These saddleries used the "cartouche" as an indication of the pride they had in their product and as a form of advertisement for the company.

Stockyards at Ogden, Utah, circa 1910. Photograph from author's collection.

Branding cattle at Wellington, Utah, circa 1900. Photograph courtesy of Lyle B. Bryner.

Lunchtime for Meathook cowboys circa 1900. Photograph courtesy of Mike Flinspach.

Meathook Ranch roundup crew at Modena, Utah, circa 1900. Photograph courtesy of Mike Flinspach.

Cattle owned by Preston Nutter being driven to the railhead at Colton, Utah, in the 1900s. Photograph courtesy of University of Utah Libraries, Special Collections Department.

Cattle roundup in eastern Utah circa 1920. Photograph courtesy of Utah State Historical Society.

K Ranch roundup crew near Jensen, Utah, in the 1880s. Photograph courtesy of Ila Cowans.

Not surprisingly, Ogden, Utah, was the home of several saddle houses which won considerable fame, both within and without the territory. The first such saddlery was the firm of Cornish and Walton. Little is known of the origins of this company, but most likely it was started in the late 1860s. The company was in business only a few years, but it is said that Butch Cassidy rode a Cornish and Walton saddle, which did much to preserve the name for future generations.[23]

The Cornish and Walton Saddle Company was purchased by W. A. Hadgman in the late 1870s. Hadgman employed a seventeen-year-old boy named J. G. Read, who in 1883 bought the firm and renamed it the J. G. Read Harness and Saddlery. In 1884 Read was joined by his brother, W. S. Read, and together they purchased the Cheyenne Harness and Saddlery, a small shop in Ogden. In 1898 Oscar L. Read joined the company and the name was changed to the J. G. Read and Brothers Company. The company continues to manufacture saddles at the present time.

In the late 1890s the Read brothers owned a champion race horse named "Nigger Boy." In honor of the animal the company produced a line of saddles and chaps that carried the cartouche "Nigger Boy Brand." This brand was very popular for a number of years until it became prudent to allow the name to die.

Another Ogden saddlery that produced a fine-quality saddle and other leather goods during the past 110 years was the C. W. Cross Company. Originally founded by Charles W. Cross in 1876, the company became known as Cross Brothers Saddlery a few years later when Alfred Cross joined his brother. The two men operated the business until the turn of the century.

In 1903 Charles Cross, Jr., incorporated the company under the name of C. W. Cross Company and it continues to operate on Washington Boulevard in the heart of Ogden. Over the years it has taken on a sporting goods line, western clothing, and hardware to complement the saddle and leather business.

In addition to firearms manufactured over the years by Browning Arms Company, the Brownings operated a saddlery and tannery in Ogden for many years. They offered a fine line of holsters, cartridge belts, saddle scabbards, leather cuffs and saddles. The Browning Saddlery was closed in 1926, but the Browning Arms Company continues.

A harness shop at Fairview, Utah, in the 1890s. Photograph courtesy of Rell Francis.

A saddle shop at Salina, Utah, in the 1890s. Photograph courtesy of Rell Francis.

A cowboy at Ogden, Utah, circa 1900. Photograph courtesy of Brent Baldwin.

Salt Lake City also had several saddle houses that provided a very good quality saddle and other leather goods which were used by cowboys throughout the territory. One of the oldest companies was founded by J. W. Jenkins soon after his arrival in the valley in 1855. It did a brisk business, particularly after Jenkins was converted to the Mormon church.[24]

Jenkins's three sons joined the company in the 1890s and the name was changed to J. W. Jenkins and Sons Saddlery. After the death of their father, the Jenkins brothers expanded into the hardware and sporting goods business and built a three-story building across from the Salt Lake City and County Building. The company continued to operate until the 1960s.

Another Salt Lake City saddlery which was prominent for a few years was W. L. Pickard and Sons Company. This firm started out as a hide and wool buyer in 1870 but soon became one of the best saddle houses in the city. In the mid-1880s Pickard took on a partner by the name of Wallin and changed the name to Wallin and Pickard Saddlery. During much of the 1880s the company advertised itself as the biggest seller of saddles, bridles, harnesses, and spurs in the territory. It closed down some time after the turn of the century.

The Salt Lake Hardware Company was established in 1879 and continued to operate until 1986. Up until the 1930s the company produced an excellent line of saddles, chaps, and gun leather. Some of the finest angora chaps or "woollies" made came out of the Salt Lake Hardware Saddlery.

Although the Newton Brothers Saddlery of Vernal was not established until after 1900, the company probably produced the most widely known saddles outside of Utah. The company was started by William Newton, blinded at the age of eleven in a freak accident involving a wagon. He became the first student to enter the State School for the Blind in Ogden and was trained in the art of boot and shoe making.

After his training at the school, William and his

Saddlemakers

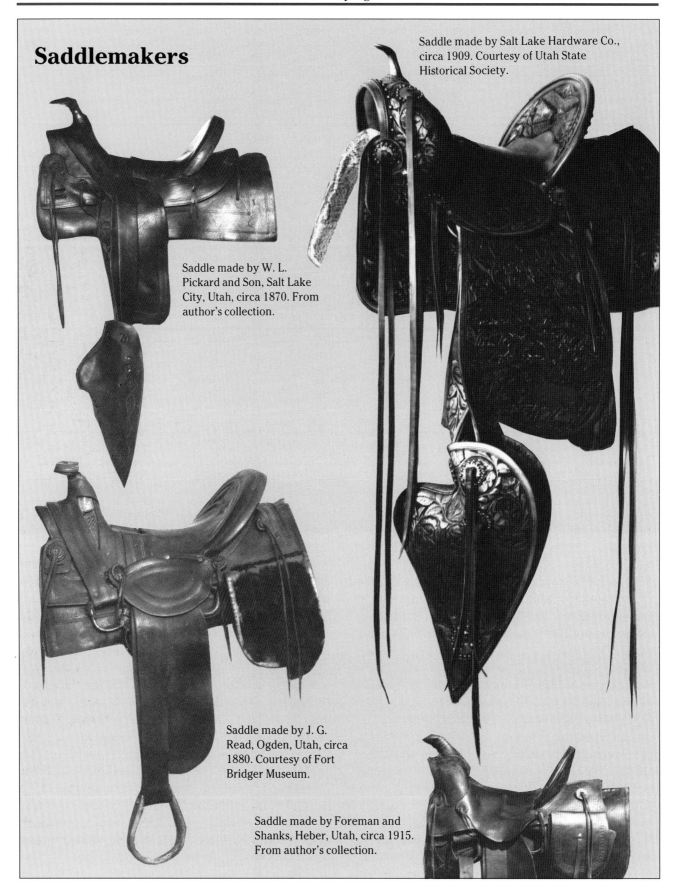

Saddle made by W. L. Pickard and Son, Salt Lake City, Utah, circa 1870. From author's collection.

Saddle made by Salt Lake Hardware Co., circa 1909. Courtesy of Utah State Historical Society.

Saddle made by J. G. Read, Ogden, Utah, circa 1880. Courtesy of Fort Bridger Museum.

Saddle made by Foreman and Shanks, Heber, Utah, circa 1915. From author's collection.

Moen Burns in the 1880s. Moen established the Burns Saddlery in Salina, Utah, in 1898. Photograph courtesy of Burns Saddlery.

brother Isaac opened a boot repair and small saddle shop in Vernal. The company soon developed into one of the best saddle shops in Utah and the surrounding states. Especially famous was the "Mother Hubbard," a full-leather covering, which fit over the saddle horn and cantle and riggings of some of the saddles produced by the company.

Newton Brothers were also famous for an outstanding saddle tree mass-produced by the company. At one time, during the 1940s, Newton saddle trees were marketed worldwide. The firm operated several years after the death of William Newton, but was finally closed down in the late 1960s.

In addition to the large saddle shops mentioned, there were several other saddle houses in the territory that rose above the "buckeye" status, but catered primarily to local cowboys. Included in this group were the Durrant Brothers and Bee Saddlery of Provo, White Saddlery of Sandy, L. Platt Saddlery of Salt Lake City, Burns Saddlery of Salina, and Foreman and Shanks Saddlery of Heber. All of these companies produced a good-quality saddle and used

the cartouche to mark their product. White Saddlery and Burns Saddlery continue to operate at the present time.

The saddle houses of Utah provided a needed commodity in the territory. Horse transportation was prominent well into the twentieth century, and in some places, like Boulder, Utah, it was the only transportation until the 1930s. Cowboys generally took good care of their leather goods because they were expensive and at times hard to come by. Riders could be pretty hard on a horse, for they were cheap and plentiful, but a good saddle was not expendable. There were never truer words spoken in the Old West than "a ten-dollar horse and a forty-dollar saddle."

Another maxim in the Old West was "a feller would never get rich punching someone else's cows." Some cowboys took this message to heart and decided to get a herd of their own. The problem was that few cowboys made enough money to buy their own cows.

131

6

The Cowboy Outlaws

In 1860 Governor Cumming reported to the legislature that the "northern part of the territory is infested by bands of cattle thieves, who commit depredations upon the ranges and dispose of their plunder in the vicinity of the military reserves."[1] When asked who was riding herd on McIntyre cattle, Samuel McIntyre curtly replied, "every son of a bitch who owns a horse."[2] At the time of the conversation the McIntyre Cattle Company was losing quite a few animals to rustlers—a problem that every other cattle baron in the Old West had to deal with at one time or another. How they dealt with the problem created some of the great legends in open-range cattle country.

The rustling of cattle became a problem soon after the Mormons arrived in Utah. Indians caused most of the problems during the first few years of settlement, but white desperadoes soon followed. The problem continued to escalate in the territory, and by 1878 Governor George W. Emery was pointing out to the legislature that one of the great risks of the Utah stock industry was "the men who drive out of Utah annually large numbers of stolen cattle and horses."[3] Much to the dismay of several succeeding

Robert Leroy Parker (alias Butch Cassidy), Ronald Wall, and Orrin Elmer at the Anderson Studio in Manti, Utah, circa 1893. Parker and Elmer grew up in Circle Valley, Utah, and were good friends. Several years after this photograph was taken Cassidy was a notorious outlaw and Elmer was the marshal of Colton, Utah. Photograph courtesy of Dennis Finch.

governors, the rustling of livestock continued to plague the industry until the late 1890s.

The Utah legislature passed a number of branding laws, the most comprehensive of which was the Branding and Herding Act of 1886, which required that no unbranded animals were to be either sold or slaughtered within the territory.[4] Heavy fines were levied against those who did not comply with the law. Honest cattlemen honored the system, but the deviant scoffed at it. Even the felony charges associated with the laws were not enough to dissuade the rustler, and at times when vigilante groups and range detectives made the rustling of livestock a capital offense by hanging or shooting a rustler, others of his ilk barely flinched.

Besides the territorial branding laws and the enforcement of them by local lawmen, cattlemen went to great lengths themselves to put an end to rustling in the territory. Livestock associations were formed and rewards were offered for the capture of rustlers. Many of these associations hired their own stock detectives to track the rustlers down. Some of the larger cattlemen hired gunfighters to scare would-be rustlers away, and many hired known rustlers in the belief that they would not steal from the hand that was feeding them. None of these means was totally effective.

For the most part, the men involved with rustling were former cowboys gone astray. There were, of course, men of other occupations who chose to be rustlers. However, once these men became rustlers

133

Angus and George Baldwin branding a horse in the Paria River country circa 1900. Photograph courtesy of Brent Baldwin.

they, in effect, became cowboys, if one applies that term to someone riding herd on cattle and horses. In any case, they had to have an ability to work with great herds of cattle and horses and were, or became, expert horsemen and ropers, as well as being experts with a gun. They also became very adept in using a running iron.

A running iron was a small iron ring or D ring or a poker-like iron that was curved on the end. When red hot, a cowboy would run the iron over the hide of an animal and alter an existing brand. The use of a running iron was not against the law in Utah, and, in fact, many honest cowboys used a running iron.[5]

During the open-range roundups, cattle were branded with a stamp brand, that is, a long-handled piece of iron that had been forged at one end to reflect a mark, number, or letter. Calves were branded according to the brand on the cow nursing them. Cattle that had missed branding on a previous year and calves that were orphans were called "mavericks," and were branded amicably by roundup crews according to the percentage of cattle an outfit was running. Because many calves were born after the spring roundup and some cattle were missed during the roundups, some cowboys carried

a ring running iron in their saddlebags. They would heat the ring and then crisscross two sticks through the ring. Using the sticks as handles, they would burn the brand into the maverick.

The temptation to brand a maverick with their own mark was too great for many cowboys who found the practice a good way to supplement their meager income. Some were able to mark enough cattle to become gentlemen cattlemen themselves. It has been said that most of the early ranchers along the Henry Fork River got their start from Judge Carter's mavericks.[6] The practice was widespread in the territory, and, because both large and small ranchers practiced mavericking, it was often winked at.

Some cowboys were not satisfied to merely brand an occasional maverick. To increase their take, these unscrupulous characters began stealing calves from their mothers. These animals were called sleeper calves. The rustler generally did not brand the calf until thoroughly weaned, thus avoiding the danger of any calf returning to its mother with the tell-tale brand on its side.[7]

Once rustling got into a cowboy's blood it was hard to turn back. He would often join rustling gangs

Angus Baldwin branding cattle in the Paria River country circa 1900. Photograph courtesy of Brent Baldwin.

who would run herds of several hundred animals off the range. These gangs would drive the animals to hideouts where they would hole up until it was safe to sell the cattle and horses. Several of these hideouts in Utah became legendary. The most famous was Robber's Roost. Brown's Park rivaled the Roost in infamy. Other hideouts included Bryce Canyon, Diamond Mountain, Snake Valley, and the San Rafael Swell.

While holed up in these hideouts, the rustlers spent the time drinking, gambling, whoring, and branding. The branding included use of the running iron to alter existing brands on the animals. Once things had cooled down, they drove the cattle and horses to the military camps and mining towns in the territory or to the mining camps of California, Nevada, and Colorado.

Utah's history is full of rustlers and outlaw gangs. Some of the gangs were short-lived and the members either ended up on Boot Hill or faded away leaving no trace as to where they went or how they died. Others became legendary and left a well-documented trail. Some of the gangs continued to rustle stock until the bitter end, while others graduated to the more lucrative art of bank and train hold-

ups. Some individual members of these gangs were cold-blooded killers and were hated and feared by every law-abiding citizen. Others were charming and affable and were looked upon as western Robin Hoods, conducting a war against the ruthless cattle barons and capitalists who were, in the eyes of many, the enemies of the little man in the West.

Many of the earliest outlaws in Utah plied their trade around the military post at Camp Floyd. There is reason to believe that the notorious Civil War guerrilla, William C. Quantrill, began his rustling and murdering ways while stationed at Camp Floyd.[8] At the outbreak of the Civil War Quantrill left Utah and organized a band of guerrillas and proceeded to ravage the pro-northern towns in Kansas. His gang, which included the James and Younger brothers, burned Lawrence, Kansas, and killed 150 citizens during one particularly violent raid. The gang was working under the auspices of the Confederacy at the time. Quantrill was killed in May of 1865 by a contingent of federal soldiers in Kentucky.[9]

One of the earliest gang leaders in Utah, William A. Hickman, was born in the State of Kentucky. Later his family moved to Missouri and, in time, Bill

Brig Larsen and Louie Fish enact a rustling scene at Moab, Utah, in the early 1900s. In reality, the rustling of livestock was a major problem in Utah. Photograph courtesy of Essie White.

married a Mormon girl and eventually joined the church. While at Nauvoo, Illinois, Bill became the personal bodyguard of Prophet Joseph Smith. Following the Prophet's death, he became a scout for the Mormons' exodus to Utah.

In 1854 Bill was appointed as Deputy United States Marshal and also sheriff of Green River County, Utah. In this capacity he encountered many outlaws who infested the country around Fort Bridger.[10]

During the invasion of Utah by Johnston's Army, Bill was called to lead a group of Mormon raiders against the federals and was successful in burning a number of army wagon trains and rustling the army's livestock. Once the army arrived at Camp

William "The Notorious" Hickman, at one time a noted lawman, became the leader of a band of renegade horse and cattle thieves. Photograph courtesy of Utah State Historical Society.

Floyd, Bill frequented Fairfield where, in his own mind, he became the eyes and ears of the church.[11]

The environment of Camp Floyd encouraged Bill to retain his rough frontier image, and before long he had organized a gang, and was rustling army livestock for a profit. On April 22, 1859, five United States marshals left Camp Floyd with orders to capture Bill Hickman, dead or alive. He escaped the marshals and laid low for several months.[12] Later Bill tried to persuade Brigham Young to allow him to lead a horse drive to California, but Brigham suspected that the horses were stolen and he would not sanction the trip.[13]

Having lost favor with Brigham Young, Bill was on the verge of losing his membership in the church. The final straw came on Christmas Day 1859. Bill and some of his gang members were chatting in a back alley in the heart of Salt Lake City when

Rockin M cowboys with a roped calf, ready for branding. Many cowboys legitimately used a running iron for branding stock. Photograph courtesy of Don Wilcox.

another gang, led by Lot Huntington, confronted them concerning some stolen property. Lot drew his revolver and shot at Bill several times, wounding him twice. Bill returned fire and wounded Lot. Gang members on both sides joined in the fracas and there was quite a running gun battle for several minutes. Several days later, as Bill lay on a hospital bed, Joe Rhodes, a member of Lot's gang, entered Bill's room and tried to knife him. Joe was killed by Jason Luce, who was standing guard in the room at the time. This gang warfare led to both Bill Hickman and Lot Huntington, who was from a prominent Mormon family, being disfellowshipped.[14]

After the altercation and being disfellowshipped, Bill tried to get back into the good graces of the church. He acted as a scout for the Superintendent of Indian Affairs and made several attempts to smooth things over with Brigham Young. Rumors persisted, however, that Bill was keeping his hand in his rustling activities. In 1864 damaging evidence against him came to light when his long-time friend and associate, Jason Luce, implicated him in a number of crimes. This damning information came on the eve of Luce's execution at the Utah Territorial Prison. Brigham wrote to Bill advising him to give up and to stand up to the charges leveled against him. Bill declined his offer and was eventually excommunicated from the church.[15]

When the transcontinental railroad was completed in 1869, certain Gentile political leaders were bent on wresting control of Utah from the Mormons. Bill became a pawn in their hands when he was arrested for a murder which took place in 1857. Together with this charge were several other charges, including the killing of a fellow called "Spanish Frank" in Rush Valley. While in prison Bill,

138

Cowboys in the Paria River area used a cabin called the "Monkey House," named after a former occupant and his pet monkey. Photograph from author's collection.

in poor health and penniless, was persuaded to write his life story. The resulting book was titled *Brigham's Destroying Angel, Being the Life and Confessions of the Notorious Bill Hickman, the Danite Chief of Utah.*

The book covered wild exploits from early times in Missouri to the heyday of his outlaw activities in Utah and implicated not only Porter Rockwell but Brigham Young as well. Bill later indicated that he "had to put in things that would make it more interesting to people who would read it and buy it, because I need the money."[16] Nevertheless, some Gentile political leaders used the book to try to ensnare the leadership of the Mormon church. Through a series of charges and trials, with some of the latter verging on kangaroo courts, Brigham Young was absolved of any wrongdoing and the anti-Mormons were stymied.[17]

Bill Hickman was finally released from prison and he returned to the Fairfield area to do some ranching. On his trips to Salt Lake City he was "shunned like a leper by every respectful man, no one pays attention."[18] In 1881 he went to Lander, Wyoming, to live with a daughter and other relatives. On August 21, 1883, at the age of sixty-eight, the notorious gunfighter, Bill Hickman, died with his boots off. The cause of death was listed as diarrhea and old bullet wounds.

Joachim Johnston was another early gang leader who preyed on the cattle and horse herds around Camp Floyd. Joachim came to Utah from California soon after the army arrived. He soon set up a gambling establishment in Fairfield. A colorful dresser, Joachim wore custom-fit buckskins elaborately embroidered with silk flowers. He used two-and-a-half-dollar gold pieces for buttons on his buckskins.[19]

A group of heavily armed men near Kanab, Utah, in the 1880s. The photographer labled the plate, "a group of toughs on Utah's Buckskin Mountains." Photograph courtesy of Utah State University Library, Special Collections.

Joachim was a typical gambler, bent on getting rich from the wages of soldiers and other low-paid types hanging around the military camp. There must have been some question concerning his honesty, because one night a group of soldiers destroyed his establishment and ran him out of town. From that time forward, he swore vengeance against the army.[20]

Joachim organized a gang of outlaws and began rustling livestock. Many of the gang's members were young, impressionable Mormon boys who nursed a hatred for the federal army and had a keen desire for adventure. The gang operated in Utah for a period of time with relative impunity, mainly because they left the Mormons alone and concentrated on the military camps. However, while riding toward California with a large number of stolen horses and mules, the gang got greedy and decided to rustle some mules which belonged to a Mormon freighter. The freighter was a friend of Porter Rockwell and asked him if he could help get the mules back.

Porter followed the rustlers out of Utah and overtook them at Las Vegas. Joachim was taken aback to think that Porter would come after him. He told Rockwell, "I didn't think your people would have followed me for stealing from your enemies."[21] Rockwell's comments are not recorded, but Joachim offered to surrender the mules without resistance if he would be allowed to continue on to California. Rockwell agreed to let Joachim go, but insisted that four Mormon members of the gang be returned to Utah. The four Mormons—Cub Johnson, Charles Flake, a youngster named Issack

Ned Ferris of Salina, Utah, in the 1890s. His clothing and guns are of 1860s vintage. The buckskin coat would be similar to one worn by the outlaw Joachim Johnston. Photograph courtesy of Rell Francis.

Neibaur, and Lot Huntington—returned to Utah with Rockwell.

In time Joachim found his way back to Utah and, along with a friend, Myron Brewer, spent a lot of time in Salt Lake's saloon district. On May 17, 1860, the two men were returning to their boardinghouse after a night on the town. As they reached the corner of Main and Second South a burst of gunfire shattered the night's silence. Both Joachim and Brewer were killed instantly. The next morning the city marshal announced that the two men had killed each other following an argument. However, rumors persisted for many years that the men were killed by Porter Rockwell.[22]

With the death of Joachim Johnston, Lot Huntington succeeded to the leadership of Joachim's rustling gang. It was a natural step for young Lot,

who had proven his fearless nature by facing the notorious Bill Hickman on Christmas Day in 1859. The gunfight with Bill Hickman had placed Lot's membership in the Mormon church in jeopardy, but instead of being repentant, he became more unruly and more of a braggart after the affair. He and his gang members continued their rustling activities and, from time to time, made themselves menaces in the saloon area of Salt Lake City.

On the night of New Year's Eve 1861, Lot and some of his men, having had a good night and being full of whiskey, set upon the new governor of the territory, John W. Dawson. Dawson was in fact fleeing the territory after having been in Utah for only three weeks. During that period he had enraged the people with indiscretions toward a prominent widow. Fearing for his life, the governor was await-

McIntyre cowboys, circa 1900, act out some western-style gun play. Most cowboys enjoyed re-creating the Wild West image associated with early-day cowboys, outlaws, and gunfighters. Photograph courtesy of Lawrence Bradfield.

ing an east-bound stage when he was attacked by Lot Huntingon, Moroni Clawson, John M. Jason, Wilford Luce, Wood Reynolds, and Issack Neibaur. The men left him unconscious and, some said, emasculated. Once out of the territory, Dawson sent a note to the *Deseret News* naming his assailants. Warrants were issued for their arrest, but two weeks later not one of the men had been apprehended.[23]

A few weeks after the Dawson attack Lot was implicated in a burglary at the Overland Mail Company office, which netted the thieves $800. Judge Elias Smith issued new warrants for the arrest of Lot and his friend, John P. Smith. With Salt Lake police officers now fully committed to apprehending the two thieves, Lot and John decided to head for Nevada. They picked up Moroni Clawson, but before leaving the Salt Lake Valley they stole a purebred horse called Brown Sal which belonged to John Bennion. Bennion notified Porter Rockwell who, together with several other posse members, set out after the three rustlers.[24]

While riding toward Faust Station, a mail and Pony Express Station, Lot saw a large herd of cattle driven by his friend Howard R. Egan. Lot told Smith and Clawson to meet him at Faust Station, twenty-two miles west of Camp Floyd. He then rode alone to the Egan camp, where he ate supper. Later Lot rode to Faust Station where he and his two outlaw friends made plans to rustle the Egan cattle.[25]

The Rockwell posse reached Faust Station early in the morning and concealed themselves around the log house. The station owner, J. J. Faust, was the first to come outside and was startled to see Rockwell beckon him over to Rockwell's place of concealment. Rockwell told Faust to go back inside and tell the outlaws to come out with their hands up. After several minutes Lot Huntington strolled out of the log house with a six-gun clenched in his fist. He did not appear to be in any hurry; he just slowly swaggered to the corral and mounted Brown Sal. Rockwell fired two warning shots in the direction of the young outlaw as he ran toward the corral. When

A cowboy near Springville, Utah, circa 1900, displays his trusty six-shooter. Photograph courtesy of Brigham Young University, Photo Archives.

Rockwell reached the corral, Lot pointed his six-gun at Rockwell and tried to squeeze off a shot, but Rockwell fired first with his Colt revolver, which was loaded with buckshot. Eight balls penetrated Lot and virtually tore his stomach apart. He slithered off the back of Brown Sal and, within four minutes, bled to death.[26]

Clawson and Smith then came out of the log house with their hands up. The posse escorted them back to Salt Lake City, where they were turned over to four city policemen. While being escorted to jail, Clawson and Smith allegedly tried to escape and were shot and killed.[27]

Another gang that met a similar fate was the Racket Gang, led by Ike Potter. Potter and his gang made a lucrative business by rustling livestock belonging to the Overland Stage Company. They operated primarily in northern Utah, concentrating on stage stations in Echo Canyon. Time and time again they would rustle horses and a while later bring the horses back to the stations under the guise that they

had captured the horses from a band of outlaws and request a reward for the return of the stock.

To end this racket company officials sent their top detective, Joseph A. Slade, better known as "Jack" Slade, to Utah from their office in Denver. Slade was not an ordinary detective—his past bordered on the criminal side as well. In 1858 he was shot five times by Overland Stage superintendent Jules Bene, who had accused Slade of stealing horses. When Slade recovered from his wounds, he tied Bene to a post with the help of friends and used his arms and legs for target practice before finally shooting him dead.

Slade spent some time in and around northern Utah, getting to know the outlaw element. He played poker with members of the Racket Gang at Echo Station and, in a moment of somber suspense, told the outlaws he was well aware of their little game. Given Slade's reputation, Ike Potter and the gang decided to leave the Overland Company alone.[28] Instead, they planned a raid on the little Mormon community of Coalville.

143

A stage station in Echo Canyon in the 1860s. Since this station was located in the general area where the Racket gang operated, perhaps this is where Overland Stage detective Jack Slade threatened gang members. Photograph courtesy of Utah State Historical Society.

Summit County Sheriff George Roundy had been informed that the Ike Potter gang was planning to raid Coalville and was prepared when they arrived. As the gang rode into town, a posse met them. During a short fight Ike Potter, John Walker, and Charley Wilson were captured. The three outlaws were put in jail and within several days they tried to escape. Ike Potter and Charley Wilson were gunned down and killed. Walker was wounded and made his way out of town, but died from the wounds.[29]

Jack Slade fared no better after leaving the Utah scene. He went to Montana, where a vigilante com-

mittee grew tired of his antics and lynched him. Slade's wife put his body in a whiskey-filled coffin and had it loaded on the train for shipment back east. By the time the train reached Salt Lake City the odor from the coffin was becoming pretty strong. At this, Mrs. Slade decided to have her husband buried in the Salt Lake City Cemetery.[30]

One of the most successful gang leaders in southwestern Utah was Ben Tasker. Little is known of his early history, but Charles Kelly, author of *The Outlaw Trail*, and a leading authority on Utah badmen, indicated that Ben was from Centerville in northern

A stagecoach and driver at Park City, Utah, early 1900s. Although the stagecoach may have been out of use at the time of the photograph, the driver's six-gun is a reminder of the precarious times for travelers going through outlaw country. Photograph courtesy of Park City Historical Society.

Utah. During the 1870s Ben set up a rustling operation in the remote mountains west of Beaver. The Tasker gang preyed on the local cattle operators and also rustled livestock from the emigrants traveling to California. There are indications as well that Ben and his men went as far as the Salt Lake Valley to rustle stock. On November 3, 1875, the *Deseret News* reported that the marshal of Beaver had recovered seventy-five head of horses which were believed to have been taken from the Salt Lake Valley by the Tasker gang.

Apparently Ben Tasker was a man without scru-

ples. He killed one of his partners, Dutch Henry, near Desert Springs and burned the body. He later made a Frenchman dig his own grave and shot him into it.[31]

In his later years Ben ran a watering station at Mountain Springs west of Milford. After supplying freighters with water and supplies, Ben would send his gang out to rob the freighters after they had traveled several miles from the station.[32] How and when Ben Tasker cashed in his chips is not known, but a man with his reputation probably did not die from old age.

Cowboys working for the Meathook outfit north of Modena, Utah, circa 1900, reenact a robbery that could have occurred when Ben Tasker was operating in the area. Photograph courtesy of Mike Flinspach.

Another outlaw gang operating in the southwestern corner of Utah was led by two Ketchum brothers, Tom "Black Jack" and Sam. The gang's headquarters was located in Snake Valley on the Utah-Nevada border, west of Milford.

During the 1890s Tom and Sam left Utah for New Mexico and Arizona and got into the more lucrative profession of train and bank robbery. On several occasions the brothers returned to Utah for short visits at the Robber's Roost—visits spurred on by hostile posses who, in most instances, would not cross the border into Utah.

In 1899 the Ketchum brothers joined up with members of Butch Cassidy's Wild Bunch and robbed a train near Folsom, New Mexico. A posse caught up with the outlaws and wounded Elzy Lay and Sam

Written on the back of this photograph, taken circa 1900, is a statement indicating that these men were outlaws. It is believed that the town was Newhouse in western Utah. Photograph courtesy of Rell Francis.

Ketchum. Ketchum later died of his wounds. Several days later Tom Ketchum tried to hold up the same train, but he was wounded in the arm and captured. Tom eventually was hanged at Clayton, New Mexico.[33]

There were several prominent rustling gangs which operated between the central Utah mountains and the Colorado border during the late 1870s through the 1880s. The Mike Cassidy gang was a loose-knit group of working cowboys who supplemented their earnings by rustling. Mike worked on the Jim Marshal ranch south of Circleville, and used the wild canyons in Bryce to hold his stolen stock until he had built up a large enough herd to drive to Colorado.

In the early 1880s Mike took a young Mormon lad by the name of Robert Leroy Parker from Circleville under his wing. For approximately four years Mike taught young Parker everything he knew about cowboying and, unfortunately, rustling. Mike had to leave Utah unexpectedly when the law started clos-

Tom McCarty was a prominent Utah cattleman who turned to cattle rustling and bank robbing. Photograph courtesy of Warner and Lacy copyright 1980.

Bill McCarty joined his brother Tom and Matt Warner to form a robbing syndicate. Photograph courtesy of Warner and Lacy copyright 1980.

ing in on him. Legend has it that he went to Mexico and was not heard from again.[34] Young Robert Parker went on to become one of the West's most famous outlaws. A fuller account of his escapades will be discussed later.

Cap Brown operated a rustling gang on the Henry Mountains and may have been one of the first outlaws to use the Robber's Roost as a hideout. As with many of the old outlaws, Cap Brown's early history and circumstances surrounding his death are mysteries. His gang did leave one note of history, however. During one cattle raid in Wayne County a posse followed Cap and two young outlaws to the outskirts of Robber's Roost. Cap stopped to fire warning shots at the posse and in the return fire one of the young outlaws was hit. He died a few hours later and Cap buried him in a shallow grave. That

Leroy Benson of Coalville, Utah, circa 1915, was not yet born when the Ike Potter gang raided the town, but no doubt he had a few relatives that settled with the outlaws. Photograph from author's collection.

burial site is now known as "Dead Man's Hill."[35]

The Blue Mountain Gang, led by Tom McCarty, operated out of La Sal, Utah. Tom and his brother Bill were the sons of William McCarty, who had moved his large family from Tennessee to the West shortly after the Civil War. A doctor by trade, William decided to go into the cattle business and established a ranch in Grass Valley, just north of present-day Antimony, Utah. In 1874 four young Navajos came to Grass Valley to trade with the Paiutes and while there killed and ate a calf belonging to the McCartys. The McCartys found the Indians eating the calf and shot and killed three of them, wounding the fourth. The wounded Indian made it back to the reservation and told of the killings. A war with the Navajos was averted only when the Mormon scout and church leader, Jacob Hamblin, went to the Navajo Reservation and convinced the chiefs that the Mormons were not responsible for the killings.[36]

A few years after the shootings the McCartys took their herd of cattle to the La Sal Mountains and es-

Bill Hitchcock was a U.S. Border Patrol officer along the U.S.–Mexican border circa 1897. Perhaps he was part of the posse that chased Warner and McCarty back to Utah. Photograph courtesy of R. G. Hitchcock.

tablished a prosperous ranch. The ranch was bought by the Pittsburgh Land and Cattle Company in 1884 and most of the family moved to Oregon. Bill went to Minnesota, where he was put in prison for shooting a man. After being released from prison, he also went to Oregon. Tom remained in Utah and organized a band of rustlers. After two or three years of this, he moved on to New Mexico, where he was involved in several scrapes around Fort Wingate with his cousin William McCarty, also known as William Bonney, alias "Billy the Kid."[37]

While in Fort Wingate Tom was joined by his brother-in-law, Willard Erastus Christianson, who

Matt Warner about the time he left Levan, Utah, to ride the outlaw trail. Photograph courtesy of Warner and Lacy copyright 1980.

would later become one of Utah's most famous outlaws, alias Matt Warner. Tom and Matt, together with another cowboy from Panguitch, Utah, called Josh Sweat, worked out a deal with the Chisholm Ranch to bring Mexican cattle across the border at $3.50 a head. They went across the border and rustled 200 head, which were paid for in cash at the Chisholm Ranch. The pickin's seemed so easy that a few days later the three were back down in Mexico rustling another couple hundred head of cattle. This time, however, the outlaws were ambushed by American Border Patrol officers. During the shooting Josh was hit three times but managed to stay on his horse. The group made it back to the Chisholm Ranch, where Josh was patched up.[38]

Within a few days of the fight at the border word reached the Chisholm Ranch that a posse of federal

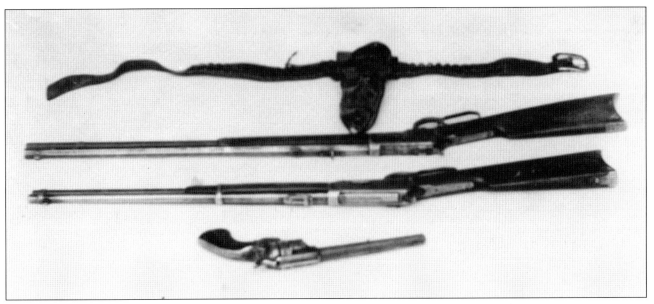

Rifles, pistol, and holster used by Matt Warner. Photograph courtesy of Warner and Lacy copyright 1980.

officers was coming in to pick up the outlaws. The posse was prepared for a long chase and had extra saddle horses and pack horses. Matt and Tom helped Josh to his horse, picked up what grub and supplies they could, and they all lit out on a dead run.

In his own words Matt described what happened next. "That was the beginning of the first chase by Federal Officers I was ever in. It covered the full length of Arizona from south to north, about half of Utah and some of Nevada—at least six hundred miles. It was like a prolonged war, with us using all of our cowboy tricks and knowledge of horses and the country against the skill, cunning and guns of the officers."[39]

The three outlaws escaped from the federal men. Josh made his way back to central Utah where he went straight and left the outlaw trail. Tom and Matt split up after spending some time around Frisco, Utah. The two met again several months later in the mining town of Telluride, Colorado. While in Telluride, Matt met up with Robert Leroy Parker and his brother Dan. They had left Utah shortly after their mentor, Mike Cassidy, left.

During this time Tom and Matt convinced Robert and Dan that bank robbing was more lucrative and much easier than rustling. In March of 1889 Tom

Matt Warner (left) and an outlaw friend. Matt had become a hardened desperado at the time the photograph was taken. Photograph courtesy of Warner and Lacy copyright 1980.

and Matt had held up the First National Bank of Denver and had escaped with $21,000. They felt the San Miguel National Bank of Telluride would be just as easy and it was. On June 24, 1889, Tom, Matt, Robert, and Dan rode out of town with $10,500 of the bank's money. The four outlaws reached Robber's Roost in Utah, where they were free from all reprisals.

After a spell at the Roost, Tom and Matt decided to go to Oregon. Robert, now using the name Cassidy, and Dan, going by Ricketts, decided to go on to the Brown's Park country. In Oregon Tom and Matt convinced Bill McCarty to hit the outlaw trail. For the next few years the three, known as the "Invincible Three," committed a number of robberies in the Northwest. Matt was captured after one robbery and placed in the Ellensburg, Washington, jail. While he was awaiting trial Tom, Bill, and Bill's son Fred rode to Delta, Colorado, where they robbed the bank. A sharp-shooting store clerk by the name of W. Ray Simpson killed both Bill and his son Fred as they were riding out of town.[40] Tom got away, and, for a time, made threats that he would return to Delta to take care of Simpson, but nothing ever happened. It was reported that Tom was later killed in a shoot-out in the Bitter Root Mountain area of Montana.

Of all of the rustlers in Utah, none could have had a stranger variety of the twists and turns of life than did Matt Warner. Matt was born in the small Mormon community of Ephraim, Utah, in 1864 and moved to Levan at a very early age. He began riding

Charlie Gibbons and a fellow called Frenchie at Hanksville, Utah, in the 1880s. Butch Cassidy worked for Gibbons after leaving Circleville, Utah. Photograph courtesy of Horace Ekker.

herd on the settlement cattle by the time he was eight, and when he was eleven years of age, he was considered one of the best bronc riders in central Utah. Many of the local ranchers paid Matt to break their horses, giving him money and prestige and a large degree of maturity at an early age.

At fourteen Matt signed on with Charley Wagner to herd three thousand head of cattle from the Mormon settlements to the high, rolling plains of Wyoming. They crossed the Strawberry Valley, which at that time belonged to the Ute Indians. The Utes had been warring until 1872 and had killed white men in the valley as late as 1876. Matt was wide-eyed as the cowboys on the trail drive told of Indian fights and savage brutality.

Matt Warner in the 1930s. Matt was living in Price, Utah, at the time and had become a respected lawman. Photograph courtesy of Warner and Lacy copyright 1980.

When the herd reached the present-day site of Roosevelt, Matt, longing for the company of a girl friend back in Levan, decided he wanted to head for home. Charley Wagner tried to talk him out of leaving, but when it appeared the young Mormon cowboy was bent on returning, he advised Matt to travel at night while crossing the Strawberry Valley alone, to make a dark camp, and to ride like hell. Matt took Charley's advice and did not encounter any Indians on the trip back.

Back in Levan Matt spent some time trying to impress a young girl, Alice Sabey. One night, as the Mormon kids met together for a church social, Matt walked Alice home. A group of boys led by the town bully, Andrew Hendrickson, who had designs on Alice himself, taunted Matt all the way. Andrew wanted to impress Alice by whipping Matt, but Matt didn't want to fight in Alice's presence. The taunting continued, and by the time they reached Alice's

Brigham Hamilton and Butch Cassidy at the Anderson Studio, Manti, Utah, in the 1880s. Photograph courtesy of Steve Lacy copyright 1990, Wild Bunch photo.

Dan Parker (sitting left) and friends at the Anderson Studio, Manti, Utah, in the 1880s. Photograph courtesy of Steve Lacy copyright 1980, Wild Bunch photo.

house, Matt was in a state of rage. He turned on Andrew, wielding a piece of fence wood and began beating him in the head. Andrew was knocked unconscious and Matt figured he had killed him. One of the boys watching the fight cried out that Andrew was dead and yelled out for someone to fetch the marshal.

Believing he had killed Andrew and that the marshal would soon be coming for him, Matt decided he had better leave town. He ran home, saddled his best horse, and went into the house to get his guns. He stopped long enough to bid his parents good-bye. He did not take the time to tell them why.[41]

Matt figured to catch up with the Wagner trail herd. He stopped a short time at a railroad camp near Indianola where a kind stranger took a liking to him and presented him with several silver dollars.

A cowboy poses in front of an adobe cabin in Brown's Park circa 1900. Photograph courtesy of Steve Lacy copyright 1980, Wild Bunch photo.

He was then waylaid by a tribe of Ute Indians in the Strawberry Valley. He was taken to their camp, but instead of being scalped, he was able to make a trade with the Indians using the silver dollars. Leaving the Indian camp on good terms, Matt rode to Diamond Mountain, a pleasant rolling highland covered by tall grass, timbered hills, and sweet water lying some thirty miles north of Vernal.

Matt found work with a rancher by the name of Jim Warren, but he soon realized that Warren's sizable herd of cattle and horses had not been acquired in the most legitimate way. Jim encouraged the boy to develop his own herd as well by using the running iron. Matt figured that since he was wanted by the law anyway, rustling would not be that bad an occupation.

By the time another young Mormon boy, a brother of Andrew Hendrickson, made his way to Diamond Mountain, Matt had established a horse ranch on Pott Creek and had accumulated around a hundred and fifty head of horses. For the first time

he learned that he had not killed Andrew and that he was not wanted by the marshal at Levan. Ironically, the news came too late, for Matt was now an established rustler along the Utah-Wyoming border.[42]

During his time on Diamond Mountain Matt had had several knock-down-drag-out fights with rough characters, had shot a Mexican called Polito in a gun-fight, and had joined "Cherokee" Bangs, leader of a cattle-rustling expedition into Wyoming. He had also managed to find time to rob a Jewish merchant who was moving goods across the Uinta Mountains. Matt left Diamond Mountain rather abruptly when he was implicated in Cherokee Bangs's venture.

From Diamond Mountain Matt and another cowboy named Joe Brooks rode south to St. Johns, Arizona, where they robbed a local store. A posse chased them back into Utah until they took refuge at the Robber's Roost. Matt stayed at the Roost for two months and then decided to look up Tom McCarty, who had married Matt's sister Teenie. It was shortly after this time that Matt, Tom, and Josh Sweat were chased all over the Southwest by federal marshals for rustling cattle across the border in Mexico.

For the next several years Matt and Tom traveled around together and made several daring holdups, including the Telluride bank job with Butch Cassidy. During their time together Matt and Tom met and married two Mormon girls from Star Valley, Wyoming. Tom's wife, Matt's sister, Teenie, had previously died. Tom's new wife, Sary Jane, was a half-sister to Matt's new wife, Rose. Matt and Rose got along well together, but Sary Jane soon tired of Tom and went to live with her mother in Salt Lake City.

Matt took Rose to Washington State, where he established a ranch and hideout known as the 7U Ranch. Rose stayed on the ranch for months on end while Matt, Tom, and Bill McCarty pulled off a number of robberies in the Northwest. When Rose became sick, Sary Jane came up to the ranch to look after her. Matt had decided to leave the outlaw trail and settle down with Rose, but he wanted to pull off just one more job to insure they would have enough money to make a new start.

Prison photo of Butch Cassidy. Photograph courtesy of Baker and Lacy copyright 1965.

The Invincible Three robbed the bank at Roselyn, Washington, which resulted in a $20,000 reward being offered for the capture of the outlaws. The temptation was too great for Sary Jane, and she turned Matt and the others in. Tom and Bill escaped, but Matt was captured and put into the Ellensburg, Washington, jail.

Matt was able to solicit one of the best criminal lawyers in the State of Washington and to beat the charges against him. It took $41,000 in outlaw gold to do the trick, however, and when he was released from jail he was penniless. The lawyer returned $500 to him to see him on his way.[43]

Matt and Rose returned to Utah, where he once again started ranching on Diamond Mountain. Rose soon became ill with cancer and had to live in Vernal. Matt spent as much time as possible in Vernal with her. While he was having a drink one day in a local saloon with a fellow cowboy, Bill Wall, they were approached by a mining promoter, Henry Coleman. Coleman had a camp in the Uinta Mountains, and he offered Matt and Bill a hundred dollars each to go and move the camp for him, which they agreed to do. Coleman, however, failed to tell the two cowboys that he had been having problems with three claim jumpers, Ike and Dick Staunton and Dave Milton. All along Coleman was hoping the cowboys would have an altercation with the claim jumpers, and, sure enough, they did.

Matt and Wall reached the camp in the Uintas and packed up. On their way out the two cowboys were ambushed by the claim jumpers. Matt's horse was shot out from under him but he instinctively grabbed his rifle as he was falling to the ground. Following a short battle, Dick Staunton and Dave Milton were mortally wounded. Ike Staunton was severely wounded. Matt had fired seven times and had hit the mark six.[44]

Matt and Bill were taken into custody by Sheriff John Pope of Vernal, but were transferred to Ogden because of unruly mobs in Vernal, friends of the Stauntons and Dave Milton. While jailed in Ogden, Matt got word to Butch Cassidy that he needed money for lawyers. Shortly thereafter Butch, Elzy Lay and Bob Meeks robbed the Montpelier, Idaho, bank and turned the entire haul of $16,500 over to a Rock Springs, Wyoming, lawyer, who was able to

The Sundance Kid and Etta Place. Photograph courtesy of Baker and Lacy copyright 1965.

Annie Rogers and Kid Curry. Photograph courtesy of Baker and Lacy copyright 1965.

get the charge of first degree murder changed to manslaughter. Although Matt and Bill had fired in self-defense, they were sentenced to five years at the Utah State Prison, primarily because they had both been outlaws in the past.[45]

Matt served his prison term and was released on January 21, 1900. He settled in Price, Utah, and lived there as an honorable citizen until his death in 1938. A final irony of Matt's life occurred when he became a deputy sheriff for the city of Price. He was also elected justice of the peace.

Butch Cassidy, like Matt Warner, was a Utah cowboy with Mormon roots. He was born Robert LeRoy Parker on April 13, 1866, in Beaver, Utah. He was the eldest of thirteen children born to Maximillian and Annie Parker, faithful and active members of the Mormon church. When Robert was twelve years old the family moved to Circleville, Utah, where they established a home. During the summers Annie

Elza or Elzy Lay was known as the educated member of the Wild Bunch. Photograph courtesy of Edwin and Roslyn Grose.

took the children to the Marshall Ranch, which lies several miles south of Circleville, where she operated a small dairy to bring in extra income for the family.[46]

The Marshall Ranch was a fairly large cattle outfit which hired a number of cowboys. One of these cowboys was Mike Cassidy, who supplemented his income by rustling cattle. Mike took to Robert and his younger brother Dan, and before long Mike was teaching his young proteges all of the arts of cowboying, including the use of the running iron. By age seventeen Robert, and Dan, age sixteen, were two of the best cowboys on the range and could hold their own with any man.

Mike left for Mexico, and shortly thereafter Robert got into trouble over some stolen stock and had to leave the Circleville area. He rode to Hanksville, Utah, where he was befriended by Charley Gibbons, who operated the local store and ran a few head of cattle. It is believed that Robert worked for Charley for a time while rustling on the side. The Wayne County sheriff picked Robert up and brought him

Several known members of the Wild Bunch can be seen in this photograph taken at Baggs, Wyoming, in the 1890s. Butch Cassidy is fourth from the left wearing a bowler hat. Photograph courtesy of Betts Ashmore.

back to Loa for questioning. There was no jail in Loa so Robert was asked to stay in town for a few days and he complied. While in Loa Robert played baseball with the local kids, endearing him to them even after he became a notorious outlaw.[47]

Nothing came from the questioning in Loa, and Robert returned to Hanksville. From there he went into the Robber's Roost, where Cap Brown helped him move some stolen horses across the Colorado River. After leaving the Roost Robert made his way to the mining town of Telluride, Colorado, where he sold the horses. Telluride was a wild town which offered all the spice and variety not obtainable in the small Mormon community of Circleville. While in

Three citizens of Mercur, Utah, in the early 1900s. Mercur was a rich mining town that would have caught the eye of Butch Cassidy. Photograph from author's collection.

Telluride, Robert met up with his brother, Dan Parker, Matt Warner, and Tom McCarty and began his outlaw career in earnest.

After robbing the Telluride bank, the four outlaws went back to the Robber's Roost. During that ride back, Matt claimed, Robert picked up the name of "Butch" when he was knocked down while shooting a sawed-off shotgun which Matt affectionately called "Butch."[48] The name Cassidy was taken from his mentor, Mike Cassidy.

Following a short stay at the Roost, Matt Warner and Tom McCarty went to the Northwest. Butch Cassidy and Dan decided to see what Brown's Park and the southern Wyoming plains were all about. Brown's Park had for years been a haven for several rustler gangs, and it was considered to be a safe place for outlaws with a price on their heads. The Park could also be a disastrous place to hide out, as

Five members of the Wild Bunch at Fort Worth, Texas, circa 1900. Sundance is sitting on the left and Cassidy is sitting on the right. Photograph courtesy of Winnemucca Bank.

was attested to by the Tip Gault and Red Sash gangs.

Tip Gault had made a lucrative living stealing cattle and horses along the Oregon Trail in Wyoming, holding them for a spell in Brown's Park, and then selling them to other emigrants along the trail or to the Mormon settlements in Utah. The gang made a mistake one time of rustling horses belonging to a tough cattle outfit from Wyoming who pursued the gang to the outskirts of Brown's Park and, in a gun battle, wiped them out with the exception of one member. The sole survivor was a black cowboy from Texas who went by the name of Isom Dart. Dart had been burying a fellow outlaw who had been kicked by a horse when the shooting started. Dart threw himself into the grave and was able to avoid the Wyoming posse.[49] After this incident he went to Brown's Park where he ranched and did a little rustling on the side.

The Red Sash gang was started by Nate Champion, who was killed during the Johnson County Range War in Wyoming. Champion's successor, Red Bob, led the gang members, who wore red sashes around their waists on a number of rustling expeditions. In 1898 the gang robbed the Union Pacific mail car near Bryan Station, Sweetwater County, Wyoming, and rode back across the state line into Utah. A Wyoming posse chased the gang into Utah, and, in a gun battle several miles west of Brown's Park, killed three members of the gang, wounded a fourth, and captured Red Bob. Red Bob thought it was highly unfair for the posse to come into Utah, but he did not have much time to think about it as he died in prison a short time later of tuberculosis.[50]

Butch Cassidy and his brother Dan made it to Brown's Park where they became friends with a cattleman named Charlie Crouse. They later established a hideout just south of Crouse's ranch on Diamond Mountain. From this hideout they spread out into the Wyoming country rustling horses and cattle. Dan, using the alias Tom Ricketts, along with fellow outlaw, William Brown, robbed the Muddy Creek stagecoach on December 29, 1889, as it made its run between Dixon and Rawlins, Wyoming. The two outlaws left Wyoming shortly thereafter for Utah. In October of 1890 Dan was captured following a gun battle with United States Marshal Joe Bush in the La Sal Mountains near Moab. Bush returned Dan to Wyoming, where he was convicted of robbing the Muddy Creek stagecoach and was sentenced to a prison term.[51]

Butch was captured by a Wyoming posse in 1894 and was committed to the Wyoming State Penitentiary for rustling horses. He spent the next year and a half there, and was released on January 10, 1896, being told in no uncertain terms to stay out of Wyoming. It was one of the few promises Butch Cassidy made and failed to keep.

Upon his release from prison Butch returned to Brown's Park, where he formulated plans to organize an outlaw gang so bold with its activities that the governors of three states, Utah, Wyoming, and Colorado, would eventually meet together to discuss ways to exterminate the gang. The Union Pacific Railroad became so tired of them it hired gunmen to ride the rails in search of the elusive outlaws. The Pinkerton National Detective Agency put its best men into the field in an effort to capture them but was totally stymied in its efforts.

For the next five years Butch and his gang, known as the Wild Bunch, kept things pretty lively in the Intermountain West. A little-known manuscript written by William T. Phillips, who most likely was a member of the gang, and, some historians believe, was in fact Butch Cassidy, indicated that the first robbery committed by Butch after his release from prison occurred in Utah.[52] A holdup did occur in Utah in April of 1896. Four masked gunmen described as typical border ruffians held up the Mercur Hotel Gambling House. Mercur at the time was one of the richest gold-producing towns in the West. The outlaws made a clean escape with an unspecified amount of money.[53]

Approximately a month later, officials of the Salt

Lake Mercur Railroad were told by an informant that a gang of outlaws was going to hold up the train on its weekly run from Mercur to Salt Lake City when it carried thousands of dollars in gold dust. Railroad officials reacted by hiring extra guards who were stationed prominently on the train. The expected holdup did not take place.[54] Whether the Wild Bunch had had a hand in the Mercur robbery and the plot to rob the gold train is purely speculative, but highly interesting.

Other robberies attributed to Butch Cassidy's Wild Bunch included the Montpelier Bank of Idaho in 1896; the Castle Gate, Utah, mine payroll in 1897; the Belle Fourche, South Dakota, bank in 1897; the Wilcox Train Robbery in Wyoming in 1899; the Colorado Southern Train robbery in New Mexico in 1899; the Tipton, Wyoming, train robbery in 1900; the Winnemucca, Nevada, bank in 1900; and the Wagner, Montana, train robbery in 1901. There were other bank and train robberies plus rustling activities going on at the time which are not directly attributed to the leadership of the Wild Bunch, but were committed by outlaws on the outer fringes of the gang and who, in their own minds, were indeed part of the Wild Bunch.

Although Butch abhorred the use of a gun, this feeling was not shared by all of the men who rode with him. Some of those in the inner circle of the gang were known to have been hot tempered and more than willing to settle things with a six-shooter. The gang itself was a loosely knit outfit which numbered anywhere from a few men to twenty or thirty. Usually only three or four gang members participated in a robbery at any given time, and the robberies were not necessarily all planned by the same gang members. Butch Cassidy, however, was the undisputed leader of the gang, and its membership included some of the most notorious outlaws of the nineteenth century.

In the beginning of Butch Cassidy's dynasty his closest associate was William Ellsway, alias Elza or Elzy Lay. Elzy was born in McArthur, Ohio, in 1868 and migrated west with his family at an early age. As a young man he found his way to Brown's Park, where he learned the cowboying trade. As a budding outlaw he participated in the holdup of a Jewish merchant in the Uinta Mountains with Matt Warner.[55]

The driver and guard on the wagon worked for Judge Harkness, who had jurisdiction in Carbon County, Utah. The black man accompanying them in the wagon is the man standing in the facing photograph. The photograph was taken at Scofield, Utah, in the 1890s. Photograph courtesy of Rell Francis.

Elzy was a tall, good-looking fellow, intelligent and often called "the educated outlaw" because his mannerisms reminded one of a Boston gentleman. Elzy was captured after the Colorado Southern train robbery in New Mexico and was sent to the New Mexico Penitentiary. He was pardoned in 1905 and eventually went to California where he lived out the remainder of his life as a respected and law-abiding citizen.

Harry Alonzo Longabaugh, alias the Sundance Kid, was, with the exception of Elzy Lay, Cassidy's closest friend, and the association between the two lasted longer than that of any other gang member.

Orrin Elmer, marshal of Colton, Utah, identified the men in this photograph as being members of the Robber's Roost gang, which may have numbered as many as thirty men. Photograph courtesy of Dennis Finch.

He was born in Phoenixville, Pennsylvania, in 1868 and moved to the New Mexico Territory while still a teenager. In 1884 he hired out as a cowboy to the Pittsburgh Land and Cattle Company at La Sal, Utah. While working on the range he spent as much time as possible practicing his quick draw and shooting. Old-timers claimed he was the fastest they had ever seen.[56] He left Utah for Wyoming in the 1880s and ended up getting arrested for horse stealing. He was committed to the jail at Sundance, Wyoming, hence his name. When he was released from jail in 1889, Sundance spent the next several years working as a cowboy and rustling on the side.

Sundance joined up with Butch Cassidy in 1896 and became an integral part of the Wild Bunch. During the time he operated with the gang he met the mysterious Etta Place. Little is known of this lady who became Sundance's companion. There is some

Miners and guards during the 1904 miners' strike at Castle Gate, Utah. The guard at far left on the rock pile is "Gunplay" Maxwell. Photograph courtesy of Utah State Historical Society.

indication that she was a schoolteacher in either Utah or Colorado prior to meeting up with him. Whatever her background, she apparently was a very beautiful woman. Maude Davis Lay, the young Mormon girl from Vernal who married Elzy Lay, often told her daughter, Marvel Lay Murdock, how beautiful Etta was—tall and stately with raven dark hair.[57]

In 1901 Etta, Sundance, and Butch Cassidy left the United States and ventured into South America. Etta returned a year or two later and, although there are indications that she later married, and resumed her life as a schoolteacher in Utah, the beautiful lady remains as mysterious today as she was in days of yore.

Sundance and Butch picked up their outlaw careers in South America and pulled off a number of successful bank robberies. They were supposedly killed in a shootout at San Vincente, Bolivia, in 1908

The man on the left is reputed to be Butch Cassidy in a photograph taken several years after he supposedly was killed in South America. Photograph courtesy of Steve Lacy copyright 1984, Wild Bunch Photo.

or 1909, but the information coming out of Bolivia was sketchy and the death of the two outlaws is surrounded with much myth and little fact. What happened to Sundance after South America is probably more factual.

One theory involving Sundance suggests that he came back to the United States and eventually settled in Utah, using the alias "Hiram Bebee." Bebee was a leather-tough old-timer living in Spring City who acted as if he had been on the outer fringes of the law most of his life. In 1945 Bebee had a run-in with the marshal of Mount Pleasant, Utah. The marshal, Lon T. Larson, tried to take Bebee in and the old-timer shot the marshal dead. Bebee was apprehended by a posse of armed men, and he eventually found himself housed at the Utah State Prison. While in prison the guards noticed that he wrote letters to the Longabaugh family in Pennsylvania, but this had no meaning to the guards at that time. Today, the fact that Bebee associated with the Longabaugh family is strong evidence that he was either Sundance or a good friend of Sundance. Bebee died at the prison on June 2, 1955.

Another theory concerning Sundance suggests

Chub Milburn, Mark Draffet, "Gunplay" Maxwell, and Peter Francis at Price, Utah, circa 1897. Maxwell and Francis were members of the Robbers Roost gang. Photograph courtesy of Vern Jeffers.

that he came back to the states and married Etta Place. An interesting trail of the two former outlaws leads to the Uinta Basin in eastern Utah, but future historians will have to follow up that trail. It would be nice if the story of Sundance and Etta ended with them riding off into the sunset together.

The deadliest and most steel-nerved member of the Wild Bunch gang was Harvey Logan, alias Kid Curry. Logan had led his own group of outlaws, known as "The Hole-in-the-Wall Gang," in Wyoming prior to joining forces with Butch Cassidy. Curry was known to have gone hundreds of miles out of his way to settle a score with suspected informants, leaving a path of dead men in his wake. Many of the dead were lawmen who had gotten in his way.

The fate of Kid Curry is also intertwined in mystery. He was captured in Tennessee and placed in the Knox County jail, but shortly thereafter he escaped. It is thought that he and two other outlaws tried to rob a train near Parachute, Colorado, in 1904. Curry was wounded during the attempt and killed himself when the posse began to close in. However, some historians dispute this account of his death and believe he made his way to Argentina, where he was killed in a gun battle on December 9, 1911.[58]

The deaths of other members of the Wild Bunch are not surrounded in as much mystery. John Logan was killed by a rancher near Landusky, Montana, in 1896. Lonny Logan was killed by officers at Dodson, Missouri, in 1900. "Flat Nose" George Curry was shot by a Utah posse in the Book Cliff Mountains in 1900. Bill Carver was killed by a sheriff at Sonora, Texas, in 1901. Camilla Hanks was killed by a posse at San Antonio, Texas, in 1902. Ben Kilpatrick was killed after an unsuccessful train robbery at Sanderson, Texas, in 1912.

Besides Elzy Lay, other members of the gang who were able to end their outlaw careers without being killed by a posse include Utah-born Henry Wilbur

170

Bob Ricker, Rufe Stoddard, and Al Starr (left to right). Ricker was a sometime cowboy and member of the Robber's Roost gang. Photograph courtesy of Baker and Lacy copyright 1965.

"Bub" Meeks, Tom "Peep" O'Day, and Walter Putney.

In addition to the inner core of the Wild Bunch, there were many more outlaws who were associated with the gang in various degrees. These cowboys were outlaws in their own right, but at times gathered horses for the gang, fed them information, and spent a good deal of time simply killing time and playing cards with gang members while they were hiding out along the outlaw trail. Many of these outlaws also met a violent end.

The black cowboy, Isom Dart, kept up his rustling activities until he was felled by a bullet in 1900. Fellow outlaw Matt Rash was killed a few weeks prior. Both men were killed by the bounty hunter Tom Horn. Numerous other graves dot the Brown's Park country and contain the bodies of outlaws and semi-outlaws who met a violent end. Included in this group are the "Speckled Nigger" Albert William, who was killed by Charley Crouse; Jesse Ewing, who was killed in a fight over a woman; John Jarvie, killed during a robbery; Cleophas Dowd, killed in a shoot-out at his ranch in Sheep Creek Canyon.

John Bennett also claimed a plot of ground six feet deep in Brown's Park. He had the misfortune to join up with Pat Johnson who, in a moment of anger, killed a young boy by the name of Willie Strang for playfully knocking a dipper of water out of his hand. Bennett was not involved in the killing but, because he was an associate of Johnson, an angry mob strung him up to a gatepost.[59]

While Bennett was being hanged, Johnson was trying to make his way out of the Park. Along the way he met up with two recent Utah Penitentiary escapees, Harry Tracy and Dave Lant. A posse caught up with the three outlaws and, during a short battle, posse member Valentine Hoy was shot and killed by Harry Tracy. Three days later the trio of outlaws was captured by the posse. Johnson was given a ten-year sentence of which he served two years. Harry

William G. Hanna, who worked for the Island Park Cattle Association, came to the area after the outlaw era was over. Photograph courtesy of Darla Gradner.

Tracy escaped from jail and went on a tear in the Northwest, killing several lawmen before killing himself. Dave Lant joined the army in 1898 and received honors for bravery in action while in the Philippines. He later returned to Utah and lived a peaceful life.[60]

A loosely knit group of cowboy outlaws that associated with the Wild Bunch operated in southern Utah and were known as the Robber's Roost gang. Many of the men operating in this section of Utah did not acquire notorious reputations outside of the region and their histories are therefore little known. As a case in point: two photographs included in this book are of a black who was believed to be a member of the Wild Bunch gang. One of the photographs, taken at Colton, Utah, shows him standing next to another outlaw; the second photograph, taken in Schofield, Utah, shows him in a wagon with an armed guard. Incidentally, the guard was employed by Judge Harkness, the justice of the peace for Carbon County, Utah. As for the black outlaw, I have

been unable to obtain any more information about him. And, there were many more shadowy and obscure outlaws during the Wild Bunch era.

On the other hand, there were some well-known Robber's Roost members who made quite a menace of themselves during the last decade of the nineteenth century. Tom Dilly came to Utah after killing a fellow in a Texas saloon. The fight was over a scarlet woman. After arriving in Utah he went to work for the Webster City Cattle Company. Dilly did not get along with one of the cowboys working for Webster City and a short time later the cowboy was killed. Tom was suspected of doing the killing and was no longer welcome on the Webster City range. From that point on, Dilly began rustling Webster City cattle and built up quite a sizable herd. The posse from Moab that killed "Flat Nose" Curry was, in fact, out looking for Tom Dilly at the time.

Dilly struck up a partnership with two fellows named Dowd and Forrester, who were running several hundred head of cattle near Sunnyside,

Utah. The three men formed the Patmos Head Land and Cattle Company. Dilly was supposed to "steal them rich," but instead he stole his partners poor. He rounded up most of the Patmos cattle and a number of others belonging to some local cattlemen. He had them shipped to Kansas City, where he sold them for a good profit. His partners expected his return, but Dilly never came back to Utah. Instead, he went to South America with the bulk of the company's assets.[61]

Joe Walker came to Utah saying that his mother was the sister of Dr. Whitmore, who had originally settled at Pipe Springs. He went to the Whitmore ranch at Sunnyside and claimed he was entitled to a share of the Whitmore holdings because Dr. Whitmore had borrowed money from his mother. The Whitmores refused the claim, and, from that point on, Joe Walker decided he would get his share by rustling Whitmore stock.[62]

Joe joined up with another rustler by the name of Johnny Herring, and together they made quite a dent in the Whitmore herds of cattle and horses. In 1898 a posse caught up with the outlaws and filled them full of holes while they were still in their bedrolls.[63]

A number of the Robber's Roost outlaws worked for J. B. Buhr, who operated the 3B Ranch right smack in the middle of the Robber's Roost region. Included in this group were Silver Tip, Blue John, Indian Ed Newcomb, and Jack Moore. These cowboys worked gratis for the 3B with the exception of food and occasional lodging. They made their pay by rustling stock from ranchers along the Henry Mountains. These outlaws fared little better than Walker and Herring. Silver Tip, whose real name was James F. Howells, was captured in 1899 and taken to Loa for trial. He was sentenced to a term of ten years in the Utah State Penitentiary but was released after one year. He went back to Wayne County where he got into more trouble. From there he went to Arizona, where he was killed by a sheriff. Indian Ed was wounded by a sheriff's posse, but managed to escape and was not heard of again. Blue John was presumed to have drowned in the Colorado River while trying to escape from a posse. Jack Moore was killed while rustling horses in Wyoming.

Dan Parker, alias Ricketts, alias Kid Parker, and

Bob Ricker were also members of the Robber's Roost gang for a time. Although Dan was Butch Cassidy's brother, he somehow never quite fit into the inner core of the Wild Bunch. As late as 1910 the Oak Saloon in Park City was held up by Kid Parker. Whether this Kid Parker was, in fact, Dan Parker has never been proven. Dan left the outlaw trail sometime after the turn of the century and lived the rest of his life as a respectable citizen. Bob Ricker went to Wyoming after rustling most of the Starr-Thompson stock on the Henry Mountains. He was shot and killed by a Baggs, Wyoming, saloon keeper not long after arriving in that small town, located just north of Brown's Park.[64]

The most famous member of the Robber's Roost gang was C. L. "Gunplay" Maxwell. Maxwell tried hard to get involved with the inner core of the Wild Bunch and might have done so if his plan to rob the U.S. Army shipment of Indian annuity funds had come off as expected. Maxwell and another outlaw, Peter A. Francis, had solicited the help of Butch Cassidy to get the money, which they believed would amount to between $30,000 and $60,000. It was to arrive on the Rio Grande train at Price, Utah, and from there it was to be escorted by five or six soldiers through the narrow, winding Nine Mile Canyon to Fort Duchesne in the Uinta Basin.

Cassidy liked the plan, and in the few weeks prior to the money's arrival at Price several associates of Cassidy, including Elzy Lay, made their way to the town. Several members of Maxwell's rustling gang also filtered into Price. With fifteen to twenty bandits taking part in the robbery, it was figured to be easy pickin's against the small number of soldiers guarding the money.

Within days of the train's arrival rumors reached Fort Duchesne that a possible holdup was being formulated. With that information in hand, the commander of the fort made preparations for a troop of Ninth Cavalry, "Buffalo Soldiers," to meet the train. When the troop of forty black soldiers, all heavily armed, came to Price to meet the train, Cassidy and Maxwell decided to call off the robbery.[65]

The outlaw careers of "Gunplay" Maxwell and Peter Francis went downhill after the aborted holdup. Francis had bought a ranch in Nine Mine Canyon prior to the planned holdup of the Indian annuity

Outlaw Guns and Wanted Posters

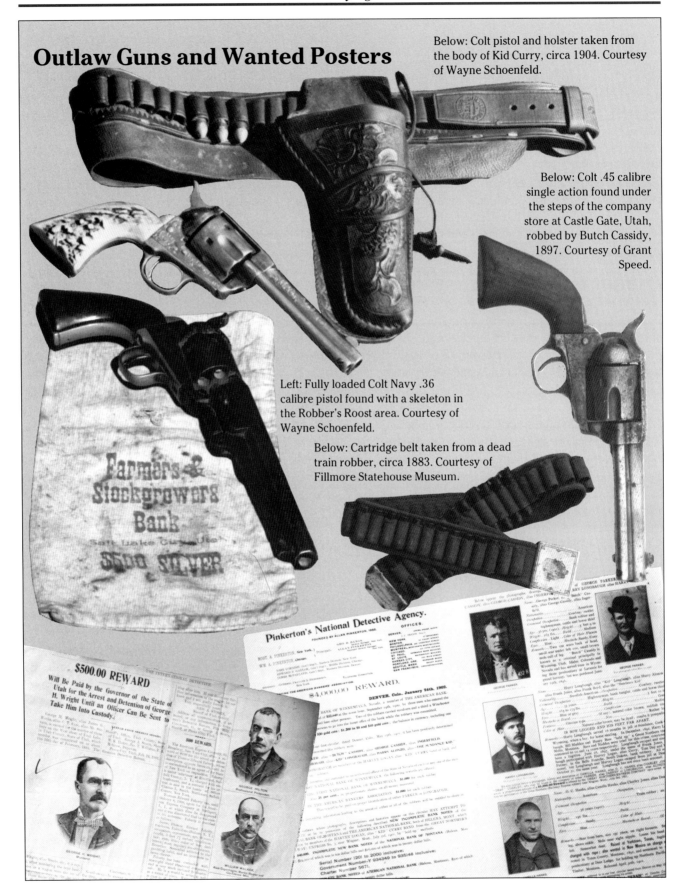

Below: Colt pistol and holster taken from the body of Kid Curry, circa 1904. Courtesy of Wayne Schoenfeld.

Below: Colt .45 calibre single action found under the steps of the company store at Castle Gate, Utah, robbed by Butch Cassidy, 1897. Courtesy of Grant Speed.

Left: Fully loaded Colt Navy .36 calibre pistol found with a skeleton in the Robber's Roost area. Courtesy of Wayne Schoenfeld.

Below: Cartridge belt taken from a dead train robber, circa 1883. Courtesy of Fillmore Statehouse Museum.

funds and also operated a small post office and saloon on his ranch, a resting place for travelers along the road. By operating the post office he was privy to information going in and out of the Uinta Basin and consequently had knowledge of the annuity shipments. After the planned holdup fell through, Francis maintained himself as a rancher and postmaster for the next several years. He was a tough character who claimed to have been a Texas Ranger at one time. Fighting appeared to be a part of his nature and he was involved in a number of altercations. He was killed during a barroom brawl in his own saloon in 1902.[66]

On May 28, 1898, Maxwell and an outlaw named Porter robbed the Springville, Utah, bank. A posse caught up to the outlaws in Hobble Creek Canyon and killed Porter in a short gun battle. One of the posse members was wounded. Maxwell was captured and, following a trial, was sent to the Utah State Penitentiary. He was released for good behavior in a little over a year and returned to the Price area. He worked as a cowboy for a time and then became a guard for the Utah Fuel Company during the labor unrest in 1904. He dabbled in prospecting and founded a few small mines bearing ore with a potential to make him wealthy.

If Maxwell had one severe drawback, it was his desire to be recognized as a tough character who was fast and deadly with a gun. In 1909 Special Deputy Edward B. Johnstone proved once and for all that Maxwell was not all that fast with a gun. The pair met in the street at Price, Utah, and Maxwell paid for his arrogance with his life in a hail of gunfire.[67]

During that same year, 1909, Butch Cassidy and the Sundance Kid were supposedly killed at San Vicente, Bolivia. Information which has come to light in recent years, however, refutes that theory.

Many people who knew Butch Cassidy, including his younger sister, Lula Parker Betensen, claimed that Butch Cassidy returned to the states and assumed a new identity. Many historians now believe that William T. Phillips, a Spokane, Washington, businessman who died in the late 1930s, was, in fact, Butch Cassidy. Other historians believe Butch returned to the United States, yet are not convinced that Phillips was Cassidy. They believe he ended up near Gold Field, Nevada, using the alias Frank Irvin. The real truth may never be known.

There is one fact concerning Butch Cassidy, however, that is little disputed. His particular style and affable nature seemed to win both law-abiding citizens and the outlaw element to his side. Matt Warner claimed "no western cowboy bandit was ever loved more by the outlaw element than Butch Cassidy."[68] Sam Adams, a Teasdale, Utah, cowboy, who lived to be in his mid-nineties and who was, for the better part of his life, a faithful and practicing Mormon, told me he had never met a finer man than Butch Cassidy.[69]

Butch managed to gain, Robin Hood image during his years as an outlaw. This image allowed him to elude the law because many otherwise law-abiding citizens were willing to help him and keep quiet concerning his whereabouts. The peasant class in South America appeared to have this same devotion for the man. There is, however, one more undisputed fact concerning Butch Cassidy. He was, beyond doubt, an outlaw—a man with a price on his head because he committed crimes.

The men who chased Butch Cassidy and other cowboy outlaws across the West—the lawmen— have been overshadowed by the exploits of the outlaws. They, too, were a tough breed of men who won the battles against colorful desperadoes.

7

The Manhunters

On leaving Hanksville one morning a traveling photographer took a snapshot of me and my horses. This photograph shows what a cowboy detective looks like when on the warpath, with bedding, grub and kitchen fixings tied to his saddle pony's tail."[1] At the time of the photograph, Charles A. Siringo was on the trail of Kid Curry through the slickrock wilderness of southeastern Utah. Siringo was a former Texas trail driver turned Pinkerton detective who estimated that he had spent four years and travelled 25,000 miles in search of Kid Curry, Butch Cassidy, and other members of the elusive Wild Bunch.[2]

Charles A. Siringo was tough, fearless, patient, and typical of the many lawmen who dedicated their lives to bringing law and order to Utah and the West. For the most part, the lawmen were low-paid and were asked to make incredible sacrifices, even giving up their lives. A typical lawman in the early days of the West could make between $100 and $150 per month.[3] In many instances he supplemented that wage by raising cattle on the side. He could also add to his yearly income with rewards offered for captured outlaws, dead or alive.

During a manhunt the peace officers organized posses made up of local citizens. If an outlaw was captured the reward money was usually split among posse members. Posses were sometimes formed to

An unidentified lawman at Price, Utah, circa 1899. Photograph courtesy of Brigham Young University, Photo Archives.

go on "hunting" expeditions because there were so many rustlers and other outlaws and lawbreakers roaming the West. No particular outlaw was being sought, but there was always a chance they might come across someone with a price on his head. It was a good way for the locals to pick up extra money, and it was an essential exercise to let lawbreakers know that their antics would not be tolerated.[4]

It would be impossible to relate the thousands of heroic deeds the lawmen accomplished in Utah. There were federal marshals, town marshals, county sheriffs, stock detectives, Indian police, and Pinkerton men, each of whom had a story to tell. It is possible, though, to relate some stories about the lawmen and manhunts that typify the spirit, character, fearless nature, and sometimes humorous side of these guardians of the frontier.

The most famous lawman to pin on a badge and strap on a revolver in Utah was Orrin Porter Rockwell. No lawman in the entire West killed as many men or was as controversial as the man the Gentiles called "The Avenging Angel." The *Salt Lake Tribune* claimed he was "brutal in his instincts and lawless in his habits."[5] The *Salt Lake Daily Herald* called him "the worst enemy that cattle thieves have ever had in Utah."[6]

Rockwell's reputation as a gunfighter and tough character began in the State of Missouri where he was at the forefront of the resistance to mob violence against the Mormons. As a member of the

Pinkerton Detective Charles Siringo at Hanksville, Utah, circa 1899.

Mormon Militia, he participated in several battles against the Missouri Militia, including the Crooked River battle in which the Mormons routed an elite force of state militiamen. This defeat led Governor Boggs to issue the famous "Exterminating Order" which effectively pushed the Mormons out of Missouri.

Several years after the Mormons had settled in Illinois, there was an assassination attempt on the life of Governor Boggs. Rockwell was in Missouri at the time and was promptly arrested for the deed. The State of Missouri did not have much of a case against Rockwell but managed to keep him in prison for nearly a year. When the haggard Rockwell finally made it back to Nauvoo, Illinois, he was greeted by Joseph Smith, who recognized Rockwell as "my long-tried, warm, but cruelly persecuted friend."[7] At the time of the meeting Joseph pronounced the

Orrin Porter Rockwell. "The worst enemy that cattle thieves in Utah ever had" according to *The Deseret News*. Photograph courtesy of LDS Church Archives.

following blessing upon Rockwell: "I prophesy, in the name of the Lord, that you—Orrin Porter Rockwell—so long as ye shall remain loyal and true to thy faith, need fear no enemy. Cut not thy hair and no bullet or blade can harm thee!"[8] For the next thirty-five years Rockwell kept his hair long, and even though he encountered many life-threatening situations involving hostile Indians and desperadoes, he managed to avoid a single physical injury at the hands of another man.

During the Mormon trek to the Salt Lake Valley Rockwell acted as a scout and game procurer. In this capacity he supplied the Mormons with antelope, deer, and buffalo meat. Rockwell especially found the hunting of buffalo to his liking. On one occasion he intended to lay to rest the rumor that a buffalo could not be brought down by a direct shot to the front of the skull. He picked out a large bull and stood his ground as the animal charged. At the opportune moment he shot the bull in the head, but, with the exception of a little dust spouting from the animal's fur, nothing happened and the bull con-

Citizens from Myton, Utah, enjoy an excursion near White Rocks, Utah, in the 1890s. The weapons indicate a real or imagined need for self-protection in the Wild West. Photograph courtesy of Alexia Cooper.

tinued its charge. At that Rockwell spurred his horse and eluded the animal.[9] It was the last time he pulled that stunt.

Once established in the Salt Lake Valley Rockwell was called upon to scout the surrounding area, and was asked by Brigham Young to make several trips to California. On March 12, 1849, he was officially appointed a deputy marshal for Utah, which at that time was called the State of Deseret. He performed his duties under this title for many years and remained in law enforcement in one capacity or another for most of the remainder of his life.

In addition to his lawman duties, Rockwell acted as a scout on occasion for the military, including the expedition to the Bear River where Colonel Patrick Connor's troops defeated the Shoshones. He ventured into the saloon business and maintained a cattle and horse ranch. He was successful in all his occupational pursuits, but he excelled as a manhunter. Legends abound concerning his cunning ability to track outlaws over the far-flung territory. He was a better tracker than most Indians and had the pa-

tience to follow trails for weeks on end. If Rockwell had a fault, it was that he brought very few of the outlaws back alive. John F. Everett claimed Rockwell "did not bother with the courts. If a man stole a horse and he had to be chased a hundred miles, he used to say, 'he deserves to be killed.' "[10]

Stories about Rockwell spread, and many visitors to Mormon country would have felt their journeys were incomplete without getting at least a glimpse of the Mormon triggerman. His ability with a gun and his mystical shield of protection were topics which spread through the outlaw camps. Many outlaws wanted nothing more than to avoid him, but a few needed to challenge Rockwell's invincibility. One such gunfighter came all the way from California to kill him. He chanced to meet Rockwell on the road to Lehi, and, from the descriptions circulating in the West, knew immediately that he had found him. The California gunfighter pulled his revolver and aimed it at Rockwell, keeping it hidden behind his saddle horn. He inquired if Rockwell was indeed the famous lawman, to which Rockwell nod-

Men at Sunnyside, Utah, circa 1899, who may have been hunters after game or a posse of bounty hunters. Local citizens sometimes joined forces to search for men with prices on their heads. Photograph courtesy of Rell Francis.

ded his head. The man thereupon raised his pistol and informed Rockwell that he had come to kill him. Rockwell stared at the fellow for a moment and then said, "You wouldn't try to shoot a man without a cap on your pistol, would you?"[11] During the split-second hesitation as the man glanced down at his gun, Rockwell drew out his revolver and shot the fellow.

It would be impossible to determine the number of men captured by Rockwell or the number killed by him in his capacity as a law officer. Utah Territory was torn between two philosophies during much of the second half of the nineteenth century. The Mormons thought little of the Gentile philosophy and the Gentiles likewise thought little of the Mormon philosophy. If Rockwell killed a horse thief, the Mormons always felt it was in the performance of his duty, and the Gentiles thought it was a wanton killing. Probably every mysterious killing in the territory was laid at his feet by the Gentiles, at least for a time. Estimates of his killings have reached over two hundred, but many of these are word-of-mouth with

little substantiation. There were enough killings which were substantiated, though, to establish the fact that Porter Rockwell was at the forefront of western gunfighters.

Aside from his gunfighter and mystical image, Rockwell was a devoted husband and father. He was also an active church member and, if not always faithful in keeping some of the commandments, he remained always willing to serve. He did indulge in alcohol and loved to frequent the local saloons. He always ordered "squar" drinks, or spirits without water. While drinking with friends, he would call out "Wheat," which to him meant "good." Sir Richard Burton had occasion to sit and enjoy the spirits with Rockwell and described him thus: "He had the manner of a jovial, reckless, devil-may-care English ruffian."[12]

For many years Gentiles sought to have Rockwell charged with committing crimes in the territory with little success. Then, in 1877, the outlaw Bill Hickman confessed to several killings and implicated Rockwell in the crimes. While awaiting trial

Jim Owens, circa 1892, was a cowboy and bounty hunter along the Utah-Arizona border. Photograph courtesy of LDS Church Archives.

Rockwell went out for a night on the town and then retired to a room he kept at the Colorado Stable in downtown Salt Lake City. Sometime during the night of June 11, 1878, Orrin Porter Rockwell died of natural causes.

Even though Porter Rockwell was the most famous of the Utah lawmen, there was enough crime in the territory to keep an entire bevy of law officers busy, even during Rockwell's tenure. Some of these lawmen became famous in their own right and some of the manhunts in which they participated became legendary. The following episodes clearly indicate what being a law officer in Utah during the 1800s was all about.

In 1860 an outlaw named Jack Cole stole several mules from Camp Floyd and drove them to his ranch

Aquilla Nebeker (left) and his deputies. Aquilla was a United States marshal for Utah. Photograph courtesy of Mary Johnson.

in Springville. A posse tracked Cole to his home and was informed by members of the family that the young outlaw was in the outhouse behind the home. The posse members surrounded the outhouse and called for Cole to surrender. Suddenly Cole burst through the door with two blazing Colt pistols and killed Levi Davis. The remaining posse members opened fire on Cole and killed him in a hail of gunfire which saw his body penetrated by no less than eight balls.[13]

In the early 1870s a United States marshal by the name of Storey accompanied a Nevada sheriff by the name of Carragram to Grantsville, Utah, to arrest a man named Hawes, who was wanted in Nevada for killing a man. During the arrest Hawes disarmed Carragram and with his gun shot and killed Marshal Storey. While a posse was being formed, Hawes went to his home, armed himself and rode out of town with the posse hot on his trail.

John Hazel Clark, circa 1900, was a rancher in Hobble Creek Canyon and known to be an excellent shot with his Colt six-shooter. Photograph courtesy of Dee Clark.

Cornered in a box canyon southwest of Grantsville, Hawes decided to make a stand. The first posse member to come into range was Erastus Sprague, who was shot from his horse and killed. Other posse members dismounted and returned the fire. Hawes was killed by a dozen bullets. When the posse went to recover the body, Hawes was wearing a gun on his belt that was rigged to discharge when it was taken hold of, and posse member John Padget was killed when he tried to remove it. Another posse member, William Everill, was shot in the hand by this same gun.[14] All in all, it was a disastrous manhunt for the citizens of Grantsville.

Corinne's marshal, Daniel D. Ryan, was wounded in the hand while trying to break up a free-for-all in the Diamond Q Billard Hall on November 11, 1872.

The fellow who shot the sheriff went by the name of Paschol. Sheriff Ryan drew his revolver and shot Paschol in the chest. Paschol eventually recovered from the wound and thereafter was much better mannered. Sheriff Ryan had to take a leave of absence from his job because of the wound to his hand.

The city fathers of Corinne found that replacing Sheriff Ryan was not an easy task. The next sheriff they hired lasted only a week. He was run out of town by some toughs. The next sheriff appointed did not ever catch on to the politics of the job and had to be replaced. It seems he arrested five prominent businessmen who had just filled a tinhorn gambler full of holes when they caught him cheating. The businessmen were put out by the inconvenience and embarrassment caused by being marched off to jail,

A very rare photograph of a citizens' posse at Corinne, Utah, circa 1875. Photograph courtesy of Utah State University Library, Special Collections.

and they demanded that the sheriff be replaced.

Fortunately for the city fathers, who were bowing to the demands of the Corinne businessmen for the removal of the sheriff, Daniel Ryan was by then healed and ready to return to service. They were only too happy to hire him back. Ryan remained the marshal of the town until its demise in the 1880s.[15]

Problems between Gentiles and Mormon officials in the territory were primarily due to the practice of polygamy by the Mormons. Laws were enacted in Washington to eradicate the practice in the territory, but it was not fully stopped by members of the church until the Manifesto in 1890. When the first antipolygamy laws were passed during the 1860s, little was done to force the Mormons to stop the practice. As subsequent laws were passed, more pressure was placed on the Mormons, and by the 1880s Mormons who were cohabiting with more than one woman could be arrested. During this time many of the church leaders were arrested and sent to the territorial prison.

Although many Mormons received prison sentences because of the antipolygamy laws, only one Mormon was killed for violating the law. Edward Dalton had successfully avoided federal marshals who had travelled to his hometown of Parowan on a number of occasions to arrest him. The marshals had been stymied in their efforts because the Mormon citizens, including local lawmen, would warn Dalton when they were in the area. Finally, in 1886, U.S. Deputy Marshal William Thompson was able to slip into town unnoticed. On the fateful day of the shooting Dalton was driving a herd of cattle through the main street of town. Marshal Thompson yelled out to Dalton that he was under arrest. Dalton disregarded the order to halt and attempted to ride off. Marshal Thompson drew a bead on the back of the fleeing Dalton and brought him down off his horse with one well-placed shot. Dalton died before he hit the ground.[16]

Violence between officers of the law was not uncommon in the Utah Territory. This usually happened when officers let their personal opinions on agency policies or political views get in the way of common sense. Such was the case when Captain Parker and Officer George Albright had an altercation in Salt Lake City during 1891. Captain Parker drew his revolver first, but Albright was the better shot. He was acquitted for killing Captain Parker on a plea of self-defense.[17]

A similar event occurred in Silver Reef when city Marshal Johnny Diamond and a mine guard, Jack Truby, had a shoot-out over a minor misunderstanding. Both men were killed. The fight started during court proceedings in a back room of a local saloon. Diamond asked Truby to remove his hat. When Truby refused to do so, the combatants went outside and began shooting at each other.[18]

Marshal Willard George "Dick" Butt became a legend in the cattle country of southeastern Utah. As the marshal of Bluff he was constantly on the lookout for outlaws trying to make their way to the Navajo Reservation on the Utah-Arizona border. On one occasion he got word that three outlaws were last seen heading for the reservation. Not wanting to waste any time gathering a posse, Butt decided to get help from the first person he saw, who happened to be a teenage boy. The two of them soon picked up the outlaws' trail and came upon their night camp. Butt left the boy with the horses and made his way into the camp, where he got the drop on the outlaws. On another occasion Butt led a posse after three renegades who had killed a rancher in Colorado. The posse captured the outlaws without a fight.

Even when old and crippled with rheumatism Dick Butt was a pretty tough fellow. Five men came into the country buying up the remnants of the L C cattle and charging five dollars for cows belonging to anyone else that were gathered in the roundup. One bunch included a gentle milch cow belonging to Dick Butt. Dick mounted his horse from a platform and tied his crutch to the back of his saddle, rode over to the cow camp, and demanded his cow. The cowboys informed him it would cost five dollars, but Dick insisted that the cow was tame and had caused them no trouble. They stated that didn't matter and that he would have to whip them to cut the cow out of the herd. At that Dick began to dismount his horse and bellowed, "I'll whip every damned one of you, but come one at a time."[19] His courage was too much for the cowboys. They relented and told Dick to cut his cow from the rest. Such was the true grit of an old sheriff called Dick Butt.

The emergence of outlaw gangs in eastern Utah

San Juan County Sheriff Dick Butt. Photograph courtesy of San Juan Historical Society.

during the 1890s kept a number of lawmen and posses active for several years. Encouraged by the Ireland Cattle Company, which had been losing numerous cattle to the outlaws, Governor Heber M. Wells, first governor of the State of Utah, offered a $500 reward for any outlaws hiding out at Robber's Roost.[20] Inspired by the possibility of reward money, a number of lawmen ventured into the wilderness which had been an outlaw sanctuary. One of the first to go into the area was United States Marshal Joe Bush, who headquartered out of Salt Lake City.[21] Bush was a tough lawman who carried a sawed-off shotgun, together with various other weapons. He was at times prone to find himself in trouble in the city and on several occasions was arrested on various charges, including frequenting a variety of area whorehouses, being drunk and disorderly, and discharging a firearm in a public building.[22]

Aside from his overindulgences, Joe Bush was a fearless lawman. During 1890 he went to Monticello, Utah, to arrest John Gibson, Robert Kelly, and William Johnson, local cowboys wanted for the crime of riot in Monticello. The men had terrorized the community and ended the night's activities of drinking and shooting by sacking Mons Peterson's store and stabling themselves and their horses inside. When Bush arrived in town, Joe Gibson was recovering from a self-inflicted bullet wound in his foot. When Gibson saw the marshal approach his sister's house where he was recuperating, he decided to fight it out. Hiding behind a curtain, he waited for Bush to enter. As Bush came through the door he saw the barrel of a Colt .45 protruding from the curtain and drew down with his shotgun. In one quick pull of the trigger, he blew the curtains and John Gibson to shreds.[23]

Joe Bush traveled to southeastern Utah on numerous occasions and was instrumental in driving a number of the Robber's Roost gang out of the state and in arresting Dan Parker. In June of 1897 he led a posse to the Granite Ranch on the Henry Mountains and succeeded in arresting the outlaw Blue John. In 1899 he captured Silver Tip. Both Blue John and Silver Tip spent very little time in jail, far less than Joe Bush spent trying to capture them.

In April of 1897 Sheriff Allred of Carbon County

187

Pinkerton Detectives Charles Siringo and W. O. Sayles at Price, Utah, circa 1899.

and Sheriff Azariah Tuttle of Castle Dale, Emery County, were on the trail of outlaw Joe Walker. They caught up with him and, during a short gun battle, Sheriff Tuttle was wounded in the leg. Walker was able to make his way to an overhanging ledge where he could look down on the two sheriffs hiding behind boulders. For several hours neither Walker nor Sheriff Allred made a move from their position for fear of being shot. Realizing that Sheriff Tuttle needed medical attention, Sheriff Allred decided to go back to Price for help.

After Allred departed, Walker and Tuttle bantered back and forth for several hours, each hoping the other would expose himself long enough to get off a shot. Finally Tuttle, weak from the loss of blood, called a truce. Walker came down to where Sheriff Tuttle lay and took his guns, then got some water for the sheriff. Tuttle told Walker that although he had made good his escape this time, Walker's day would come. On that note Walker bid the sheriff adieu.[24]

Approximately a year later Joe Walker and an

Emery County Sheriff Azariah Tuttle. Photograph courtesy of Steve Lacy copyright 1980, Wild Bunch Photo.

outlaw by the name of Johnny Herring were rustling cattle belonging to the Whitmore outfit when the foreman, Billy McGuire, and one of the Whitmore sons came upon them. Joe Walker beat Billy McGuire up pretty bad and put a good scare into the young Whitmore. Soon thereafter a posse, including Sheriff Tuttle, went into the field looking for the outlaws. They found them still sleeping in their bedrolls and, rather than give them a chance to escape, proceeded to fire a fusillade of bullets into the sleeping men.[25]

In 1899 the famous Pinkerton detective Charles Siringo and the equally famous Pinkerton man W. O. Sayles came to Salt Lake City and outfitted themselves for a trip into eastern Utah to look for outlaws who had held up the Union Pacific train near Wilcox, Wyoming. While heading toward Brown's Park, the detectives received a telegram at Fort Duchesne that outlaws fitting the description of the robbers were seen heading for Robber's Roost. Siringo and Sayles turned south at Fort Duchesne and made their way through Nine Mile Canyon to Price.[26]

In a Price hotel the editor of the local paper came

Two Emery County, Utah, lawmen in the early 1900s. Photograph courtesy of Emily Howard.

to the detectives' room and informed them that the hotel was surrounded by a heavily armed posse, and that the local sheriff had sent him up to inform them they were being arrested for the robbery of the Union Pacific train. The agents always traveled incognito and would not reveal their true identities to the sheriff but were able to convince him they were merely on a prospecting trip, showing him the mining equipment they carried on their pack horses. The sheriff felt good about the explanation and allowed them to go free. The next morning, prior to leaving Price, Siringo and Sayles allowed their pictures to be taken by a local photographer who was amused by the antics of the previous evening.[27]

From Price the agents rode to Hanksville, where they picked up the trail of Kid Curry. They crossed the Colorado River and followed Curry's trail up White Canyon to a rocky bluff several hundred feet high, which Siringo said "looked to be an impossible feat,"[28] but Curry knew the country well and was up to the task. Sayles went back to Hanksville to get supplies while Siringo made his way slowly up the

bluff. By nightfall Siringo decided to return to where he had left Sayles, finding out later that he was within a half-mile of Curry's camp. He was told this by a miner who had been sitting on a knoll watching every move the riders made. Siringo felt he was actually better off to have quit when he did because Curry was probably also aware of his movements and would have been able to ambush him.

The next day Sayles and Siringo followed the outlaw's trail through White Canyon. Siringo described the next leg of the trip in the following manner. "To recite our ups and downs in finding water and keeping the dim trail and of having our pack horse killed by a rattlesnake bite would require too much space. Suffice it to say that we reached Bluff City, a little Mormon settlement on the San Juan River, in good health, the distance being about one hundred and twenty miles with not a habitation on the route."[29]

Kid Curry had been in Bluff City but had gone east into Colorado just a few days before the agents arrived. From Bluff City the agents went to Colorado, where the trail grew cold. Siringo went to New Mex-

Lawmen at Castle Gate, Utah, circa 1904. Photograph courtesy of Cloud Baker.

ico and then to Kansas, trying to pick up the trail. Sayles traveled to Montana to see if he could pick up any leads.

In Kansas Siringo was given a message to return to Utah and to drift around for awhile. He came back to San Juan County and met up with Carlisle Cattle Company foreman Latigo Gordon. Gordon told Siringo that Kid Curry and some other outlaws had been in the area for several weeks, but had left the country in the past few days. Siringo drifted in the Utah country for several days, then rode into New Mexico where he had heard the outlaws might have gone.

In Alma, New Mexico, Siringo was able to infiltrate into the Wild Bunch. He gained the confidence of a fellow named Jim Lowe, who Siringo later learned was Butch Cassidy. He had concentrated so hard on Kid Curry that he had had right in his hand the top dog of the Wild Bunch and didn't even know it.

Siringo was finally called off the Wild Bunch case after spending the best part of four years and travel-ing some 25,000 miles in search of the gang.[30] Had Siringo gone that extra half-mile to Curry's camp in White Canyon, he might have gotten his man. Instead, Curry was free to roam the West for several more years, taking several more lives, including that of Grand County Sheriff Jesse Tyler and Deputy Sam Jenkins.

Jesse Tyler was born in Beaver County, Utah, in 1857 or 1858. His parents died while he was still a boy and he was raised by cattleman John King. Jesse worked as a cowboy for a number of years in Millard and Wayne counties before settling in Moab, Utah, where he was elected county sheriff in the late 1890s.

In 1899 Tyler led a posse into the heart of Robber's Roost while chasing Blue John and Silver Tip, who had stolen a number of horses in Moab. The posse surprised the outlaws, who had joined up with Indian Ed Newcomb and another outlaw. During a brisk gun battle over 200 shots were fired but, because both sides were well covered in the rocky terrain, only Indian Ed received a wound to the leg.

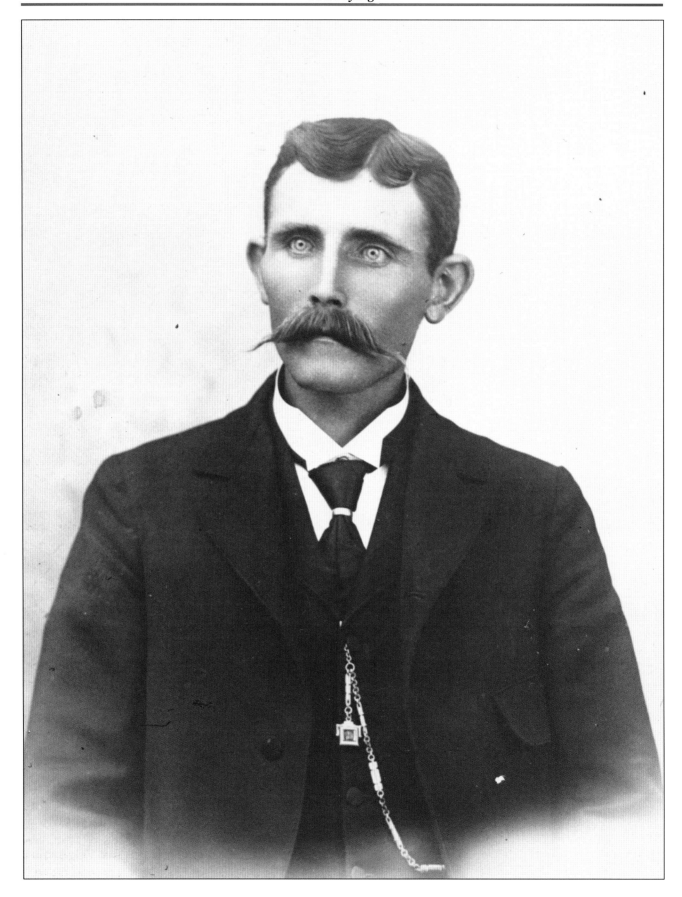

Indian Police at Fort Duchesne, Utah, in the 1890s. Photograph courtesy of Thorne Studio.

Indian policeman at Fort Duchesne, Utah, in the 1890s. Photograph courtesy of Thorne Studio.

The outlaws made their way to a high ridge and were able to escape from the posse. Although they got away, the Battle of Roost Canyon served notice that from that time on the law was willing to go into the impregnable outlaw sanctuary, and that Sheriff Jesse Tyler was a force to be reckoned with.

In April of 1900 Sheriff Tyler and Sheriff William Preece from Vernal, Utah, led a posse into the Book Cliff Mountains in search of Tom Dilly, who had been rustling cattle belonging to the Webster City Cattle Company. The posse came upon an outlaw believed to be Dilly, but was in fact "Flat Nose" George Curry. During a short gun battle Curry was killed by a bullet fired by Sheriff Tyler. The killing of George Curry caused quite a bit of excitement in the Intermountain West, which did not go unnoticed by Curry's nephew, Kid Curry, and he swore to avenge the killing.

Grand County Sheriff Jesse Tyler. Tyler was killed by the notorious Kid Curry. Photograph courtesy of Emma Walker.

In May of 1900 Sheriff Tyler was back in the Book Cliff Mountains looking for Tom Dilly. He and Deputy Sam Jenkins rode into what they thought was an Indian camp to see if they could get some information. When the two lawmen dismounted and took a few steps toward the three men sitting around a fire, they suddenly realized that the men, wrapped in Indian blankets, were not Indians but Kid Curry and two outlaw companions. Before the two lawmen could reach for their guns, Curry and the others shot them down in a hail of gunfire.[31]

The deaths of Sheriff Tyler and Deputy Jenkins were a small victory for the outlaws of southeastern Utah, but it occurred in the twilight of that country's sanctuary for outlaws. Pressures brought by lawmen such as Tyler, Bush, and Tuttle eventually forced the outlaws out of the country. Similar pressures cleaned up the outlaw element in Brown's Park.

Unlike Robber's Roost, with its deep, dark canyons and thousands of slickrock mazes, Brown's

Uintah County Sheriff John Pope. Pope was the first lawman to enter the outlaw stronghold of Brown's Park. Photograph courtesy of Doris Burton.

David Lant (right) was an escapee from the Utah State Prison at the time he became involved with the notorious Harry Tracy in Brown's Park. Photograph courtesy of Aileen Lant.

Park was a long, narrow valley with the Green River running through its middle. It had long been a cattle range for several hardy ranchers who, at times, were suspected of rustling by the bigger cow outfits of the surrounding area. Its reputation as a sanctuary or hideout for hardened outlaws came about because the Park was centrally located in a three-state area that included Utah, Colorado, and Wyoming. If the law ventured into the area, the outlaws could go into a different state other than that which the posse represented. Local lawmen had no jurisdiction in another state. The Park was also situated in a remote region far away from towns of any size.

The first record of a lawman entering Brown's Park was Sheriff John T. Pope of Uintah County,

A lawman in Salina, Utah, in the 1890s, wears a five-star badge. Most five-star badges during this period were encircled; those not encircled were usually six-star badges. Photograph courtesy of Rell Francis.

Utah. He was a tough sheriff who had been elected to the office without his knowledge after capturing a fellow who had held up a Vernal, Utah, store. Pope first entered Brown's Park in pursuit of an outlaw named Buckskin Ed. He captured Ed without a fight, but as they forded the Green River in a boat, Ed proceeded to untie himself and attack Pope with a knife. Pope succeeded in drawing his gun and shot the outlaw, whose body fell into the river.[32]

Sheriff Pope was severely wounded in the throat during the fight with Buckskin Ed, but managed to make his way back to Vernal, where he recovered. In 1897 he returned to Brown's Park to arrest Joe Tolliver, who had murdered a fellow named Charles Seger. A few months later, he and a Colorado sheriff killed three Mexican horse thieves in the Park.[33]

Pope remained sheriff of Uintah County until 1898. During that year his successor, William Preece, asked Pope to join a posse going into Brown's Park to capture an outlaw named Patrick

195

Louis Johnson who had killed a young boy, Willie Strang. Strang and Johnson were in fact friends, but when the young Strang playfully knocked a cup of water out of Johnson's hand, Johnson decided to teach him a lesson by putting a shot close to the boy. The shot was too close, and Strang was killed by a bullet in his back.

As word of the killing went out, posses from Utah, Colorado, and Wyoming converged on the Park to capture the killer. An associate of Johnson, John Bennett, was captured by the Colorado posse and was held under guard at the Bassett Ranch. Johnson, trying to work his way southward out of the Park, met up with two recent escapees from the Utah State Penitentiary, Harry Tracy and David Lant. With all of the law running around in the Park, Tracy and Lant decided to leave the area with Johnson.

The Colorado posse caught up with the trio and, in a short gun battle, Harry Tracy killed a member of the posse, Valentine Hoy. The posse retreated to the Bassett Ranch, and that night several masked men lynched the prisoner, John Bennett. The following day a combined posse from the three states captured the three outlaws following a short gun battle. After some deliberation it was decided that the Colorado posse would take Tracy and Lant and that the Wyoming posse would get Johnson. The Utah posse wanted all three of the men, but was voted down for the reason that the outlaws would most likely escape from prison again if they remained in Utah.

The optimism shared by the Wyoming and Colorado posses was soon laid to rest because Johnson was acquitted by a Wyoming jury and Tracy and Lant escaped from a Colorado jail. Lant returned to Utah and decided to leave the outlaw trail. Tracy went to Oregon, where he continued his outlaw life. He was incarcerated in the Oregon State Penitentiary but escaped, killing three prison guards. He was chased by a posse and wounded and took his own life to avoid being captured and returned to prison.[34]

Although lawmen penetrated the heart of Brown's Park, the area continued to be a sanctuary for out-

laws until the turn of the century. This all changed when a famous Indian scout turned bounty hunter appeared on the scene. His name was Tom Horn, and in a matter of a few months during 1900 he put such a scare into the remaining outlaws they packed up and left the country.

Horn had spent many years on the Arizona and New Mexico frontier acting as a guide and Indian interpreter for the U.S. Army. In this capacity he hunted and killed many Apaches and was involved in the final surrender of Geronimo. With the end of hostilities he worked as a cowboy on several ranches. His skills were so good he once won the roping championship at the Arizona Territorial Fair.

By 1894 Horn had drifted into Colorado, where he joined up with the Pinkerton National Detective Agency. Working out of the Denver office of the company, Horn started on the trail of an outlaw named Joe McCoy. He followed McCoy to Ashley, Utah, where he was able to capture the outlaw without a fight. It was one of the few arrests made by Horn while in the employ of the Pinkerton Agency.

Horn left Pinkerton soon after his arrest of Joe McCoy and went to Wyoming where he went to work for the Swan Land and Cattle Company. His reputation as a gunfighter and tracker soon put him in the employ of a number of Cheyenne, Wyoming, cattle barons who wanted to put an end to the rustling of their cattle. Working under their orders Horn went to Brown's Park using the alias of James Hicks and pretending to be a cattle buyer. After gaining a great deal of information concerning the local rustlers Horn decided to eliminate one of them and on the morning of July 8, 1900, he put three well-placed bullets into the carcass of Matt Rash.[35]

He then rode to Ogden, Utah, where he spent the next couple of months. In October of 1900 he returned to Brown's Park and killed the black cowboy Isom Dart, who had escaped being killed with the Tip Gault gang by diving into a freshly dug grave many years before.[36] The killings effectively stopped the rustling activities which had, for years, been the lifeblood of Brown's Park because, following the death of Isom Dart, several Brown's Park characters known to be free with a running iron packed up and left.

Tom Horn stayed in the Wyoming cattle country

The town marshal of Helper, Utah, in the early 1900s. Photograph courtesy of Helper City Mine Museum.

Fred George and Patrick "Patsy" Coughlin in prison clothing. Coughlin was executed at Randolph, Utah. Photograph courtesy of Wayne Dickson.

after the killings in Brown's Park and was involved in several fracases, including a wild knife fight in the Bull Dog Saloon at Baggs, Wyoming, where he was cut up pretty good. A short time later he was arrested for the killing of a young sheepherder, Willie Nickells. Many people felt that Horn did not kill the lad and that he had been set up by local county officials. Horn denied the killing, but was found guilty by a Wyoming jury and was sentenced to hang. On the morning of November 20, 1903, Tom Horn was hanged in the courtyard of the Laramie County jail.[37]

One of the most intense manhunts ever to occur in Utah began on a spring morning in Park City in 1896. Youthful pranksters, Patrick "Patsy" Coughlin and Fred George, had made a name for themselves

A Salt Lake City Mounted Police officer in the 1890s. Photograph courtesy of Beehive Collector's Gallery.

around the Park City area by being unruly and incorrigible, so when they stole some strawberries from a local vendor, Sheriff Harrington publicly vowed that he would punish them severely. When word reached Coughlin and George that the sheriff intended to make examples of them, they decided to get out of Park City. To hasten their journey the two strawberry thieves decided to steal a pair of horses from a local rancher.

Coughlin and George rode to a sheep camp fifteen miles north of Park City and decided to rest before heading for Wyoming country. Sheriff Harrington and a Deputy Williams followed them and, in a brief gunfight, Sheriff Harrington was slightly wounded. Harrington and Williams rode back to Park City and telegraphed several marshals to be on the lookout for the now-dangerous desperadoes. In the meantime Couglin and George rode into Wanship, Utah, where they purchased 300 rounds of ammunition.

Armed men preparing for the execution of Patrick "Patsy" Coughlin. Photograph courtesy of Wayne Dickson.

Leaving Wanship, Coughlin and George rode to the Palmer's shack, an old line cabin on the Wasatch Flats several miles west of the border town of Evanston, Wyoming. There they holed up for the night and in the morning when Coughlin opened the shack door, a bullet whizzed by his head. Sheriff Thomas Stagg of Echo, Utah, a deputy and two men from Evanston had surrounded the shack during the night and, fearing the two men inside, decided to shoot first and ask questions later. Coughlin dove back into the shack and commenced firing, while George alternately reloaded their rifles.

Coughlin's second shot mortally wounded N. E. Dawes of Evanston. When Sheriff Stagg was killed in the gunfire, the remaining two members of the posse decided to hightail it back to Evanston. During the battle George received flesh wounds in both thighs, and Coughlin removed most of the lead with his pocketknife. Then, before leaving the shack,

Coughlin made a crude apology to the dying Dawes.

Deciding at this point to abandon the idea of going to Wyoming, Coughlin and George rode across Monte Cristo Peak and down into Huntsville, Utah. From there they went into Ogden, Utah. When the Salt Lake City police force received a tip that the desperadoes were seen riding south out of Ogden, they sent fourteen men on horseback north to intercept them. Later Captain Donovan followed with five more officers in a paddy wagon.

Upon reaching the city of Bountiful, the officers were caught off-guard when they saw the heavily armed lawbreakers riding along with a small convoy of vegetable wagons in the dawn light. While the police officers were scrambling around to draw their weapons, Coughlin and George rode off toward the mountains southeast of Bountiful. Obtaining horses for Captain Donovan and the five officers from the paddy wagon, the nineteen-man

Patrick "Patsy" Coughlin awaits his execution. Photograph courtesy of Wayne Dickson.

posse followed the trail of the desperadoes to the head of City Creek Canyon. Spotting Coughlin and George riding to the ridge of the canyon, the posse opened fire. Coughlin's horse was shot out from under him and George's horse came up lame. Both fellows took time to remove the saddles and bridles as bullets flew all around them. With saddles, bridles, and guns in hand, they made their way to the top of the ridge and dropped down over the other side. By the time the posse reached the ridge Coughlin and George were well hidden in the thick underbrush. The posse strafed the foliage-clad slopes below but were unable to flush out their prey.

Coughlin and George spent the next two nights at the Mt. Olivet Cemetery and at Jack Gilmer's ranch on the eastern outskirts of Salt Lake City. By the time they left the Gilmer Ranch, posses from Salt Lake, Weber, Summit, Davis, Utah, Wasatch, Morgan, and Rich counties were in the field searching for them. They made their way to the Union Pacific Saloon at Murray and stole two horses tied to the hitching rail in front of the saloon. From Murray they rode to Grantsville, some forty miles west of Salt Lake City.

By that evening they had made their way to a miner's camp west of Grantsville and asked the miner, Ruel Barres, for food. Coughlin and George ate hastily and rode off. Immediately Barres rode into Grantsville and informed the citizens that he had sighted the two fugitives. The Grantsville posse rode out and by morning reached the camp of Coughlin and George. A volley of bullets warned the two youngsters that they were surrounded and Coughlin immediately raised his hands and yelled out, "Don't shoot!" He then spoke out bitterly: "This is the first time we've had a chance to surrender like men without being shot down like dogs! It was shoot or die at Wasatch and City Creek."[38]

Colton, Utah, Marshal Orrin Elmer and friends in the 1890s. Elmer was good friends with Butch Cassidy in his younger years. Photograph courtesy of Dennis Finch.

Orrin Elmer doing a little fishing from a raft at Colton, Utah, in the 1890s. Photograph courtesy of Dennis Finch.

Garfield County Sheriff George Dodds (horseback) in the 1890s. Photograph courtesy of Garfield County Daughters of the Utah Pioneers.

Coughlin and George were returned to Randolph, Utah, and a jury found them guilty of murder in the first degree for the shooting of Dawes. Coughlin was sentenced to be shot, and the jury recommended mercy on behalf of Fred George. Fred spent several years in prison and was then released. On December 4, 1896, Coughlin was taken to Sage Hollow, a mile north of Woodruff, Utah, and executed by a firing squad. Just before the execution Father Galligan from Park City told Coughlin to "keep up your courage," and Coughlin replied, "Oh, you bet your life I will."[39]

Even rock-hard lawmen of Utah may have been sympathetic toward Patrick "Patsy" Coughlin, whose last words to his mother were, "As I'll never see you again, believe me, Mother, the first shot was fired at me by Sheriff Harrington."[40] Nevertheless, the lawmen were sworn to uphold the laws of the territory and did so to the best of their abilities.

Another lawman who died while upholding the laws of the territory was James "Jim" Burns, mar-shal of Spring City, Utah. Marshal Burns had ridden to the co-op sheep corrals in the mountains east of Spring City on September 26, 1894, to arrest Jim Mickel and Moen Kofford, who were suspected of rustling sheep from the Manti Co-op herd. When confronted by the marshal, Mickel and Kofford asked to see a warrant for their arrest. Marshal Burns put his hand on the Colt .45 he was wearing and said, "I don't need one, this .45 is all I need to take a couple of beardless kids!"[41] The two rustlers decided Burns's arrest warrant was not sufficient and drew on the lawman. Burns managed to wound Mickel, but Kofford shot and killed the marshal. The two outlaws then made their way out of the territory.

Several other lawmen were killed in the line of duty during the cowboy-outlaw era. William Strong was fatally shot in Provo in 1899, the same year William A. Brown was killed in Ogden. Perhaps one of the most tragic deaths occurred in 1873, when Albert H. Bowen, Provo City chief of police, attempted

Tools of the Lawman

Colt single action pistol shipped to Salt Lake Hardware Co. in 1914, used by Texas Sheriff Jack Dutton. Courtesy of Southwest Indian Traders, Park City, Utah.

Below: Telegram to outlaw turned judge, Matt Warner, and Wyoming penitentiary identification of his friend, Butch Cassidy. Courtesy of Steve Lacy.

Above: Alta, Utah, marshall badge, circa 1880; and the badge thought to have been worn by Sheriff Tyler, circa 1900. Courtesy of Wayne Schoenfeld.

Below: Affidavit of witness signed by the notorious Gunplay Maxwell. Courtesy of Steve Lacy.

Sheriff Joe Farrer is the man sitting in front of the saloon door. The Sundance Kid is standing in front of the tree and Butch Cassidy is sitting next to him. Interestingly, as this photo at Green River, Utah, in the 1890s shows, outlaws and lawmen were at times friendly. Photograph courtesy of Warner and Lacy copyright 1980.

to arrest the notorious Harrison Carter as he was engaged in shooting up a local saloon. Harrison had bragged that no lawman could take his guns from him, and backed up this boast when Chief Bowen confronted him.[42]

Fortunately, not all of the lawman-outlaw confrontations in the territory ended in tragedy. Some of the confrontations were even, at times, quite humorous. Like the time Sheriff Tom Fares of Green River, Utah, and two of his deputies came across Matt Warner, Tom McCarty, and Butch Cassidy. The outlaws got the drop on the lawmen and decided to teach Fares a lesson. The way Matt told it, "We got their guns and stars and Fares' saddle. Then we took Fares' pants off, put him on his horse bareback, and herded the three of 'em into the canyon and started 'em back the way they had come."[43]

Then there was the time when two posses, one from Price and one from Green River, came upon each other at dusk as they were searching for the bandits who had robbed the payroll at Castle Gate. Each posse thought the other was the outlaws and a lively little gunfight ensued until both sides retreated. It wasn't until the next day when the posses met and began telling about the fight that they realized they had been shooting at each other.[44]

There were many other such humorous events, but it is better to dwell on the courageous nature of the lawmen—such as the type of courage it took for Deputy David Bulloch of Cedar City, Utah, to ride alone to the wild mining town of Pioche, Nevada, to arrest a horse thief wanted in Utah. He walked into a local saloon and informed the outlaw he was taking him back to Cedar City. Four friends of the outlaw arose from a nearby gambling table and surrounded the deputy with their guns drawn. The outlaw told his friends to back off; the deputy was an old friend and he did not want to see him hurt. The outlaw then rode back to Cedar City with the brave deputy, was convicted of grand larceny, and served a sentence in the Utah State Prison.[45]

It was the courage of the David Bullochs, the Jesse Tylers, and others that beat the cowboy outlaws by running them out of the country, providing them with a stay in prison, or giving them a permanent view from Boot Hill. The credit was not all theirs, though; the lawmen had help from the old cowmen's curse—woolly sheep.

8

The Finis of the Wild West

No man engaged in walking sheep could be a decent citizen. He was a low-down, miserable being, whom it was correct to terrify or kill."[1] Those sentiments were shared by many cowboys during the 1880s and 1890s. It was a feeling that permeated the open range and led to a number of bloody conflicts between the cowboy and sheepman. Because of the unique character of Utah, the sheep wars were held to a minimum, but conflict did occur within her borders, and, at times, the stench of death was the end result.

During the first twenty years of Mormon colonization there was little conflict between cattlemen and sheepmen. The ranges were big enough to accommodate both. Most Mormon settlements developed sheep co-ops right along with cattle co-ops, and there was the general feeling that under proper management it would be possible for both species to occupy the same range. In reality, this theory was true. Sheep are primarily browsers and, although they eat grass in abundance, they prefer shrubs and brush. Cattle, on the other hand, will eat brush and shrubs, but prefer grass. Under proper management both sheep and cattle can share the same range.

There were some problems with sheep raising that created a reasonable conflict for the cattlemen. Sheep will eat grass much closer to the ground and their small hooves have a tendency to tear up the

roots of grasses that have been grazed too short. Because five sheep can graze in the same area as one cow, the number of hooves cutting through the soil are greatly multiplied. So long as the herder kept his herd at a reasonable number and moved it constantly over the range, damage could be kept to a minimum. But if the herder paid no attention to these basic range management skills, great damage was done. Neither the sheepmen nor the cattlemen paid much attention to range management skills during the nineteenth century, so the potential for range damage ran high.

As early as 1869 conflicts concerning sheep began to appear in the settlement papers. The *Ogden Daily* noted that pastures between Ogden and Salt Lake City had been "poisoned by the breath of sheep."[2] However, as with most Mormon vs. Mormon conflicts, the rhetoric rarely led to any kind of violence. The potential for violence increased dramatically though, as the large cattle companies began developing away from the core-Mormon settlements during the 1870s.

Through most of the 1870s and early 1880s the cattlemen were able to maintain the integrity of their cow range, but by the late 1880s a number of events developed which began pushing sheep onto the cattle ranges. New Mexico sheepmen were overcrowding their territory with sheep and were venturing northward in search of new range. At the same time the northern cattlemen had experienced some of the most severe winters in memory, fol-

Sheepmen gather in central Utah in the 1890s. Photograph courtesy of Rell Francis.

207

A cowboy and a sheepherder meet in the border country of Utah and Idaho in the 1890s. Photograph courtesy of Lynne Clark Photography.

lowed by a series of droughts and low cattle prices. Many smaller ranchers were completely wiped out, while others were hanging on by a thread. In an effort to recover, many of these cattlemen began looking to sheep as a way to stay in the livestock business. It took four good years for a calf to mature on the open range and become ready for market, yet a sheep could produce two cash crops each year—lambs and wool.

The dramatic increase in the number of sheep coming into Utah is indicated by government census reports, and while the numbers themselves may not be accurate, the rate of growth is acknowledged. In 1887 there were 658,285 sheep in the territory. One year later there were 1,335,000.[3] Wyoming and other northern territories also showed this rate of growth. With the increase in the number of sheep crowding the cattle ranges, there were bound to be problems. The *Wasatch Wave*, published in Heber, Utah, responded to the problem. The article stated:

> Sheep are destroying the range for cattle and are a nuisance generally to everybody except the tariff-protected owners of the sheep. There seems to be no protection for Wasatch County people against sheep, unless they protect themselves. Common decency and respect for the rights of others should induce them to take their sheep at least far enough away from the settlements so as not to eat out the cow range. The tariff protects the wool, but may not protect the sheep.[4]

Throughout the territories cowboys did more than print warnings to the sheepmen. From time to time bloody range wars flared up in the region and Utah was not excluded. Deadlines were posted and herders moved their sheep over those deadlines at a peril to their lives. A deadline existed on the small mountain range, known locally as the Sawtooths, which separated the Pahvant Valley from Snake Valley in western Utah. A white herder and his Chinese companion disregarded the warning and took their sheep across the deadline into Snake Valley. Cowboys rode into the camp, killed the two herders, and scattered the sheep.[5]

In eastern Utah cowboys took over a sheep camp near Vernal, and tied and blindfolded the herders.

Robert Olson and Claude Meecham of Snake Valley, Utah, were local cattle ranchers called on several times to run undesirables out of the valley. Photograph courtesy of Emerson Gonder.

The cowboys then proceeded to kill 800 head of buck sheep. One of the Basque herders disappeared during the attack and it was assumed he was killed by the cowboys.[6]

Cattlemen set up deadlines on the north slopes of the Uinta Mountains along the Henry's Fork River and dared sheepmen to cross the line. Deadlines were also set on the Utah-Idaho border near the Raft River Mountains.

On the south slopes of the Book Cliff Mountains the outlaw Tom Dilly, foreman of the Patmos Head Cattle Company, had a continuing feud with a sheepherder from American Fork, Utah, by the name of Steve Chipman. This feud came to a head when Chipman moved his sheep onto Dilly's horse pasture. An argument ensued and Dilly shot and killed Chipman.[7]

There were probably several other killings which took place on the vast Utah frontier. Transient herders were especially susceptible to the cowboys' hostility and in the event of their deaths, it is probable they were never missed. A lonely grave mar-

ker, high in the San Rafael Swell of southeastern Utah, still stands as a sentinel over a forgotten grave. The weathered wooden marker simply reads, "He was told to leave the country with his sheep or else."[8]

The killing of herders and bands of sheep did not deter the sheepmen. With the law on their side the sheep owners continued to occupy the public ranges, which had for years been held exclusively by the cattle barons. As cattle prices continued to dip, many of the long-established cattlemen began dismantling the barriers and began bringing sheep onto their ranges. In 1895 the Taylor outfit near Moab decided to run both cattle and sheep on the range. U.S. Marshal Joe Bush came down from Salt Lake City and patrolled the Taylor range until the clamor settled down.[9] Shortly after this Carpenter and Cunningham, managers of the old Pittsburgh outfit, purchased sheep and put them on their range.

It was during this time that many of the giant corporate cattle companies decided to get out of the cattle business entirely.[10] Bad livestock markets,

A group of well-armed sheepmen in western Utah appear to be ready for any range war between cowboys and themselves. Photograph courtesy of University of Utah Libraries, Special Collections Department.

competition for the depleted "green gold," and the legal issues involving land occupied by them appeared to be too much of a problem. As these large cattle companies left Utah, new companies came in to occupy the land. Those new companies were formed primarily by Mormons who were willing to work under the legal and political systems of the territory.

The cowboy-sheepman conflict spilled over into the twentieth century as some cattle areas fought hard and long to keep sheep off the range. Some of the old cattle barons managed to keep their cattle ranges intact over the years, but they were able to do it through the courts, not through force. Such was

John Whiting and friend in the 1890s. Whiting was a cattle rancher near Heber, Utah, and may have been one of the citizens of the area that resisted the invasion by sheepmen and their herds in 1889. Photograph courtesy of Rell Francis.

the case with Preston Nutter and Samuel McIntyre. But, by and large, the sheep industry in Utah and other Intermountain states continued to grow until, for a number of years, it was the main livestock industry. The trend continued until the industry reached its peak in the 1940s. Since then, it has declined and cattle are once again prominent.

Although the cattle industry suffered during the turbulent time between 1887 and 1915 because of sheep encroachment, it was not given a knockout blow. Many of the large ranches established in that era were in fact cattle ranches. Other ranches were established that ran sizable numbers of both cattle and sheep. It would appear the livestock barons just got smarter and those that survived were willing to work under the new economy.

One of the bigger, if not the biggest, pure cattle companies established at this time was the "TY" outfit owned by Al and Jim Scorup. In 1891 Al left Sa-

Loading bales of wool from the Henry Webster Esplin ranch in Orderville, Utah, circa 1920. Photograph courtesy of Fred Esplin.

Cowboys at Indian Creek circa 1900. Photograph courtesy of Lena Stocks.

Bales of wool being readied for shipment at Marysvale, Utah, circa 1920. Photograph courtesy of Fred Esplin.

lina, Utah, to go to the remote White Canyon east of the Henry Mountains to take care of 150 longhorn cattle for a man named Claude Sanford. After arriving there Al soon ran out of money and was forced to sell a steer to a miner for twenty dollars. With the money he rode to Hite Ferry on the Colorado River and purchased a sack of flour from Cass Hite for eleven dollars. That was all Al needed to know. At those prices, he would never survive in the remote country without money.[11]

Leaving the cattle, Al rode to Blanding, Utah, where he hired on with a Texas outfit that was trailing cattle from the Elk Mountains to Ridgeway, Colorado. During the trail drive to the mining towns of Colorado, the hardened, gunslinging Texas cowboys nicknamed the nineteen-year-old Scorup "the Mormon cowboy," and although they were not impressed with his particular habits of not drinking or smoking, they did respect his ability to ride a horse and work with cattle.[12] Even at this tender age Al had learned the trade of cowboying while riding for the Salina Cattle Co-op. He had gone on trail drives as far as Omaha, Nebraska, with that company.

Once Al got a little money in his pockets he returned to White Canyon, only to find five Texas cowboys who told him to move on because they had taken over the White Canyon range. There was little Al could do against the heavily armed Texans, so he headed back to Salina. Once in Salina he wrote to Sanford and told him what had happened. Sanford replied that he would give him half of the cattle if he would return. Al liked the idea and determined to go back.

He decided to lease a herd of cattle belonging to a Mr. Hugentobler and take them back to White Canyon. He also talked his brother Jim into going with him and taking along Jim's cattle. The two Scorups returned to White Canyon driving about 300 head of cattle. Just prior to entering the canyon Al told Jim about the Texas cowboys who had sent him packin'. Jim was mad, but there was nothing he could do about the matter then.

Once inside, Al and Jim found that the Texans were staying pretty close to the south side of the canyon and, with the help of homesteader Charley Fry and an outlaw named Billy Sawtell, the Scorups were able to gather up most of the Sanford cattle and take them to the north side of the canyon where they would be out of the way of the Texans. Here the Scorups began their cattle empire.[13]

After a couple of years the Texans decided that the country was too tough for their type of cowboy-

Harve Williams was foreman and later part owner of the Scorup-Somerville Cattle Company. Photograph courtesy of Heda B. S. N. Williams.

ing and pulled out, leaving White Canyon exclusively to the Scorups. During the next few years there were many hardships and disappointments, but the brothers hung in there and gradually forged a cattle empire which saw thousands of head of cattle wearing the "TY" brand.

In 1918 the Scorups sold their White Canyon holdings and bought out the Indian Creek Cattle Company, established by businessmen from Moab, Utah, on the north slopes of the Blue Mountains in the 1890s. As the years passed, the Scorups bought more ranches and, in 1926, formed a partnership with the Somerville brothers and Jacob Adams. Combining the assets of the men involved, the

A shepherd and his dog near Moab, Utah, in the 1890s. Photograph courtesy of G. Ballard.

newly formed Scorup-Somerville Cattle Company owned or leased nearly 2 million acres of rangelands and ran upward of 14,000 head of cattle.[14] Brands used by this company included the "TY," the "Flying V Bar," and the "Bar X Bar."

The S S Cattle Company continued to operate for the next thirty-five years and was one of the last big outfits to drive cattle overland to the railhead at Thompson. The company continued the hundred-mile drives until the mid-1950s, and in 1965 the S S Company was sold to the Redd family.

The Redd Ranch was established by L. H. Redd, one of the first Mormon pioneers in San Juan County. He began buying up land occupied by the large cattle companies in San Juan County, including deeded acreage owned by the Bluff City Pool when that cattle co-op broke up in the 1890s, the

Employees of the La Sal Cattle Company circa 1920. Photograph courtesy of Cosme Chacon.

Carlisles's, and the LC Cattle Company when they left the country.

In 1914 Redd helped establish the La Sal Livestock Company, which bought out the Carpenter and Cunningham holdings. Redd's son Charles became the manager of the company, and under his direction the La Sal Company and several other ranching companies were merged into what was known as the Redd Ranches. In 1965 the Redd Ranches became even bigger when the Scorup-Somerville Cattle Company was purchased.

In recent years the Redd Ranches have been divided among Charles Redd's three sons. Paul Redd owns the Redd Ranch, headquartered at Paradox, Colorado, encompassing land in both Utah and Colorado. Robert Redd runs the Indian Creek Ranch on the north side of the Blue Mountains, and Hardy Redd owns the La Sal Livestock Company, operating out of La Sal. The grazing lands utilized by the Redds totals more than three quarters of a million deeded and leased acres, and approximately 6,000 mother cows are run on this land.[15]

In 1910 a group of ranchers in the vicinity of Verdure formed the K-Lazy T Ranch on the south slope of the Blue Mountains. At peak times this outfit ran 10,000 head of cattle. This ranch is currently operated by the Dalton family of Monticello, Utah.[16]

It should be pointed out at this time that the manner in which cattle are counted on the range has changed over the years. In olden days, cattle were held on the range for four to five years before they were taken to market. It took that long for the steers to grow and fatten on the range. Therefore, the tendency to count all cattle on the range was common before the turn of the century.

Today, many of the cattle ranches in Utah are cow-calf operations. Calves are born and stay on the range until they are nine months to a year old. They are then sold to feed lots where they are fattened for market. When determining the size of a cow-calf operation, only the cows are counted. If an operator had 2,000 mother cows and the calving rate was 80 percent, the operation would have 2,000 mother cows and 1,600 calves on the range for part of the year. In this type of operation it would be proper to count only the cows on the range, excluding bulls and calves.

Some ranches in Utah run a cow operation and additionally run older steers year round. In this case, for statistical purposes, both the cow herd and steer herd would be counted. In addition, most ranchers who keep replacement heifers add this number to their total operation.

A group of forest rangers on the La Sal Mountains circa 1905. These men were former cowboys who took advantage of the opportunity to work for the government. Photograph courtesy of Carol Hines.

Branding a steer on the Browning Ranch circa 1920. Photograph courtesy of Jess Cook.

A third type of outfit operating in Utah would be a "steer only" operation. These outfits buy yearling steers and run them on the range for part of the year. During the winter months these outfits keep the steers at feed lots around the main ranch headquarters. When discussing the size of these operations it is common to quote the number of animals being fed during the winter.

When determining the size of large cattle operations like the Crocker outfit and the Carlisles's, it is assumed all of the cattle on the range were counted. When talking about modern outfits such as the Redds', only mother cows are counted. When talking about the numbers of cattle run by the big ranches which sprang up in the late 1890s and early 1900s, a little guesswork must be applied.

Early in the 1900s the United States government began setting aside large tracts of land as forest reserves and controlling the number of animals which could graze on these lands. It is generally understood that, at that time, many more cattle were

put on the land than those scheduled. It took many years for the forest service to gain control over the millions of acres presently held. In the interim cattle companies claimed to run a certain amount of cattle but could, in actuality, have many more on the range.

The change between pure cow-calf operations and those operations that ran cows and steers took a long time to evolve. The Scorup-Somerville Cattle Company ended up being a cow-calf operation, as did the Redd Ranches, but for many years after the turn of the century these companies were running steers on the range much longer than the year or less that modern operators keep their calves. Therefore, when the S S Cattle Company was issued 11,000 government permits in the 1920s, were they permits for cows only, with calves not counted, or were they keeping steers on the range long enough to take up an allotment?

Realizing that accurate records were not available during the 1890–1920 period, the author has chosen

218

Breaking a horse at the Browning Ranch circa 1920. Photograph courtesy of Jess Cook.

to assume the numbers of cattle belonging to the "big ranches" during that period of time were mother cows, heifers and yearlings, or older steers and do not reflect calves and bulls.

The "big ranches" in northern Utah took over lands which, for many years, were controlled by the Crocker, White, and Wells Fargo interests. The first to come on the scene was the Lindsay Land and Livestock Company, which was founded by Walter J. Lindsay in the 1890s. Headquarters for the company was located at Avon, but the range extended over a number of counties, including Weber, Cache, and Box Elder.

The Lindsay outfit ran 22,000 sheep, 5,000 cows, and 300 horses on their range, which extended from the Bear River Mountains to Skull Valley.[17] The company branded their cattle with the WJ.

The Lindsay Land and Livestock Company became financially troubled during the First World War and had to break up this vast livestock empire. A number of investors bought parcels of the opera-

tion, including the Benson and Browning families.

Much of the old Crocker property and parts of the Lindsay property were bought up by the Browning brothers of gun-making fame in the early 1900s. By 1916 the Browning Ranch was running 10,000 head of cattle on 300,000 deeded acres of land in northern Utah and on 30,000 acres of land in Montana.[18]

The bulk of this ranching empire was broken up during the 1950s. Today 1,000 mother cows graze on the remnants of the Bar B Ranch at Eden, Utah.

Several large ranches running both sheep and cattle took over lands in the Bear River Mountains west of Woodruff in the late 1800s. The Neponset Livestock Company ran as many as 50,000 sheep and several thousand cattle. This outfit hired gunmen to protect their range and was known to use violence to keep outsiders away. The company broke up prior to the turn of the century.[19]

The Deseret Land and Livestock Company, with headquarters at Woodruff, Utah, was established by a group of Mormon sheepmen in the 1890s. Through

Bar Z cowboys getting ready to brand circa 1909. Photograph courtesy of LDS Church Archives.

a series of land deals the Deseret was able to buy up vast amounts of land including lands claimed by the Neponset outfit. By the early 1900s the sheepmen decided to run cattle on parts of their range and in time the outfit became primarily a cattle operation. Cattle brands used by the company include the "Bar S," "IX," and "Quarter Circle J."

At one time the Deseret outfit owned over 300,000 acres of grazing land and leased another 300,000 acres of government land from the Wyoming border to Skull Valley in Tooele County. It was sold during the early 1980s, first to foreign interests and then to the Mormon church. The ranch is currently run by the church, which maintains 201,000 deeded acres in Rich and Weber counties. Currently the Deseret Land and Livestock Company runs 3,500 mother cows and 6,000 steers. Counting replacement heifers, the outfit at peak times is ranging 12,000 cattle.[20]

The Skull Valley Ranch, operated by the Blackburn family, was at one time part of the old Deseret outfit. Today this ranch is operating on 350,000 acres of deeded and leased land. Counting mother cows, replacement heifers and steers, the Skull Valley Ranch runs approximately 4,000 cattle.[21]

The Rees Land and Livestock Company began operating at Woodruff, Utah, in the early 1900s on lands once occupied by the Crawford and Thompson Company. At peak times this outfit ran 20,000 sheep and 5,000 cattle. In recent years the ranch has been divided. The Woodruff ranch is currently running 1,500 mother cows.[22]

The Weston Livestock Company began operating on the south shore of Bear Lake in the 1890s. Over the years the company has expanded onto lands once occupied by the B Q outfit in the Bear River Valley near Randolph, Utah, and is currently running 3,500 mother cows and 500 steers.[23]

In 1908 the huge Sparks Tinnin Cattle Company was sold to a group of Ogden, Utah, businessmen, who changed the name of the operation to the Vineyard Land and Livestock Company. The company was then sold to the Utah Construction Company, headed by the Eccles family, in 1912. Sheep were introduced to this ranching operation at that time, but it continued to run horses and cattle.

Cowboys at the Rees Ranch near Randolph, Utah, circa 1900. Photograph courtesy of Barbara Peart.

The U C C continued as a ranching operation until the 1950s. At peak times the ranch comprised some 3 million acres in Nevada, Utah, and Idaho and ran 50,000 mother cows, 3,000 horses and 42,000 sheep.[24]

The Paxton Livestock Company of Kanosh, Utah, was started in the 1860s by Anthony Paxton. He later sold out to his son, Frank Paxton. Frank at one time was foreman for the B. F. Saunders outfit on the Arizona Strip and also was foreman for the Saunders-Haley outfit. In time, Frank settled on the ranch at Kanosh and formed it into a pretty big outfit. At peak times, the AP controlled over a million and a half acres of grazing land in Utah, Nevada, and Colorado and ranged 31,000 sheep and 4,200 cattle. The ranch was sold in 1986 to the Platt brothers of Arizona. They currently run 1,200 mother cows on the Utah ranch.[25]

The Wood Land and Livestock Company had its beginnings in the 1890s in the Cedar City area. Much of the range on which this company operates was controlled by Homer Duncan. Over the years several generations of the Wood family have operated the ranch and today the company comprises some 150,000 deeded acres in Utah and Arizona and currently runs some 2,500 mother cows.[26]

The Strawberry Water Users Association was formed in the early 1900s to utilize the waters being backed up by the newly constructed Strawberry Dam and to graze cattle during the summer months in the lush Strawberry Valley. The association was formulated by Utah County cattlemen who owned rights to the Strawberry water.

During the spring of each year the cattlemen gathered between 8,000 and 10,000 cattle and drove them from Utah County ranges to the Strawberry Valley by way of Spanish Fork Canyon and then through Sheep Creek Canyon. The cattle were rounded up in October and driven back to Utah County.

The Association has operated in the Strawberry Valley for the past eighty years but the increased size of the lake and pressures from sportsmen have diminished the amount of range available to the cattlemen.[27]

During the 1890s and early 1900s the Hatch fam-

221

Utah Construction Company cowboys circa 1918. Photograph courtesy of Utah State University Library, Special Collections.

ily established a vast sheep and cattle operation that utilized grazing lands in western Utah and along the northwestern portion of the Uinta Mountains. Most of this ranching enterprise was purchased by the Anchutes Company out of Denver, Colorado, in 1960. At its peak the Anchutes Ranch owned 300,000 acres and had range rights to an additional 500,000 acres of government land. The Anchutes was primarily a cattle company and ran in excess of 9,000 mother cows. Currently the ranch runs 3,000 mother cows and leases portions of its property to other ranchers.[28]

The Grand Canyon Cattle Company, better known as the "Bar Z" outfit, began operating along the Utah-Arizona border during the late 1890s on land acquired from B. F. Saunders. The Bar Z brand was originally established by Saunders when he began buying up land on the Arizona Strip. Headquarters for the ranch was at Cane Beds, Arizona, just a mile

or two below the Utah line. Many of the cowboys who worked for this cattle company were from the southern Utah area and the town of Kanab was the main supply point for the outfit.

The Bar Z operated for approximately twenty years, and at peak times the outfit was running 60,000 cows.[29] The company was disbanded in the 1920s as the land surrounding Grand Canyon National Park became more and more restricted for grazing use.

The JR Livestock Company currently operates on lands once claimed by the Carter Cattle Company on the north slopes of the Uinta Mountains along the Utah-Wyoming border. The company was originally established by the Broadbent family during the early 1900s and has continued to grow into one of the finest ranches in the region. It runs 1,800 mother cows, pastures 5,000 steers, and keeps 15,000 sheep on the range.[30]

A group of cowboys at Ogden, Utah, circa 1910. Photograph courtesy of Brent Baldwin.

The Robber's Roost Ranch was established in 1909 by Joe Biddlecome, who ventured into the area not long after the outlaw element had been run out of the country. At Joe's death in 1928, Pearl Baker, Joe's daughter, took over and operated the ranch until 1940, when she sold it to Arthur and Hazel Ekker, Pearl's sister and brother-in-law. Currently owned and operated by A. C. Ekker, the ranch is a cow-calf operation which utilizes the limited grazing lands contained in the hundreds of thousand acres of slickrock and canyon mazes running along the Colorado River.[31]

The breakup of the old cattle empires helped bring the colorful saga of the cowboy-outlaw gangs to an end. The cowboy outlaws were as free and as wild as the open range on which they plied their trade. Many of these outlaws were involved with the life because it provided excitement, adventure, and the thrill of danger. As barbed wire began sectioning off the range, as sheep began taking over the cattle range, and as forest permits limited the numbers of cattle on the range, the opportunities for wholesale rustling diminished. Faced with these problems, plus the pressure from local lawmen, the old-time horseback outlaws, at least those who were still alive and free, began moving to greener pastures in South America.

The finis of the Wild West, however, did not come easily. From time to time events occurred which stoked up the dying embers of the wild, turbulent country for several decades into the twentieth century. In many areas of Utah these Wild West lingerings seemed to crop up on a regular basis, and, in fact, some of the most colorful manhunts and feuds to occur in Utah happened at a time when most of the West had been tamed.

On the night of January 2, 1911, two men held up the Union Pacific train at Reese, Utah, a station

223

Edna Gibbons and Cornelius Ekker (left) and friends circa 1900. Edna and Cornelius married shortly after the photograph was taken at Hanksville, Utah. Photograph courtesy of Horace Ekker.

Cowboys and some visitors near Modena, Utah, circa 1920. Photograph courtesy of Mike Flinspach.

Warren Allred on the right and another sheepherder get ready to go to the sheep corrals above Spring City, Utah, circa 1900. Photograph courtesy of Gloria Chappell.

twelve miles west of Ogden. The holdup was extremely violent. The men killed one black porter who resisted and wounded another black porter. The bandits pistol-whipped three passengers who protested when their valuables were taken.[32]

A manhunt for them centered in the Ogden-Salt Lake City region where it was thought they had holed up. The two men, former workers for the Union Pacific Railroad, were finally captured and sent to prison.

The most intense manhunt to occur in Utah began on the evening of November 21, 1913, in the mining town of Bingham Canyon. A Mexican miner by the name of Rafael Lopez drew his pistol and killed a fellow miner in front of his sweetheart's cabin during a fit of jealousy. Following the shooting Lopez went to his own cabin, gathered up his cartridges, and left town on foot. A light snow had fallen and Lopez left a clear path as he walked through the night toward Lehi.

Because of the snow and the clear tracks, Bingham Police Chief J. W. Grant decided to wait until morning light to follow Lopez. At dawn Grant and

three Salt Lake County deputy sheriffs assigned to Bingham, Otto Witbeck, Nephi Jensen, and Julius Sorenson, mounted their horses and started toward Lehi, following the tracks laid down in the hard-crusted snow. By sundown the four lawmen had reached the southern shores of Utah Lake without catching a glimpse of Lopez and were openly questioning their earlier decision to wait for morning to follow the fugitive.

As the posse viewed the surrounding area, they saw some movement in the tall brush. Splitting up, Grant and Jensen rode toward the movement and Sorenson and Witbeck made a wide circle to the side. When Grant and Jensen drew close to the high brush, Lopez opened fire on the two lawmen. Within seconds both had been shot from their horses with mortal wounds. Upon hearing the shots and seeing the flashes from the barrel of Lopez's gun Sorenson and Witbeck spurred their horses and rode into the fray. Shots again rang out and Deputy Witbeck was mortally wounded. Sorenson dismounted and, following several minutes of silence, decided to go to a nearby farm where he could summon help.[33]

225

Bingham City police circa 1909. Chief J. W. Grant, who was killed by Rafael Lopez, is sitting third from left. Photograph courtesy of Utah State Historical Society.

A Bingham Canyon posse in the early 1900s. Photograph courtesy of Utah State Historical Society.

Rafael Lopez. Photograph courtesy of George Abplanalp.

By morning a large posse of men gathered at the farm and preparations were made to get the sharp-shooting Lopez. The initial posse was headed by Riley Mathew Beckstead, an old, tough Salt Lake County deputy sheriff, who, incidently, was this author's great-grandfather. Several other posses from the surrounding towns also got involved in the chase for Lopez, and at one time more than a hundred men were scouring the hills for the desperado.

One posse came under fire from Lopez in the Lakeside Mountains southwest of Lehi. Lopez kept the posse pinned down and, at times, carried on a conversation with posse members. He wanted to know if Sorenson was with the group and said he had a bullet waiting for the lawman. It seems that in the past Lopez and Sorenson had had words and that there was no love lost between the two.[34]

The posse waited for the cover of darkness and then retreated down the mountain. The next day the lawmen returned with reinforcements to the spot where Lopez had fired on them. They found several spent pistol cartridges, and it was apparent that Lopez had run out of rifle cartridges and had opted to use his less-accurate pistol to fire on the posse at Lakeside Mountain.

The chase moved into western Utah where Lopez had been sighted on several occasions; however, the trail came up cold and it was feared he had hopped a train and was California-bound. Authorities in Nevada and California were notified to be on the lookout for the man-killer, and the bulk of the Utah posses disbanded.

Lawmen were wary when word came from Bingham a few days later that Lopez was back in town. The rumors were verified and witnesses indicated that Lopez had picked up supplies and had made his way deep into the Minnie Mine. Under the leadership of Deputy Sorenson, all entrances to the mine were placed under guard by armed men. Miners were allowed in and out of the mine and on several occasions miners told tales of being robbed of their tobacco and food by Lopez.

Deputy Sorenson decided it would be foolish to enter the mine, with its miles of unlighted tunnels, and he proposed a plan to smoke the fugitive out. Once the miners vacated the mine, guards built

huge fires at the entrances and directed the smoke to the shaft openings. As the fires burned, guards kept an eye open for any sign of Lopez, but after several hours there was nothing to indicate Lopez was even in the mine.

As the fires began to burn out, the guards ventured a short distance into the shaft openings. At an opening known as the Andy Incline, four deputies entered and walked about thirty feet into the dingy shaft. Suddenly shots rang out and two of the deputies were hit. One of the men died instantly, the other fellow lay wounded in the shaft for several hours before dying. The other deputies managed to make their way out of the shaft.

Once again, fearful of taking men into the miles of tunnels which Lopez knew so well, Sorenson decided to smoke the mine again. The smoking continued for several days until it was believed no living thing could survive in the mine. When the mine was cleared of smoke deputies combed the mine but no evidence of Lopez was found. At that, the mine was reopened and miners went back to work.

And again they found themselves being robbed by Lopez. One miner claimed to have been held at gunpoint by Lopez and that the fugitive had given him a message to give to Deputy Sorenson. The message was that Lopez would meet Sorenson at the same spot, at the same time, on the next day, and that he intended to kill the lawman. The miner was persuaded to return the next day to deliver a message from Sorenson to Lopez, but Lopez never showed up for the meeting.

To the present day the whereabouts of Lopez is a mystery. Rumors spread he had been seen in California and New York, but these were never substantiated. The hunt for him cost Salt Lake County some $25,000 in expenses and took the lives of five lawmen.[35]

Two years after the Lopez incident, violence flared again, this time in San Juan County. An Indian named Tse-ne-gat robbed and killed a Mexican sheepherder, Juan Chacon. A posse was formed to apprehend Tse-ne-gat, but his father, Chief Poke, refused to let the boy be taken. A fight began and three

Indians were killed as was one member of the posse.

Learning of the fight, another Indian named Posey decided to get in on the action. Taking his rifle he rode toward Poke's camp. On the way there he saw two white men riding nearby and raised a white flag to attract their attention. When they approached, Posey shot and killed one of them. He then made his way to Poke's camp and told him of the killing.[36]

When word of the killings reached Bluff City, a posse was formed and men were talking about an all-out war with the Indians. The Indians must have sensed their precarious position, and Poke and Posey gathered their tribes and headed toward Navajo Mountain. Once entrenched on the mountain, it would have taken a regiment of soldiers to defeat them and, realizing this, the men of Bluff sent word to Washington, D.C., requesting that federal troops be sent to the area. Instead of complying, government officials sent General Hugh L. Scott to San Juan.[37]

General Scott was familiar with Utah's San Juan region since he had been stationed at Fort Wingate, New Mexico, in 1907, and he had led a troop of soldiers to Aneth, Utah, to quell a small uprising of Navajos. During that foray two Indians were killed and several others arrested. This time, rather than fight with Poke and Posey, General Scott successfully convinced the two old chiefs and Tse-ne-gat to surrender. With the assistance of U.S. Marshal Aquilla Nebeker, the Indians were escorted to Salt Lake City, where they were met with a great deal of excitement. Word of the small Indian war had traveled throughout the nation and the Indians emerged as heroes.

For several days they were the toast of the town. Crowds came to see them and reporters flocked around. Incredibly, Posey and Poke were released and allowed to return to San Juan. Tse-ne-gat was taken to Denver, where he stood trial in a federal court for the murder of Juan Chacon, which occurred on an Indian reservation. His reception in Denver was the same as in Salt Lake City. He was wined and dined and treated as a hero. The city was filled with Indian rights people. Their presence, plus the influence of the local papers, which glorified the Indian, must have influenced the courts, for he was set free.

Ute Indians in the vicinity of Thompson, Utah, circa 1923. Photograph courtesy of Baker and Lacy copyright 1979.

A posse from Bluff, Utah, and one of the Indians who was killed during the fight in 1915. Photograph courtesy of Heda B. S. N. Williams.

Some captured Indians at the Bluff City jail circa 1915. The white man on the right was not involved in the fight. Photograph courtesy of Carol Hines.

Posey and Poke circa 1915. Photograph courtesy of Baker and Lacy copyright 1979.

Sheriff William Oliver circa 1923. Photograph courtesy of Baker and Lacy copyright 1979.

Tse-ne-gat took in the pleasures of Denver, including several women who threw themselves at him. When his fame died down, he returned to Utah's San Juan, where he continued to scoff at the law. A year later he died from a white man's disease, tuberculosis.[38] His death appeared to take the fight out of Poke. From that day on he was a mere shell of a man. Not so for Posey; buoyed up by the treatment he received in Salt Lake City, he made a real menace of himself in the San Juan country.

Eight years passed and the relationship between Posey and the Mormons of San Juan did not improve. In fact, it got worse. In 1923 Posey and five of his warriors rode hell-bent-for-leather toward three Blanding, Utah, cowboys, emitting war whoops and acting as if they intended to kill the cowboys. Upon reaching them the Indians stopped, with the exception of one Indian who began whipping one of the cowboys with his quirt. Posey soon stopped the Indian and told the cowboys that they were just playing a little joke, but the cowboys were not amused.

The Indian doing the whipping was the son of Joe Bishop, and even though Posey tried to quiet him down, Bishop taunted the cowboys, saying, "What's the matter of you blank-blank Mormon cowards, all time heap talk, no fight, heap scairt!"[39] Within a few weeks of the incident Bishop and two other Indians robbed a sheep camp belonging to the city of Blanding. Sheriff William H. Oliver and a posse went to the Indian camp and arrested Bishop and one of the other robbers.

On the day of the trial Posey rode into town and tied his horse to the steps of the courthouse, then pushed himself into the crowded courtroom. There he made several outbursts against the prosecuting lawyer that disrupted the trial. When the court adjourned for noon, Bishop managed to break away from Sheriff Oliver and jumped onto Posey's horse. The sheriff took hold of the reins, but Bishop pulled the gun from Oliver's holster and fired point blank into the sheriff's chest. The gun misfired, but the shock of having the pistol crammed into his body

was enough to cause the sheriff to let go of the reins.

As Bishop rode off, Sheriff Oliver jumped onto his own horse and soon caught up with the fugitive. Riding side-by-side the sheriff tried to wrestle Bishop off his horse, and all the while Bishop was shooting the pistol at Oliver. The pistol misfired several times, and then went off. The bullet hit Oliver's horse and the sheriff found himself tumbling to the ground in a cloud of dust.[40]

Bishop rode to the Indian camp at West Water, several miles west of Blanding. Posey soon followed and hastily gathered the clan together. Leaving most of their possessions behind, the Indians began moving toward the Bear's Ears on Elk Ridge. A posse of men from Blanding was soon on the Indians' trail with an intent to put an end once and for all to the Indian threat in San Juan.

In an effort to give his people time to reach the mountain, Posey remained behind the group and laid an ambush for the posse. The first posse member to ride into range of Posey's long gun was John D. Rogers. Posey, who for years had prided himself on his shooting ability, missed his mark and shot the horse out from under Rogers. The other members of the posse dismounted and took cover. For several minutes there was dead silence, each man too leery to poke his head up. Suddenly the silence was broken by the sound of a Ford car chugging along the road filled with more posse members who had elected to use the comfort of modern transportation.

Posey took a bead on the car and began firing. A bullet ripped a hole through the back seat, just missing three men. The driver stepped on the gas, but another bullet blew out one of the tires. The car came to a screeching halt, but before Posey could pick off the men scampering from the car, the horseback posse, able to see Posey's position, began shooting at the old chief. With bullets flying all around him, Posey mounted his horse and rode out to catch up with his people.[41]

The main body of Indians made it to Comb Reef, a high, slickrock uplift west of Blanding, where they decided to wait for Posey. In the meantime, Posey rode to the camp of Jack Fly and warned him and

Robert Lee Newman led the posse that captured the Indians during the Posey War of 1923. Photograph courtesy of Ellen Lefler.

two other Indians of the fight which was taking place. He told them to gather their belongings as soon as possible and then to join the fight. He then rode off toward Comb Reef. Upon reaching the reef Posey found the posse between him and his people. He spurred his horse and rode past the posse. In an effort to protect himself from the posse's bullets, Posey swung down on the side of his horse and, aiming from under its neck, shot at the posse with his pistol. The posse was reluctant to shoot the horse, but aimed at the leg and buttocks of Posey. One or two of the bullets found their mark, causing Posey to abandon the effort to reach the Indians at the top of Comb Reef. Instead, he veered off and rode out of sight.

Within minutes of the shooting the posse spotted Jack Fly and two other Indians riding toward the reef. They left Bill Young in charge of the horses and ran to a position where they could get open shots at the Indians. Bishop and another Indian saw the posse move toward Fly and decided to ride down off the reef to take care of Bill Young and steal the posse's horses. The Indians gave piercing war cries as they rode toward the lone white guard. Young ran for cover, pulled his gun, and shot Bishop through the heart. Bishop gave one final bloodthirsty howl as he plummeted from his horse. The remaining Indian, not wanting the same bad medicine, turned his horse and rode back to the reef.[42]

Seeing Bishop drop from his horse, general panic struck the Indians on Comb Reef. They abandoned most of their provisions to lighten the load and fled. After several days in flight, they realized Posey was not going to rejoin them, so they threw down their weapons and surrendered to the pursuing posse. After returning to Blanding the sheriff allowed Posey's wife and two sons to go look for him. After a few days they returned and reported seeing no sign of him.

A federal marshal who was sent to Blanding to oversee the confinement of the Indians and to restore peace talked with Posey's sons and got them to admit they had found their father. They told him that Posey had been severely wounded in the fight, but was alive when they found him. They and Posey's wife had made him as comfortable as possible and buried him when he died of his wounds.

A sheep camp in the Bear River Mountains near Lake Town, Utah, circa 1900. Photograph courtesy of T. Weston.

A cowboy and his two sons at Parowan, Utah, in the 1890s. Most cowboys eventually settled down and raised families. Photograph courtesy of Carma Smith and Steve Lacy copyright 1990.

Charlie Glass at the Turner Ranch circa 1920. Photograph courtesy of Joyce Cunningham.

The marshal persuaded the two Indian men to take him to the place where they had buried Posey so he could verify the death and could close the matter. The Indians agreed on the condition that no men from Blanding would be allowed to go to the burial site. The marshal consented to these terms and was taken to the site, where he verified that Posey had died. The men of Blanding waited until the marshal returned to Salt Lake City and then followed his tracks to the burial site. They wanted to see for themselves that Posey was dead, so they dug up his body and photographed it. Posey indeed had made his last raid.[43]

Two years prior to the Posey uprising, the cattle range near Cisco, Utah, was engulfed in a range war when sheepmen from Colorado moved their herds of sheep onto the range of the Lazy Y Cross Ranch, owned by Oscar L. Turner. The border country between Utah and Colorado had been engaged in range wars as Utah sheepmen moved onto the Colorado ranges in 1911. Between that year and 1920, a number of hostilities occurred as the Colorado cattlemen fought to keep the sheep off the range. Then, in 1921, the roles were reversed when Turner went to the courts for restraining orders to keep Colorado sheep off his Utah cattle range.[44]

The Utah courts took action to protect Turner's cattle range from being "sheeped," and set up quarantine lines which prevented the Colorado sheep from moving onto the range claimed by the Lazy Y Cross. This did not stop the Basque sheep-herders, however, for they understood very little English and used the excuse of misunderstanding the quarantine lines. When told to get off the land, the Basques moved the herds peacefully, but would soon again return to the range. This was a constant occurrence, condoned and encouraged by the Colorado sheep barons.

Charlie Glass was foreman of the Lazy Y Cross outfit, a tall, good-looking black man who was also one-fourth Indian. He always wore a six-shooter and was reputed to be the best shot along the border country. He had come to the Utah-Colorado region in 1909 from Indian Territory, where it was rumored he had killed a man in a range war.[45] He was well liked in the country, but was not a man one would want to tangle with.

Glass had warned several sheepherders during the winter of 1920–21 that there would be trouble if they did not stay off the Lazy Y Cross range. Finally, on the morning of February 20, 1921, the verbal warnings ended and gunplay began. A French sheepherder and camp mover, one Felix Jesui, was told by Glass to get off the range. Jesui refused, guns were drawn, and Jesui was shot and killed by Glass.[46]

Glass was brought to trial at Moab, Utah, in March of 1921 for the death of Jesui and although evidence indicated that both Glass and Jesui had fired shots, Glass was found guilty for the felonious death of the sheepherder. It was an unpopular decision and several prominent cattlemen, including Turner and Latigo Gordon, were able to raise enough money to obtain Glass's release on bond while awaiting an appeal of the second-degree murder charges. While awaiting the outcome of a second trial, cowboys rode to the headquarters of the sheepman who had employed Jesui and killed thirty-five horses. It was never proven that Glass was a member of the raiding party or that the raiders came from Utah.[47]

During the second trial affidavits were given to show that a feud existed between the cattlemen and the transient sheepmen which would mitigate the charges against Glass. The court agreed and Glass was acquitted of the murder charges. The sheepmen, though, finally got even. In 1937 Charlie Glass spent the night gambling and drinking in a Thompson Springs, Utah, saloon with two Basque sheepherders. The three men left the saloon together in an old truck and drove to Cisco, Utah, where they intended to continue their party. Along the way the truck crashed and Glass died from a broken neck. Neither sheepman was hurt and the circumstances behind the wreck were considered mighty suspicious.[48]

Following Glass's funeral, one that many prominent white people from Utah and Colorado attended, the black cowboy was buried in the exclusively white cemetery at Fruita, Colorado, even though the town charter prohibited the burial of blacks, thereby testifying to Glass's popularity.

Robert Marshall hangs from a tree at Price, Utah. Photograph courtesy of Steve Lacy copyright 1978 Wild Bunch Photo.

At the other end of the popularity spectrum was another black by the name of Robert Marshall. He has the dubious distinction of being the last victim of a lynching in Utah.

On the evening of June 15, 1925, Robert was seen walking along the railroad tracks in the mining town of Castle Gate by two young men on their way home. The boys taunted Robert as they passed him, calling him names. They then proceeded across the bridge which spanned the Price River and came upon Deputy Sheriff J. Milton Burns (the son of James Burns, the deceased marshal of Spring City), who was making his nightly rounds. Burns and the boys spoke briefly and then the boys walked away.

Robert Marshall also made his way to the bridge and encountered Deputy Burns. Without warning Marshall pulled out a pistol and shot the lawman twice. As Burns slowly fell to the ground, Marshall shot him three more times. Then he took the deputy's gun and the money he was carrying.

The two boys who had just talked with Burns witnessed the shooting and, in a panic, ran for help. Within minutes of the shooting a posse was formed under the leadership of Sheriff Ray Deming, and the manhunt was on.

Marshall successfully eluded the posse the first night in the rugged mountains surrounding Castle Gate. Meanwhile, Deputy Burns clung to life in his hospital bed, but his condition was hopeless. He died from the bullet wounds some twenty-four hours after he was shot.

Tired and hungry, Marshall made his way out of the mountains several days later and found shelter in an old cabin belonging to a black man called George. George suspected something was wrong, but gave Marshall food and provided him with sleeping quarters. While Marshall slept, George went into Castle Gate to purchase supplies and there learned that Marshall was wanted for the killing of Deputy Burns. George notified the authorities that Marshall was at his cabin, and a posse was immediately formed. They surrounded the cabin and Marshall gave up without a fight.

Because of the possibility of a lynching, Marshall was escorted by vehicle to Price. As the car carrying him made its way down the road, a number of cars fell in behind. By the time the vehicle reached Price,

The Clash between Cattlemen and Sheepmen

Model 73 Winchester. Courtesy of Bob Fehr.

Right: A .38 long Colt single action. Courtesy of Southwest Indian Traders, Park City, Utah.

Left: Back and front views of pommel holster made by Pickard and Son, Salt Lake City, circa 1880. From author's collection.

Right: Advertisement for the maker of the holster above.

Charles H. Esplin, Orderville, Utah, circa 1919. Photograph courtesy of Fred Esplin.

over forty carloads of irate people had joined the procession. Sheriff Deming tried to reason with the mob, but was soon overpowered. The mob then proceeded to hang Robert Marshall to a tree.[49]

The lynching of Robert Marshall on June 18, 1925, was the last lynching to take place in the Wild West. The Indian battle which took place at Blanding, Utah, in 1923 was the last Indian-white battle in the country. There would be more violence in Utah and the rest of the nation after these two events when the 1920s ushered in the gangster era; however, the day of horseback manhunts had come to an end.

By the 1920s most of the vices associated with the Wild West had been curtailed, regulated, or stopped. Gone were the days when local politicians and law officers were willing to allow prostitution to flourish. As early as 1911 laws were being formulated to stop gambling in the saloons. Utah was one of the last "Wet States" to fall into line when the Eighteenth

Amendment to the Constitution went into effect on January 16, 1920. Utah was the thirty-sixth and deciding state to repeal national prohibition in December of 1933. Today alcohol is legal in Utah, prostitution and gambling are not.

The end of the open-range cattle industry came with the passage of the Taylor Grazing Act in 1934. It established grazing districts and permits to graze on all federal land not in the National Forest. This affected a considerable amount of land in Utah. With the passage of this act, cattle barons were no longer able to move their cattle where the grass stood tall or control the range with the barrel of a gun. Small-time ranchers could now line up, pay their allotment fees, and use the range without fear of reprisal.

Finis was written to the Wild West because of human progress, but there was a degree of sadness in its passing. Even before the final death bell tolled, enterprising people were preserving its heritage.

9

The Legacy Preserved

According to Alexander Toponce, Lot Smith was "a rough and ready type. He would have passed as a cattleman in any country."[1] It was the ultimate compliment from one cowboy to another. It not only showed respect for his cowboying skills, but acknowledged his tough and determined character. The same could be said about Howard Egan and his sons, the McIntyre brothers, Preston Nutter, Al Scorup, Robert LeRoy Parker, and the hundreds of other cowboys who rode the Utah range.

Cowboying in Utah was not easy. The rugged and semiarid land made sure of that. Cowboying in any type of country was not particularly easy. Each region of the West could produce its hardships. The treeless and windswept plains were ruthless during the winter. The scorching heat and dust were just as ruthless in the Southwest. It took a lot of determination to be a cowboy in any part of the country.

There were not many occupations in the Old West that required the physical and mental stamina that being a cowboy did. On the long drives he was subjected to the cold rain and snow without shelter. He was often wet for days on end and he could count himself lucky if he had more than one set of clothes to wear. If the cowboy was not subjected to the cold,

George Muir was a true working cowboy near Heber, Utah, during the 1880s. His pose is classic: standing tall, with a stern look and a trusty six-shooter at his side. Photograph courtesy of Mildred Muir.

then most likely he was battling the heat and the dust and a lack of cold water.

A cowboy's life could end abruptly at the end of a bronco's hooves, a steer's horns, or an Indian's lance. Flash floods, prairie fires, and stampedes were likewise hazardous to life and limb. The elements, the human dangers, all were part of a cowboy's life and most likely every cowboy complained about them from time to time, but rarely would he give up cowboy life for another occupation. Cowboying was something he loved, even though the pay was low and the job was, in the eyes of many, demeaning and reserved for second-class citizens.

The cowboy created many of his own problems by hell-raising, women-chasing, drunken brawls, and gunplay at the end of the trail. Many citizens of the towns wanted to bring civilization to the West and to emulate eastern standards. They imported finery and clothing from the East in an effort to create better surroundings. The uncivilized cowboy, with his evil ways and frontier dress, simply did not fit in. For a time in the West a cowboy was considered vermin. Even the great cowboy artist Charles Russell once wrote of them that they were "careless, homeless, hard-drinking men."[2] That image did not last because there were forces at work which would transform the cowboy from America's villain to America's hero.

By the 1870s eastern journalists were coming west to get a firsthand look at the western character. They wrote bigger-than-life stories about these men

242

William "Buffalo Bill" Cody and some of his friends in the 1890s. Photograph courtesy of Brigham Young University, Photo Archives.

of the West and sent them back to newspapers and publishers who flooded the eastern market with dime novels. Exaggerated stories were published concerning gunfighters and buffalo hunters, but no character got more adulating press than the American cowboy. In the mind of the eastern public, he was emerging as the "Knight of the Plains." He could shoot straighter, fight harder, cuss louder, and spit farther than any other character on the frontier. Yet, with all these harsh attributes, when it came to the ladies, the cowboy was chivalrous, gentle, and downright shy. At least, that is how the easterners viewed him.

By the 1880s eastern schoolboys were running away from home to travel west and become cow-

A working cowboy poses in a Salt Lake City studio circa 1920. Photograph from author's collection.

boys. This eastern love affair with the cowboy soon began catching on in the West. The cowboy, himself, began to be caught up in the mystique of the cowboy image. Trips to town became an opportunity to capture that image at the local photo studio. The backdrops varied, but the pose was unmistakable. Standing tall, the cowboy always had a stern look on his face, was ready for action, and had his trusty six-shooter prominently displayed on his hip. If his six-shooter happened to be locked up in the sheriff's office, the photo studio usually had a prop or two.[3] If he wasn't wearing the right clothing, the studio could usually provide that as well.

The cowboy mystique soon crossed the Atlantic Ocean and Europeans began a love affair with the American cowboy. Wild West shows with real cowboys and Indians were organized and transported to eastern and European audiences, where they

The cowboys who participated in Buffalo Bill Cody's show at Evanston, Wyoming. Oscar Quinn is sitting just behind the supine man's shoulders and George Herford is to the right of Quinn. Photograph courtesy of Wyoming State Archives, Museums and Historical Department.

received standing ovations from commoners and royalty alike. The first of these Wild West shows was established by William Cody, better known as "Buffalo Bill."[4]

Cody had lived in real life the very events which he was now performing. He came west at an early age and got a job as a mule skinner with Johnston's Army on the march to Utah. He saw firsthand the Mormon cowboys, Lot Smith and Porter Rockwell, drive off herds of the army's cattle and horses and burn the supply trains. Cody later made a reputation for killing buffalo for the railroad. He became a scout for the army and reached the pinnacle of frontier glory when he bested Chief Yellow Hand in a fight to the death.[5] No one was better suited to carry the cowboy heritage east than was Buffalo Bill Cody.

Buffalo Bill's Wild West show depicted all phases of western life from Indian warfare to bronco riding. He hired real Indians and real cowboys to perform in the show. At least one native Utah cowboy be-

came a part of the show. His name was Oscar Quinn and, for a time in the 1890s, was billed as the "Prince of Cowboys." Quinn was born in Salt Lake City and as a teenager decided to become a cowboy. He worked on several cattle ranches in Utah and Wyoming and was the acknowledged bronco-riding champion of those two states.[6]

Quinn's opportunity to work with Buffalo Bill came about because of the misfortune of another Utah cowboy. In 1887 Buffalo Bill took his Wild West show to Evanston, Wyoming, and put out the word that he was looking for the best bronc rider in the area to perform with his show in Europe. Cowboys from the surrounding areas came to Evanston where the ride-off was to take place. One of those participating was Salt Lake City-born George Hereford, who at that time was cowboying for the Lige Driscoll outfit at Manila, Utah.

During the competition the cowboys rode long and hard, and one by one were eliminated. Finally George Hereford and Oscar Quinn emerged as the

Buffalo Bill Cody stands in front of a group of Kanab, Utah, cowboys in 1892. The cowboys broke horses so Cody could continue his journey to the Grand Canyon. It was a chance for the local boys to perform for the West's greatest showman. Photograph courtesy of LDS Church Archives.

very best of the lot. A ride-off between the two took place and Hereford came out the winner. He was offered the job with the Wild West show but, due to his brother's untimely death, he had to decline.[7] The job was then offered to Quinn, and for the next several years he traveled around America and Europe with the show.

In 1892 Buffalo Bill brought a party of eastern and foreign dignitaries on a tour of the Southwest. The group traveled through Utah on their way to the Grand Canyon. By the time the party reached Kanab most of the horses were pretty worn, especially those ridden by the tenderfeet in the party. Bill hired a number of Kanab cowboys to round up some range stock he had purchased and to take some of the wild out of them. The Kanab cowboys put on a pretty good show for the party as they took the fight out of the horses. Whether or not Buffalo Bill offered any of these cowboys a chance at stardom with his show is not known, but for a brief moment even these hard-working cowboys must have been

caught up in the glory of riding in the presence of the West's first and greatest showman.

The Wild West shows perpetuated to an adoring public the western mystique that had been spawned by the dime novels. The cowboys, Indians, and shooting exhibitions put on by the likes of Annie Oakley, Pawnee Bill, and Cody himself, plus the pageantry of the Wild West shows left an indelible image of the cowboy West in the eyes of the viewers. That colorful image also was not lost on the men who actually rode the western rangelands.

By the late 1890s the cowboy himself was fully aware of his public image. His occupation, no longer considered menial, conjured up all kinds of dashing and romantic thoughts, and the cowboy was more than willing to perpetuate the image. His particular style of clothing, although functional and necessary, had become a uniform to inform society that the wearer was indeed a Knight of the Range.[8] The cowboy had finally passed from frontier vermin to the greatest of American legends.

A wild west show troupe rides down a Salt Lake City, Utah, street in 1911. Photograph courtesy of Utah State Historical Society.

There were imitators of the cowboy image. Many men and women who were not associated with the cattle business adorned themselves with the finest cowboy clothing the photo studios could provide and had their photos taken while posing in typical cowboy fashion. This was an accepted practice started in the 1880s that continues to the present. It indicates only the public's infatuation with the cowboy. The discerning eye can separate the real Knights of the Range from the counterfeits. The cowboy, somehow, wore his uniform in a more convincing manner.

Aside from the glamorous image of the cowboy and away from the photo studio, the reality of cowboying had changed very little since the first trail

Two working cowboys in a Heber, Utah, photo studio circa 1900. Photograph courtesy of Dr. R. R. Green.

drives came north out of Texas. Long days in the saddle, cold, lonely nights, bawling calves, and the smell of branded flesh were all reasons why many more people dreamed of being cowboys than were actual cowboys.

The heyday of the American cowboy lasted from 1866 until 1900, and, in some isolated spots, especially in the Rocky Mountains where much of the land was open and free, it was possible for the old-style cowboys to practice open-range traditions until the closing of the public range in 1934. The closing, however, did not kill the spirit of the cowboy, for his image was meant to be preserved.

Beginning in 1898, the famous inventor, Thomas Edison, began capturing the cowboy image in a new and exciting medium known as the motion picture. He filmed a little tableau called *Cripple Creek Bar-Room,* in which some western dandies, a barmaid,

Two cowboys working for the Becwith Quinn outfit act out the image of the Wild West in the 1890s. Photograph courtesy of Ralph Nebeker.

Two make-believe cowboys at the Liberty Photo studio in Salt Lake City, Utah, circa 1915. Photograph from author's collection.

and a cowboy appeared while enjoying a little "red eye." He followed that tableau with a story film called *The Great Train Robbery* in 1903. These two rudimentary films were the first of thousands which would create a lasting, although somewhat fanciful, image of the American cowboy.

The first motion pictures were filmed in studios, but in time the film moguls and picture directors opted for the wide open spaces where they could capture the beauty and vastness of cowboy country. More often than not, Utah was chosen as the backdrop for a western movie. Over two hundred movies and several long-standing television series have been filmed in the area.[9] Kanab and Moab have been host for the majority of these movies. Many of them have been western classics and include such favorites as *The Searchers, Cheyenne Autumn,*

A make-believe cowboy in a Price, Utah, photo studio circa 1910. Somehow the real cowboys wore the clothing with more authority. Photograph courtesy of Steve Lacy and J. Bracken Lee copyright 1989.

Drums Along the Mohawk, My Friend Flicka, Smokey, She Wore a Yellow Ribbon, Stagecoach, and *Butch Cassidy and the Sundance Kid.*

Utah also starred in several other westerns: *Hills of Utah,* starring Gene Autry; *Utah,* with Roy Rogers; *Utah Blaine,* with Rory Calhoun; *The Utah Kid,* with Hoot Gibson; and *Utah Trail,* starring Tex Ritter. Tyrone Power and Dean Jagger starred in *Brigham Young;* Allan Lane starred in *Salt Lake Raiders,* and Rex Lease starred in *Robber's Roost.* Zane Grey's original book about the Utah frontier, *Riders of the Purple Sage,* was filmed four times. The second starred Tom Mix.

The "Duke," John Wayne, played a Utah cowboy turned lawman in *Man from Utah,* with Gabby Hayes playing his sidekick. Ben Johnson and Harry Carey, Jr., acted as Utah cowboys when they helped Ward Bond, acting as a crusty Mormon, in *Wagon Master.* Paul Newman played the lovable Utah cowboy outlaw, Butch Cassidy, in *Butch Cassidy and the Sundance Kid,* and Robert Redford played an uncompromising Utah cowboy in *Electric Horseman.*

With Sincere Wish
Art Acord.

Hollywood actors at a movie location in southern Utah, circa 1930. The man third from the left could easily be a young John Wayne. Photograph courtesy of Lynne Clark Photography.

The heyday of the western movies ended in the early 1970s as younger viewing audiences were caught up in futuristic films and cops and robbers capers. Consequently, fewer and fewer western movies have been made recently. This trend will surely change in the future—at least, there are many who hope so. In the meantime, rodeo, which is increasing in popularity, continues to preserve the heritage of the cowboy.

Certain forms of rodeo began as early as 1869 when cowboys coming in off the range participated in roping and riding competitions to pass the time.[10] Soon after, fairs began offering rodeo competition and the Wild West shows provided a number of riding and roping events for the audiences. Today there are hundreds of professional and amateur rodeos throughout the country. Many of the towns in Utah put on an annual rodeo and some of these are on the "must" list for the professional cowboys who, every year, compete for the chance to go to the National Finals Rodeo. Included in these rodeos

are the Days of '47 in Salt Lake City, Pioneer Days in Ogden, and the Lehi Roundup.

Over the years Utah has produced several quality rodeo cowboys. One of the best during the 1930s was Matt Cropper from Deseret, Utah. Known as "Mosquito Jack," Matt won many rodeo events on the Rocky Mountain circuit and succeeded in riding the unridable bull "Escalante One Eye" and the famous bucking horse "Kingfisher."[11] The most famous of Utah's cowboys is Lewis Feild from Elk Ridge, Utah. He won the All-Around Cowboy title in the National Finals in 1985, 1986, and 1987. Another Utah cowboy, Lance Robinson, was runner-up to Feild in 1987.

The books, movies, rodeos, and western pageants have helped to keep alive the spirit of the cowboy. Another source of preservation for the cowboy heritage comes from the writings and humorous stories of men and women who lived on the wild frontier. One of my favorite stories was told by Richard "Ras" Egan. The cattle range on the western border of Utah was engulfed in an Indian war and Egan, who was cowboying in the country, took some time to help build a Pony Express station near lbapah. One day he rode off to look for a log big enough and

Art Acord was a prominent actor and stunt man during the silent-film era. He was born and raised in Emery County, Utah. Photograph courtesy of Emery County Museum.

251

Rodeo was a yearly occurrence in most Utah towns. This action took place at Randolph, Utah, circa 1900. Photograph courtesy of Barbara Peart.

Another rodeo scene at Cannonville, Utah. Photograph courtesy of Brent Baldwin.

Moses Beckstead was a top rodeo bronc rider at the turn of the century. He was born and raised in Spanish Fork, Utah. Photograph courtesy of Robert M. Beckstead.

long enough to make a ridgepole, and soon found himself about eight miles from the construction site. While riding along, Egan dragged his rawhide lasso, an act which cowboys did from time to time to keep the rawhide pliable. He was enjoying the solitude when he suddenly came upon a camp of Indians. Fortunately the Indians were friendly and they invited him to sit down at their fire.

After sharing food and talk Egan mounted his horse and intended to ride off. He began looping his lasso and, in a moment of frivolity, decided to lasso several of the Indians sitting around the fire. It was all taken in stride and the chief jokingly indicated that it would be a good way to catch a squaw. Egan then threw the lasso again and caught the chief's daughter.

Laughing, the young girl claimed that Egan could not catch her again and she began to run. Egan spurred his horse and galloped after her, swinging the loop of his lasso. Just as he prepared to throw the lasso, the girl dodged behind a tree. Egan's pony was a well-trained cow horse and gave a quick jump to go around the tree to cut her off. In doing so, the horse went under a low limb of the tree which snagged under the rim of Egan's saddle, breaking the cinch and throwing Egan to the ground. The cow pony didn't stop running until it had reached the Pony Express site. Egan had to walk the eight miles back. By the time he reached the camp, his feet were mighty swollen, but they didn't hurt near as much as his pride.[12]

Lige Moore was a Texas cowboy who came to Utah in the 1890s to capture wild horses. He never returned to Texas, but instead became a prominent cattleman in the Bryce Canyon region. Lige lived to be close to a hundred years of age and was still cowboying in his nineties. He was a favorite storyteller and could keep the citizens of Henrieville, Utah, on the edge of their seats for hours on end.

One of Lige's favorite stories happened during

A cowgirl in Jensen, Utah, circa 1915. Many women on the ranches of the West worked with the cattle and horses alongside the men. Photograph courtesy of Doris Burton.

Clarence W. Rogers worked as a cowboy in Idaho and Utah. He and his new bride settled in Thompson, Utah, in the early 1900s. Photograph courtesy of L. W. Rogers.

roundup on the high cliffs overlooking Bryce. A fellow cowboy roped a big steer that must have been ten years old. The steer fought his way to the edge of a cliff and fell over. The horse and rider were being pulled to the edge of the cliff and it looked like both horse and rider were goners. Lige pulled out his six-shooter and shot through the rope, saving the horse and rider, and the old steer fell to its death.[13]

Earl and Cass Mulford were nine and seven years old, respectively, in 1898, but still old enough to be helping their father round up steers west of Boulder Mountain. While they were sitting around the night

Erastus Egan was a Pony Express rider and cowboy who worked on the ranges at Ibapah, Utah. He was a great storyteller. Photograph courtesy of Utah State Historical Society.

campfire several well-armed men rode in and asked the father if he could spare some food. Little was said at the campfire as the men sipped coffee and ate bread and beans. When they left, the boys' father cautioned them not to let anyone know when they got home that the men who stopped to rest and eat were members of Butch Cassidy's Wild Bunch gang.[14]

Ten years later Earl Mulford got into trouble with a local rancher when he got too familiar with the rancher's daughter. The rancher's son and a friend came to the Mulford ranch and called Earl out. Guns were drawn and Earl shot the rancher's son twice. He was acquitted for the shootings when it was determined it was done in self-defense, but it wasn't long before he had to leave Wayne County because of numerous threats on his life.[15]

255

Jack Strange at Price, Utah, 1899. Although cowboying was a tough job, rarely would a cowboy want to do any other kind of work. Photograph courtesy of Brigham Young University, Photo Archives.

Earl went to Grand County where he got involved in the Utah-Colorado sheep war and from there he moved on into Wyoming and Montana. He punched cows and herded sheep for the next fifty years, and, when he was too old to throw a leg up over a horse, he returned to Wayne County and lived out the remainder of his days in a little one-room cabin which had neither electricity nor plumbing.

I had the good fortune to meet Earl at his cabin several times during the 1960s. He was in his late 80s at the time, but still capable of telling some good stories. One time while sitting outside his cabin I noticed that about twenty yards away there were some aspen trees which had been cut most of the way through, but which were still standing. I asked Earl how that had come about and he explained that he used the trees for firewood but that he was not nimble enough to get out of the way of the falling

trees. He therefore cut the trees most of the way through and then waited for a big wind to come along and knock them over.

I also had the good fortune to meet Sid and Ellen Rymer during the late 1960s. Sid was in his nineties at the time, but he had a very crisp memory. He and Ellen had grown up in Wayne County, married, had a fine family, retired, and became temple workers at the Manti Temple. They were typical faithful and good Latter-day Saints. That is why I was somewhat taken aback when Sid recited the story about Butch Cassidy playing baseball with the kids in Loa. Here was Sid, a fine, upstanding churchman and yet, with a twinkle in his eye, he spoke about one of the most celebrated outlaws in the annals of the West. Sid had actually thought that Butch Cassidy was a heck of a nice guy.

Ellen's experience with outlaws was not so nice.

256

Wells Robins left his Scipio, Utah, home at the age of seventeen to drive cattle from the Arizona Strip to Milford, Utah, in 1905. He died at the age of 100. Photograph courtesy of Wells Robins.

She lived on an isolated ranch in Wayne County and recalls the night when, as a little girl, she heard a knock on the cabin door. Her father opened the door and standing outside were U.S. Marshal Joe Bush and his prisoner, the notorious "Silver Tip." Joe asked if they could spend the night and, true to the hospitality in those days, her father welcomed them in and fed them. The family spent the night in the loft, while the marshal and his prisoner slept on the main floor. Ellen lay awake the whole night fearing that Silver Tip was going to get loose.

Most of the old-timers are gone now. Hopefully, their stories have been recorded. Occasionally one runs into a holdout, though. Wells Robins was in his ninety-ninth year but still had a mind sharp as a tack. At his home in Scipio, Utah, he recalled for me driving 5,000 head of cattle from the Arizona Strip to the railhead at Milford, Utah. The year was 1905 and he

was working for B. F. Saunders. Robins was a Mormon boy, just barely seventeen, while most of the men were a little older and spoke with Texas accents. When they reached Milford the cowboys did up the town at the local saloons, that is, all of the cowboys except Wells. He did admit, however, that the other fellows looked like they were having a heck of a lot of fun.[16]

J. P. Gonzales of Monticello, Utah, is alive and well at the splendid age of 106. He came to San Juan County in the 1890s and started working for Al Scorup. For a time he was the cow boss for the sprawling Scorup-Somerville outfit at Indian Creek. J. P. was sitting on the edge of his bed in a very small but unusually clean bedroom when I was first introduced to him by his son William. We talked briefly about his cowboy days riding side by side with the likes of "Latigo" Gordon. When I was about

Two cowboys at Circleville, Utah, circa 1900. Most cowboys were just hard-working, ordinary fellows. Photograph courtesy of Oscar Wiltshire.

to leave, William said he wanted to show me something. Lifting up J. P.'s pillow, William revealed to me a six-shooter. As I looked at the frail white-haired man sitting on the bed next to the six-shooter, I suddenly realized how special this interview was. Here before me was a man who had lived the life I was writing about. He was a cowboy. Even though time had warped his body, the six-shooter under his pillow was a testament that his frontier spirit was still alive.[17]

The days of thousand-mile drives are gone. So are the end-of-the-trail towns and the wild gunfights. There are still some cow towns which cater to the local cowboys, but society is much more apt to make the cowboys toe the line now. The heritage of the range is still alive, though. Many changes have taken place in the cow business, but many of the old traditions have remained. Buckaroos along the Utah-Nevada border dress in garb reminiscent of earlier times. They shun the convenience of trucks, preferring to drive cattle to distant grazing grounds. Grouse Creek cowboys in northwestern Utah annually drive 2,000 cattle to the winter range at Wendover, a distance of seventy-five miles. Their preference for roping calves and branding from an open fire rather than using modern calf chutes and electric brands is reflected by the remarks of a typical Grouse Creek buckaroo, Barney McWilliams, who says, "Hell, it just feels better to do it the old way."[18]

Occasionally things happen in our modern times which remind one of a more wild and turbulent

William Chynoweth at Henrieville, Utah, in the early 1900s. He rode the range with the great storyteller Lige Moore. Photograph courtesy of Melba D. Smith.

time. A few years ago Claude Dallas gunned down two Fish and Game officers in Idaho. That shoot-out was reminiscent of a bygone era, and, not unlike the outlaws of the Old West, Dallas became somewhat of a local folk hero.

Even more recently the Bureau of Land Management held a wild horse roundup on lands adjacent to the Ute Indian reservation in Utah's Uinta Basin near Ouray. The Indians accused the government's cowboys of rounding up some of their horses and tempers flared. The matter was later resolved in court. The Utes claimed that the horses were an integral part of their spiritual heritage, and that the government had no right to interfere. The court agreed and the horses, although wild and unbranded, were returned to the land of the Utes.

On January 27, 1988, the *Salt Lake Tribune* published an article which they entitled, "Trio Faces Sentencing for Cattle Rustling." The story related that the men were surprised in the act of rustling cattle in a remote region of Robber's Roost, northeast of Hanksville, Utah—proclaiming once again "Robber's Roost, where the Old West remains young."

Today there are many cattle ranches in the State of Utah and the number of cattle fluctuates between 800,000 and a million head. The open range no longer exists; the land is all in private hands or under the control of the Bureau of Land Management or the National Forest Service. Gone, too, are the giant cattle companies that ran 20,000 to 75,000 head of cattle. Instead there are hundreds of operators who

A cowboy at Jensen, Utah, circa 1900. Photograph courtesy of Ila Cowans.

may run anywhere from 25 to 1,500 head of cattle. Many of these ranchers come from pioneer stock raisers who settled the wild lands of Utah. The Yardley family of Beaver has raised cattle for 130 years and is working on their fifth generation of cowboys. The Deardon family of Garrison has carved out a living on the western deserts of Utah for four generations.

There are a few operations that run considerably more than 1,500 cows. The largest cattle operations currently in Utah are the Deseret Land and Livestock Company and the Escalante Ranch, operating out of Jensen, Utah. Cattle numbers fluctuate according to wet and dry years, but the Deseret consistently runs between 10,000 and 12,000 cattle. The Escalante Ranch is a "steer only" outfit; however, it feeds between 11,000 and 15,000 steers.

Combining mother cows and steers, there are several 4,000-cattle outfits operating in Utah. Included in this group are the Anchutes Land and Livestock Company, the Skull Valley Ranch, the Weston Livestock Company, the Ute Livestock En-terprises, and the Carter Ranch of Minersville, Utah.

Two-thousand-cow outfits in the state would include the Redd Ranch, the La Sal Livestock Company, the Rees Ranch, the Cunningham Cattle Company, the JR Livestock Company, the M & O Ranches, the Wood Land and Cattle Company, the Simplot Land and Cattle Company, and Thousand Peak Ranches.

In addition to the ranches there are several feed lots and packing companies in the state. One of the largest in the entire country is Miller Brothers at Hyrum, Utah.

There are several county livestock associations operating, some of which have been organized for more than one hundred years. The granddaddy of all livestock organizations is the Utah Cattlemen's Association, which was first organized in 1870. The first president of this prestigious organization was Howard Egan. He held this position until 1900 when the reins were turned over to John White. The current president of the organization is Glen Larsen of Spanish Fork, Utah.

Cowboys prepare a meal at their camp near Colton, Utah, circa 1920. Photograph courtesy of Dennis Finch.

The importance of Utah as a livestock center was recognized very early in her history. The first cattlemen's convention was held at Ogden, Utah, on April 29, 1892. Fifteen states and territories were represented at the convention. The Fourth Annual Convention of the National Livestock Association was held in Salt Lake City in 1901. A follow-up newsletter on the convention indicated that some 7,000 delegates attended the convention. The article also pointed out what a great host the city had been to the stockmen and their families. The Mormon church gave the use of its church buildings to the convention, and the houses of the leading citizens were thrown open to the entertainment of visitors. The article stated, "The great Tabernacle Choir gave one of its world-famous concerts, and it was a revelation to see this wonderful building crowded with stockmen listening with rapture to the most classical music, popularly supposed to be unintelligible to the average man of the plains. Yet it was noticed that the applause was spontaneous and intelligent."[19]

Utahns can be proud of their ranching and cowboy traditions which have been in the making for over 200 years. The ranchers and cowboys currently working the vast rangelands of Utah will continue to keep the cowboy heritage of the state alive. It is the land itself, however, that will assure the cowboy heritage of Utah being a living entity. After all, it was the land itself which, in a sense, gave birth to the American cowboy. Cattle grazed on the green fertile grasses of the eastern and southern states long before the first longhorn cattle were driven out of Texas. The eastern cattle were domesticated and fairly content on their grass-rich enclosures. Cattle on the semiarid lands of the West had to range over vast distances that at times provided far too little feed. Spreading out to get the available feed, the cattle roamed far and wide. Cowboys were needed to round them up and get them to market. As long as Utah has vast amounts of land with cattle grazing upon it, roundups will have to be made and the cowboying way of life will be preserved.

Utah is a big, wild land which is, for the most part,

Left: Buffalo-head bit by August Buermann, circa 1900. Courtesy of Bob Fehr.

Right: The band on this hat is marked Blyth and Fargo, Park City, Utah, circa 1900. Courtesy of Roslyn Grose.

Right: Hat worn by a Monroe, Utah, cowboy, circa 1880. Courtesy of Bumbleberry Inn.

Below: Cowboy's rawhide lariet. Courtesy of Bob Fehr.

Above: Custom cuffs designed by owner, circa 1920. From author's collection.

Grouse Creek cowboys driving cattle to Wendover, Utah, circa 1989. Photograph from author's collection.

unpopulated. The lack of water has always been a problem and has limited the growth of the population. One can drive west on the old Pony Express Trail from the western edge of the Wasatch Mountains and find little civilization for the next 120 miles. It is as if the land has stood still for a thousand years. Riding along in an automobile, one can envision encountering a savage Indian or a desperado. The open, wild land creates that type of dreaming for travelers on the road.

There are hundreds of similar roads in Utah where one can relive history. Be careful, though, for you might suddenly encounter a herd of range cattle moving at their leisure smack dab in the middle of the road. You will slow down and shoo them out of the way as you pass. You'll pick up speed again as you watch the cattle through your rear-view mirror, and, if you give it some thought, you will realize that when the cold winds begin to blow and the first light snow falls, a cowboy on horseback will be rounding up those cattle. Such is the way of the cowboy.

Notes

Chapter 1

1. T. A. Davis, "Story of Early Life in Box Elder County," in *History of Box Elder County* (Salt Lake City: Daughters of the Utah Pioneers, 1937), 42.

2. Richard C. Roberts and Richard W. Sadler, *Ogden, Junction City* (Ogden, Utah: Windsor Publications, History Book Division, 1985) 19.

3. Don D. Walker, "The Cattle Industry of Utah, 1850–1900: An Historical Profile," *Utah Historical Quarterly* 32 (Summer 1964): 183.

4. J. Cecil Alter, *Utah the Storied Domain* (Chicago and New York: American Historical Society, 1961).

5. John R. Evans, Gordon S. Thompson, Harold W. Lee, Osmond L. Harline, *Beef Cattle in the Utah Economy* (Salt Lake City: University of Utah College of Business, The Bureau of Economic and Business Research, 1967), 10.

6. Orson Hyde, conference remarks of October 7, 1865, cited in *History of Utah, 1847 to 1869*, Andrew Love Neff (Salt Lake City: Deseret News Press, 1940), 766.

7. J. J. Watson, interview, Delta, Utah, September 1940, Utah State Historical Society, manuscript, A2320.

8. Richard F. Burton, *City of the Saints* (New York: Alfred A. Knopf, 1963), 314.

9. Harold Schindler, *Orrin Porter Rockwell: Man of God, Son of Thunder*, 2d ed. (Salt Lake City: University of Utah Press, 1983), 172.

10. Howard R. Egan Estate, *Pioneering the West* (Salt Lake City: Skelton Publishing Co., 1917), 182.

11. Leonard J. Arrington, *Great Basin Kingdom: An Economic History of the Latter-day Saints, 1830–1900* (Lincoln: University of Nebraska Press, 1958), 136.

12. Garnet M. Brayer and Herbert O. Brayer, *American Cattle Trails 1540–1900* (Bayside, N.Y.: Western Range Cattle Industry Study in cooperation with the American Pioneer Trails Association, 1952), 40.

13. Andrew Love Neff, *History of Utah, 1847 to 1869* (Salt Lake City: Deseret News Press, 1940), 270.

14. Arrington, *Great Basin Kingdom*, 207.

15. Burton, *City of the Saints*, 32.

16. Don Ward, *Cowboys and Cattle Country* (New York: American Heritage Publishing Co., 1961), 10.

17. Ibid., 30.

18. Paul I. Wellman, *The Trampling Herd* (New York: Carrick and Evans, 1939), 127.

19. Burton, *City of the Saints*, 504.

20. Kate B. Carter, *Heart Throbs of the West* 12 (no. 6, 1966): 264.

21. *Journal of Discourses* (Liverpool, England: Church of Jesus Christ of Latter-day Saints, 26 vols., 1854–1886), 1:251–52.

22. State of Utah, *Laws of Utah*, act of January 18, 1854, cited in "The Development of Utah Livestock Law, 1848–1896," Levi S. Petrson, *Utah Historical Quarterly* 32 (Summer 1964): 205.

23. Alter, *The Storied Domain*, 140.

24. Neff, *History of Utah*, 264.

25. Ibid., 272.

26. Arrington, *Great Basin Kingdom*, 136.

27. Ibid., 196.

28. Juanita Brooks, ed., *On the Mormon Frontier, The Diary of Hosea Stout, 1844–1861*, 2 vols. (Salt Lake City: University of Utah Press and Utah State Historical Society, 1982), 2:700.

29. At least eight men were killed in Cedar Valley between August 1854 and February 1856. A Mormon colonization party dispatched to the Elk Mountains (LaSal Mountains) in 1855 gave up the attempt to form a permanent settlement when three herders were killed by Utes. Two herders were killed by Indians at Kimball Creek in 1856, three men and a woman were killed at Salt Creek Canyon, and two herders were killed at Chicken Creek in 1858.

30. Ronald R. Bateman, "Deep Creek Reflections" (n.p.: copyright in author's name, 1984), 54.

CHAPTER 2

1. Albert R. Lyman, "The Fort on the Firing Line," *Improvement Era,* 52 (December, 1949), 820.

2. William Jones Bowen, "The Memories of William Jones Bowen," typescript in possession of author.

3. The Charles Ashael Perry Family Organization, "The History and Genealogy of John Chapman Duncan and Teresa Ann Ferrell" (Provo, Utah: n.p., 1980), 22.

4. Don Ward, *Cowboys and Cattle Country* (New York: American Heritage Publishing Co., 1961), 24.

5. *Story of the Great American West* (Pleasantville, New York, and Montreal: The Reader's Digest Association, 1977), 275.

6. Ibid., 276.

7. Ibid.

8. Cyrus C. Loveland, *The California Trail Herd* (Los Gatos, Calif.: Talisman Press, 1961), 15.

9. Ibid., 15.

10. Don D. Walker, "Longhorns Come to Utah," *Utah Historical Quarterly* 30 (Spring 1962), 139.

11. J. Marvin Hunter, *The Trail Drivers of Texas* (New York: Argosy-Antiquarian Ltd., 1963), 135–36.

12. Ibid., 33.

13. Ibid., 45.

14. Ibid., 522.

15. Joseph G. McCoy, *Historical Sketches of the Cattle Trade of the West and Southwest*, Ralph P. Bieber, ed. (Glendale, Calif.: Arthur H. Clark Co., 1940), 76–77.

16. Leonard J. Arrington, *Great Basin Kingdom: An Economic History of the Latter-day Saints, 1830–1900* (Lincoln: University of Nebraska Press, 1958), 293–98.

17. Ibid., 296.

18. York Jones and Evelyn Jones (Cedar City, Utah: Lehi Willard Jones, 1972), 65–66.

19. Herman Pollick, interview with author, Tropic, Utah, 1988. Mr. Pollick's grandfather was John Davis, who managed the Kanarra Cattle Company.

20. Andrew Karl Larson, *I Was Called to Dixie* (Salt Lake City: Deseret News Press, 1961), 241–46.

21. John K. Rollinson, *Wyoming Cattle Trails* (Caldwell, Idaho: Caxton Printers, 1948), 334.

22. Charles S. Peterson, *Look to the Mountains* (Provo, Utah: Brigham Young University Press, 1975), 84.

23. Ibid.

24. John Rolfe Burroughs, *Where the Old West Stayed Young* (New York: Bonanza Books, 1962), 15.

25. McCoy, *Historical Sketches*, 76–77.

26. U.S. Bureau of the Census, *Report on Cattle, Sheep, and Swine* cited in the "Cattle Industry of Utah, 1850–1900: An Historic Profile," Don D. Walker, *Utah Historical Quarterly* 32 (Summer 1964): 186.

27. Don D. Walker, "Cattle Industry of Utah", *Utah Historical Quarterly* 32 (Summer 1964): 193.

28. Ibid., 194.

CHAPTER 3

1. Daughters of the Utah Pioneers, Kane County, *History of Kane County* (Salt Lake City: Daughters of the Utah Pioneers, 1960), 106.

2. James Cox, *Historical and Biographical Record of the Cattle Industry and Cattlemen of Texas and the Adjacent Territory* vol. 2, p. 14, cited in Don D.Walker, "The Cattle Industry of Utah, 1850–1900: An Historical Profile," *Utah Historical Quarterly* 32 (Summer 1964): 189.

3. Jesse L. Embry, ed., *La Sal Reflections: A Redd Family Journal* (Provo, Utah: Charles Redd Foundation, 1984), 35.

4. Charles S. Peterson, *Look to the Mountains* (Provo, Utah: Brigham Young University Press, 1975), 91.

5. Alexander Toponce, *Reminiscences of Alexander Toponce, Written by Himself* (Norman: University of Oklahoma Press, 1971), 22.

6. Ibid., 126–32.

7. Ibid., 152.

8. Ibid., 156.

9. Ibid., 188.

10. Dick Dunham and Vivian Dunham, *Flaming Gorge Country: The Story of Daggett County, Utah* (Denver: Eastwood Printing and Publishing Co., 1977), 97.

11. William H. McIntyre, Jr., "A Brief History of the McIntyre Ranch," *Canadian Cattlemen* (September 1947), 86.

12. Floyd Bradfield, interview with author, Leamington, Utah, 1987.

13. Steel McIntyre, interview with author, Silver City, Utah, 1987.

14. Edna D. Patterson and Louise A. Beebe, *Halleck County— Story of Its Land and People* (Reno: University of Nevada, 1982), 73.

15. Daughters of the Utah Pioneers, North Davis County Company, *East of Antelope Island* (Salt Lake City: Publishers Press, 1948), 34–35.

16. Ouida Nuhn Blanthorn, "In Old Paradise (Avon), Stansbury Park, Utah," chap. 13, p. 2, Utah State Historical Society, manuscript.

17. Walker, "Cattle Industry of Utah," 193.

18. Blanthorn, "In Old Paradise," chap. 13, p. 1.

19. Ibid., p. 6.

20. David Lavender, *Pipe Springs and the Arizona Strip* (Springdale, Utah: Zion National Park, Natural History Association, 1948), 18.

21. Clarence Pilling, interview with author, Price, Utah, 1987. Mr. Pilling's father worked for the Whitmore Cattle Company.

22. Ibid.

23. Woodrow Pilling (Clarence Pilling's brother), interview with author, Big Springs Ranch, Sunnyside, Utah, 1987. Mr. Pilling is the current owner of the ranch.

24. Clarence Pilling, interview.

25. Ibid.

26. Virginia Price and John T. Darby, "Preston Nutter: Utah Cattleman, 1886–1936," *Utah Historical Quarterly* 32 (Summer 1964): 234.

27. Ibid., 236.

28. Ibid., 237.

29. Ibid., 239.

30. Ibid., 242.

31. Ibid., 245.

32. William H. McDougall, "End of an Era," *Utah Cattleman* 25 (November 1981): 8.

33. Wells Robbins, interview with author, Scipio, Utah, 1988. Mr. Robbins helped drive Saunders's cattle to Lund, Utah, in 1905.

34. Andrew Karl Larson, *I Was Called to Dixie* (Salt Lake City: Deseret News Press, 1961), 243–46.

35. Frank Paxton, interview with author, Kanosh, Utah, 1989. Mr. Paxton is the grandson of Frank Paxton.

36. Joseph Yates, interview with author, Tremonton, Utah, 1987. Mr. Yates is the grandson of Joseph Yates.

37. John Rolfe Burroughs, *Where the Old West Stayed Young* (New York: Bonanza Books, 1962), 10.

38. Nora Linjer Bowman, *Only the Mountains Remain* (Caldwell, Idaho: Caxton Printers, 1958), 56.

39. Ibid.

40. James A. Young and Abbott B. Sparks, *Cattle in the Cold Desert* (Logan: Utah State University Press, 1985), 102.

41. Bowman, *Only the Mountains Remain*, 58.

42. Edward Mix (Brig) Crandall, "Autobiography," unpublished ms.

43. Orson F. Whitney, *History of Utah* (Salt Lake City: George Q. Cannon and Sons Co., 1904), 23–25.

CHAPTER 4

1. Gene M. Gressley, *Bankers and Cattlemen* (New York: Alfred A. Knopf, 1966), p. 63.

2. Edgar Beecher Bronson, *Reminiscences of a Ranchman* (Lincoln: University of Nebraska Press, 1962), 293–94.

3. John Rolfe Burroughs, *Where the Old West Stayed Young* (New York: Bonanza Books, 1962), 227.

4. *Breeder's Gazette* 6 (October 23, 1884): 608.

5. Charles S. Peterson, *Look to the Mountains* (Provo, Utah: Brigham Young University Press, 1975), 91.

6. Ibid., 93–96.

7. Ibid., 96.

8. Albert R. Lyman, *Indians and Outlaws: Settling of the San Juan Frontier* (Salt Lake City: Bookcraft, 1962), 104.

9. Peterson, *Look to the Mountains*, 96.

10. Don D. Walker, "The Carlisles: Cattle Barons of the Upper Basin," *Utah Historical Quarterly* 32 (Summer 1964): 270.

11. Peterson, *Look to the Mountains*, 88.

12. Elaine Gordon Turner, interview with author, Moab, Utah 1987. Mrs. Turner is the daughter of "Latigo" Gordon.

13. Governor Ross to J. D. Warner, February 16, 1886, cited in Walker, "Carlisles," *Utah Historical Quarterly* 32 (Summer 1964): 281.

14. Peterson, *Look to the Mountains*, 98.

15. Ibid.

16. Ibid., 99.

17. Lyman, *Indians and Outlaws*, 109.

18. Ibid., 107.

19. Ibid., 105.

20. Peterson, *Look to the Mountains*, 90.

21. Walker, "The Carlisles," 276.

22. Franklin D. Day, "The Cattle Industry of San Juan County, Utah, 1875–1900" (Master's thesis, Brigham Young University, 1958), 37.

23. Turner, interview.

24. Peterson, *Look to the Mountains*, 86.

25. Hardy Redd, interview with author, Monticello, Utah, 1987. Mr. Redd is the grandson of Lemuel H. Redd.

26. Pearl Baker, interview with author, Green River, Utah, 1986.

27. Pearl Baker, *The Wild Bunch at Robbers Roost* (New York, Toronto, and London: Abelard-Schuman, 1971), 68.

28. Don Wilcox, interview with author, Green River, Utah, 1987. Mr. Wilcox is the son of Ray Wilcox.

29. George E. Stewart, "Utah's Book Cliffs Look Down on the Outlaw City," *Salt Lake Tribune*, October 19, 1975.

30. *The Life of Stephen Washburn (Wash) Chipman* (Salt Lake City: Utah Printing Co., 1969), 25.

31. Nutter Collection, Special Collections, Marriott Library, University of Utah, Salt Lake City.

32. Stewart, "Utah's Book Cliffs."

33. George A. Thompson to author, letter, June 6, 1987.

34. Wilcox, interview.

35. Dennis V. Finch, interview with author, Colton, Utah, 1988.

36. Doris Karren Burton, *Blue Mountain Folks: Their Lives and Legends* (Salt Lake City: K/P Graphics, 1987), 15–19.

37. Ibid., 25–28.

38. Burroughs, *Where the Old West Stayed Young*, 270.

39. Burton, *Blue Mountain Folks*, 12–14.

40. Ibid., 33–34.

41. Burroughs, *Where the Old West Stayed Young*, 267.

42. Burton, *Blue Mountain Folks*, 38.

43. John J. Stewart, *The Iron Trail to the Golden Spike* (Salt Lake City: Deseret Book Co., 1969), 258.

44. Ibid., 259.

45. T. A. Davis. "Story of Early Life in Box Elder County," in *History of Box Elder County* (Salt Lake City: Daughters of the Utah Pioneers, 1937), 43.

46. Ibid.

47. Leonard J. Arrington, *David Eccles, Pioneer Western Industrialist* (Logan, Utah: Utah State University Press, 1975), 263.

48. Ibid.

49. Ouida Nuhn Blanthorn, "In Old Paradise (Avon), Stansbury Park, Utah," chap. 13, p. 2, Utah State Historical Society, manuscript.

50. Norman Weston, interview with author, Laketown, Utah, 1987. Weston now operates a ranch on lands that at one time were used by the Beckwith and Quinn Cattle Company.

267

51. Theris "Slash" Cornia, interview with author, Woodruff, Utah, 1989. Mr. Cornia worked briefly with the B Q Outfit in the early 1900s.

52. *Salt Lake Herald*, June 6, 1893.

53. Fern Ereckson, interview with author, Murray, Utah, 1988.

54. Ward J. Roylance, *Utah: A Guide to the State* (Salt Lake City: A Guide to the State Foundation, 1982), 630.

55. *Deseret News*, March 25, 1885.

56. Daughters of the Utah Pioneers, Beaver County, *Monuments to Courage: A History of Beaver County,* 2d. ed. (Beaver, Utah: Beaver Printing Co., 1974), 236.

57. Charles Kelly, *The Outlaw Trail: A History of Butch Cassidy and the "Wild Bunch"* (New York: Bonanza Books, 1959), 51.

58. Daisey Rowley, interview with author, Milford, Utah, 1989. Mrs. Rowley grew up on a small ranch in Garrison, Utah.

59. Horace Allred, personal history, manuscript in author's possession.

60. Tom Anderson, interview with author, Gunnison, Utah, 1987. Dr. Anderson's father was involved with the ownership of the M & O Ranches in the early 1900s.

61. Charles S. Peterson, "Albert F. Potter's Wasatch Survey, 1902: A Beginning for Public Management of Natural Resources in Utah," *Utah Historical Quarterly* 39 (Summer 1971): 245.

62. Allred, personal history.

CHAPTER 5

1. John K. Rollinson, *Wyoming Cattle Trails* (Caldwell, Idaho: Caxton Printers, 1948), 63.

2. Richard Lloyd Dewey, *Porter Rockwell: A Biography* (New York: Paramount Books, 1986), 472.

3. Newell Knight, interview with author, Salt Lake City, Utah, 1975. Mr. Knight at the time was the Salt Lake City historian.

4. Ward J. Roylance, *Utah: A Guide to the State* (Salt Lake City: A Guide to the State Foundation, 1982), 483.

5. Harold R. Hickman, "Frisco, Utah: Voice of a Ghost Town" (a film for television) (Master's thesis, University of Utah, 1960), 12–13.

6. Larry R. Gerlach, "Ogden's 'Horrible Tragedy': The Lynching of George Segal," *Utah Historical Quarterly* 49 (Spring 1981): 159–60.

7. Ibid.

8. Ibid.

9. Ibid.

10. Ibid.

11. Aldon Rachele, "The Strip, a Rough, Wild Town of the Old West," *Vernal Express*, June 15, 1983.

12. Elizabeth Farrer Leman, interview, Green River, Utah, 1937, Harold B. Lee Library, Brigham Young University, microfilm 920.

13. Albert R. Lyman, *Indians and Outlaws: Settling of the San Juan Frontier* (Salt Lake City: Bookcraft, 1962), 104.

14. Gerlach, "Ogden's 'Horrible Tragedy'," 159–60.

15. Ibid.

16. Juanita Brooks, ed., *On the Mormon Frontier: The Diary of Hosea Stout, 1844–1861,* 2 vols. (Salt Lake City: University of Utah Press and Utah State Historical Society, 1982), 2:706.

17. Thomas G. Alexander and James B. Allen, *Mormons and Gentiles: A History of Salt Lake City*, The Western Urban History Series vol. 5 (Boulder, Colo.: Pruett Publishing Co., 1984), 120.

18. Gerlach, "Ogden's 'Horrible Tragedy'," 166.

19. Ora Brooks Peake, *The Colorado Range Cattle Industry* (Glendale, Calif.: Arthur H. Clark Co., 1937), 28.

20. George A. Thompson, *Some Dreams Die: Utah's Ghost Towns and Lost Treasures* (Salt Lake City: Dream Garden Press, 1982), 142.

21. George A. Horton, Jr., "An Early History of Milford and Its Incorporation as a Town" (Master's thesis, Brigham Young University, 1957), 69.

22. Wells Robbins, interview with author, Scipio, Utah, 1988. Mr. Robbins worked for B. F. Saunders in 1905.

23. Lee M. Rice and Glenn R. Vernam, *They Saddled the West* (Cambridge, Md.: Cornell Maritime Press, 1975), 101.

24. Ibid., 100.

CHAPTER 6

1. Governors' Messages, November 12, 1860, pp. 82.14–82.21 (Salt Lake City: State Archives).

2. Edna D. Patterson and Louise A. Beebe, *Halleck County: Story of Its Land and People* (Reno: University of Nevada, 1982), 7.

3. Governor's Messages, in *Journals of the Legislative Assembly . . . for the Year 1878*, cited in "The Development of Utah Livestock Law, 1848–1896," Levi S. Peterson, *Utah Historical Quarterly* 32 (Summer 1964): 209.

4. Peterson, "Utah Livestock Law," *Utah Historical Quarterly* 32 (Summer 1964): 209.

5. Richard H. Cracroft, "The Heraldry of the Range: Utah Cattle Brands." *Utah Historical Quarterly* 32 (Summer 1964): 230.

6. John Rolfe Burroughs, *Where the Old West Stayed Young* (New York: Bonanza Books, 1962), 10.

7. Kate B. Carter, *Heart Throbs of the West* 12 (no. 6, 1966): 342.

8. Robert Elman, *Badmen of the West* (Secaucus, N.J.: Castle Books, 1974), 49.

9. Peter Newark, *Illustrated Encyclopedia of the Old West* (New York: Gallery Books, 1980), 201.

10. Leonard J. Arrington and Hope A. Hilton, "Setting the Record Straight: Profiles of William A. Hickman," The Wm. A. Hickman Family Organization, 1980, p. 7.

11. Ibid., p. 20.

12. Ibid.

13. Ibid., p. 21.

14. Ibid., p. 23.

15. Ibid., p. 30.

16. Ibid., p. 36.

17. Ibid.

18. Ibid.

19. Harold Schindler, *Orrin Porter Rockwell: Man of God, Son of Thunder*, 2d ed. (Salt Lake City: University of Utah Press, 1983), 306.

20. Ibid., 302.

21. Ibid.

22. Ibid., 308.

23. Ibid., 316.

24. Ibid.

25. Ibid., 318.

26. Ibid.

27. Ibid.

28. Dick C. Clayton, interview, Coalville, Utah, January 22, 1937, Harold B. Lee Library, Brigham Young University, microfilm 920.

29. Thomas L. Beech, interview with C. Bryant Copley, Coalville, Utah, period of 1926–28, copy in author's possession.

30. George A. Thompson, *Throw Down the Box* (Salt Lake City, Utah: Dream Garden Press, 1989), 31.

31. Charles Kelly, *The Outlaw Trail: A History of Butch Cassidy and the "Wild Bunch"* (New York: Bonanza Books, 1959), 111.

32. George A. Horton, Jr., "An Early History of Milford and Its Incorporation as a Town" (Master's thesis, Brigham Young University, 1957), 29.

33. Kelly, *Outlaw Trail*, 254.

34. Ibid., 12.

35. Pearl Baker, *The Wild Bunch at Robbers Roost* (New York, Toronto, and London: Abelard-Schuman, 1971), 17.

36. Pearson H. Corbett, *Jacob Hamblin, the Peacemaker* (Salt Lake City: Deseret Book Co., 1952), 343–49.

37. Steve Lacy, interview with author, Salt Lake City, Utah, 1989. Dr. Lacy is an outlaw historian.

38. Matt Warner, as told to Murray E. King, *The Last of the Bandit Riders* (New York: Bonanza Books, 1940), 81–85.

39. Ibid., 87.

40. E. Richard Churchill, *The McCartys: They Rode with Butch Cassidy* (Leadville, Colo.: Timberline Books, 1972), 34–39.

41. Warner, *Last of the Bandit Riders*, 21–28.

42. Ibid., 52.

43. Ibid., 288.

44. Ibid., 301.

45. Ibid., 306–8.

46. Lula Parker Betenson, as told to Dora Flack, *Butch Cassidy, My Brother* (Provo, Utah: Brigham Young University Press, 1984), 40.

47. Sidney Rymer, interview with author, Manti, Utah, 1967. Mr. Rymer was in his nineties at the time. He was one of the boys who played ball with Butch Cassidy.

48. Warner, *Last of the Bandit Riders*, 110.

49. Dick Dunham and Vivian Dunham, *Flaming Gorge Country: The Story of Daggett County, Utah* (Denver: Eastwood Printing and Publishing Company, 1977), 87.

50. George A. Thompson, *Some Dreams Die: Utah's Ghost Towns and Lost Treasures* (Salt Lake City: Dream Garden Press, 1982), 117–18.

51. Larry Pointer, *In Search of Butch Cassidy* (Norman: University of Oklahoma Press, 1977), 60–62.

52. Ibid., 103.

53. *The Daily Tribune*, Salt Lake City, Utah, April 14, 1896.

54. Ibid., May 10, 1896.

55. Warner, *Last of the Bandit Riders*, 54.

56. Edward M. Kirby, *The Rise and Fall of the Sundance Kid* (Iola, Wisc.: Western Publications, 1983), 29.

57. Betenson, *Butch Cassidy*, 121.

58. Pointer, *In Search of Butch Cassidy*, 203.

59. Burroughs, *Where the Old West Stayed Young*, 165.

60. Ibid., 163.

61. Lamont Johnson, "Last of the Rustlers," *Deseret News Magazine* (Salt Lake City, Utah), May 27, 1951, pp. 9–10.

62. Baker, *Wild Bunch*, 67.

63. Ibid., 81.

64. Ibid., 131.

65. *Salt Lake Tribune*, March 1, 5, 1898.

66. Virginia N. Price and John T. Darby, "Preston Nutter: Utah Cattleman, 1886–1936," *Utah Historical Quarterly* 32 (Summer 1964): 246.

67. Earl Mulford, interview with author, Grover, Utah, 1968. Mr. Mulford was in Price at the time of the killing.

68. Warner, *Last of the Bandit Riders*, 323.

69. Sam Adams, interview with author, Teasdale, Utah, 1968.

CHAPTER 7

1. Charles A. Siringo, *A Cowboy Detective* (Chicago: W. B. Conkey Co., 1912), 348.

2. Ibid., 379.

3. Paul Trachtman, *The Old West: The Gunfighters* (New York: Time-Life Books, 1974), 109.

4. Earl Mulford, interview with author, Grover, Utah, 1968.

5. *Salt Lake Tribune*, June 11, 1878.

6. *Salt Lake Daily Herald*, June 11, 1878.

7. Joseph Smith, Jr., *History of the Church*, vol. 6 (Salt Lake City, 1902–1912), 134–35.

8. Harold Schindler, *Orrin Porter Rockwell: Man of God, Son of Thunder*, 2d ed. (Salt Lake City: University of Utah Press, 1983), 102. Local legends suggest that Rockwell refused to cut his hair for the rest of his life, with one exception. He allowed his hair to be cut and made into a wig for a lady friend who lost her hair because of a serious illness.

9. Ibid., 155.

10. Richard Lloyd Dewey, *Porter Rockwell, a Biography*, (New York: Paramount Books, 1986), 472.

11. Ibid., 331.

12. Richard F. Burton, *The City of the Saints* (New York: Alfred A. Knopf, 1963), 503.

13. Don Carlos Johnson, *A Brief History of Springville, Utah* (Springville: William F. Gibson and D. C. Johnson, 1900), 59.

14. Edward W. Tullidge, *Tullidge's Histories*, vol. 2 (Salt Lake City: Juvenile Instructor, 1889), 101.

15. Brigham D. Madsen, *Corinne, The Gentile Capital of Utah* (Salt Lake City: The Utah State Historical Society, 1980), 40–43.

16. Orson F. Whitney, *Popular History of Utah* (Salt Lake City: The Deseret News, 1916), 432.

17. Cleon Skousen, compiler, "History of Law and Order in Salt Lake City," copy on file, Utah State Historical Society.

18. Louis Slack, "Life Sketch of Lorenzo Jefferies Slack," Harold B. Lee Library, Brigham Young University, microfilm 920, no. 89.

19. Albert R. Lyman, *Indians and Outlaws: Settling of the San Juan Frontier* (Salt Lake City: Bookcraft, 1962), 135.

20. Charles Kelly, *The Outlaw Trail: A History of Butch Cassidy and the "Wild Bunch"* (New York: Bonanza Books, 1959), 174.

21. Ibid., 156.

22. Thomas E. Austin and Robert S. McPherson, "Murder, Mayhem, and Mormons: The Evolution of Law Enforcement on the San Juan Frontier, 1880–1900," *Utah Historical Quarterly* 55 (Winter 1987): 46.

23. Ibid., 47.

24. Pearl Baker, *The Wild Bunch at Robbers Roost* (New York, Toronto, and London: Abelard-Schuman, 1971), 72–76.

25. Ibid., 80.

26. Siringo, *Cowboy Detective*, 307.

27. Ibid., 310.

28. Ibid.

29. Ibid., 311–12.

30. Ibid., 379.

31. *The Times-Independent* (Moab, Utah), May 29, 1980.

32. Kelly, *Outlaw Trail*, 337–40.

33. Ibid., 341.

34. John Rolfe Burroughs, *Where the Old West Stayed Young* (New York: Bonanza Books, 1962), 157–69.

35. Ibid., 207.

36. Ibid., 210.

37. Ibid., 214.

38. *The Salt Lake Tribune, Home Magazine,* March 5, 1961, p. 4.

39. Ibid.

40. Ibid.

41. Kay C. Watson, *Life under the Horseshoe* (Spring City, Utah: Daughters of the Utah Pioneers, 1987), 102.

42. Provo City Records, October 21, 1873, Utah Territory, cited in *The Story of Provo, Utah,* John C. Moffitt (Provo: Press Publishing, 1975).

43. Matt Warner, as told to Murray E. King, *The Last of the Bandit Riders* (New York: Bonanza Books, 1940), 141.

44. Baker, *Wild Bunch at Robbers Roost*, 208–9.

45. Ray Haueter, "Early Law Enforcement," *The Utah Peace Officer*, 60 (4), 1983:14.

CHAPTER 8

1. Charles M. Sypolt, "Keepers of the Rocky Mountain Flocks: A History of the Sheep Industry in Colorado, New Mexico, Utah and Wyoming to 1900" (Ph.D. diss., University of Wyoming, 1974), 222–23.

2. *Salt Lake Daily Telegram*, May 14, 1869. The *Daily Telegram* had recently been transferred to Ogden in anticipation of the new importance the transcontinental railroad would give that city.

3. Compiled from U.S. Department of Interior and U.S. Department of Agriculture yearbooks and statistical reports, governors' annual reports, and census reports as stated in Sypolt, "Keepers of the Rocky Mountain Flocks," 324.

4. *Wasatch Wave* (Heber, Utah), April 20, 1889.

5. Mary Lyman Reeve, interview, Hinckley, Utah, January 22, 1937, Harold B. Lee Library, Brigham Young University, microfilm 920, no. 92.

6. *Manti Messenger* (Manti, Utah), July 31, 1897.

7. Lamont Johnson, "Last of the Rustlers," *Deseret News Magazine*, Salt Lake City, May 27, 1951.

8. I have interviewed several people who have seen the grave site.

9. Allan Kent Powell, *San Juan County, Utah: People, Resources, and History* (Salt Lake City: The Utah State Historical Society, 1983), 181.

10. Ibid., 180.

11. Neal Lambert, "Al Scorup: Cattleman of the Canyons," *Utah Historical Quarterly* 32 (Summer 1964): 303.

12. Ibid., 304.

13. Ibid., 304–6.

14. Ross A. "Rusty" Musselman, interview with author, Monticello, Utah, 1988. Mr. Musselman worked for the S S Cattle Company during the 1930s.

15. Hardy Redd, interview with author, La Sal, Utah, 1987.

16. Max Dalton, interview with author, Monticello, Utah, 1988.

17. Ouida Nuhn Blanthorn, "In Old Paradise (Avon), Stansbury Park, Utah," chap. 13, p. 3, Utah State Historical Society, manuscript.

18. Mathew Browning, interview with author, Ogden, Utah, 1986.

19. Theris "Slash" Cornia, interview with author, Woodruff, Utah, 1989.

20. Greg Simonds, interview with author, Deseret Land and Livestock headquarters, Woodruff, Utah, 1988.

21. Jerry Blackburn, interview with author, Skull Valley, Utah, 1987.

22. Connie Rees Rex, interview with author, Woodruff, Utah, 1989.

23. Norman Weston, interview with author, Laketown, Utah, 1987.

24. Leonard J. Arrington, *David Eccles, Pioneer Western Industrialist* (Logan, Utah: Utah State University Press, 1975), 253.

25. Frank Paxton, interview with author, Kanosh, Utah, 1989.

26. Jerry Wood, interview with author, Salt Lake City, Utah, 1987.

27. Vern Jeffers, interview with author, Springville, Utah, 1987. Mr. Jeffers is a historian of the Spanish Fork Canyon area.

28. Max Arneson, interview with author, at ranch, Echo Canyon, Utah, 1987. Mr Arneson is the manager of the Anchutes operation in Utah.

29. Rowland W. Rider, as told to Deirdre Paulsen, *Sixshooters and Sagebrush* (Provo, Utah: Brigham Young University Press 1979), 82.

30. J. R. Broadbent, interview with author, Salt Lake City, Utah, 1987.

31. Pearl Baker, interview with author, Green River, Utah, 1987.

32. *The Salt Lake Tribune*, January 4, 1911.

33. *Deseret Evening News*, November 22, 1913.

34. Bertrand E. Gallagher, *Utah's Greatest Manhunt: The True Story of the Hunt for Rafael Lopez by an Eyewitness* (Salt Lake City: G. W. Gardiner Co., 1913), 40.

35. Ibid., 139.

36. Albert R. Lyman, *Indians and Outlaws: Settling of the San Juan Frontier* (Salt Lake City: Bookcraft, 1962), 161.

37. Ibid., 163.

38. Ibid., 167.

39. Ibid., 170.

40. John D. Rogers, interview, Paradox, Colorado, 1975, manuscript. Mr. Rogers was part of the posse that chased the Indians.

41. Ibid.

42. Ibid.

43. Ibid.

44. Walker D. Wyman and John D. Hart, "The Legend of Charlie Glass," *The Colorado Magazine* 46 (no. 1, 1969): 44.

45. Ibid., 41.

46. Ibid., 45.

47. Ibid., 46.

48. Ibid., 52.

49. Steve Lacy, *The Lynching of Robert Marshall* (n.p.: Castle Press, 1978), 21.

CHAPTER 9

1. Alexander Toponce, *Reminiscences of Alexander Toponce, Written by Himself* (Norman: University of Oklahoma Press, 1971), 21.

2. Don Ward, *Cowboys and Cattle Country* (New York: American Heritage Publishing Co., 1961), 111.

3. William H. Forbis, *The Old West: The Cowboys* (New York: Time-Life Books, 1973), 29.

4. Paul O'Neil, *The Old West: The End and the Myth* (Alexandria, Va.: Time-Life Books, 1979), 44.

5. Keith Wheeler, *The Old West, The Scouts* (Alexandria, Va.: Time-Life Books, 1978), 225.

6. Dick Dunham and Vivian Dunham, *Flaming Gorge Country, The Story of Daggett County* (Denver: Eastwood Printing and Publishing Co., 1977), 147.

7. Ibid.

8. Forbis, *The Old West: The Cowboys*, 29.

9. Utah State Film Commission, *Utah Statewide Film History: List of National Release Theatrical and Television Productions Shot in Utah as of April 11, 1986.*

10. O'Neil, *The Old West: The End and the Myth*, 99.

11. Lincoln Eliason, *Matt: The Story of a Utah Cowboy* (Salt Lake City: Deseret, 1986), 31.

12. Howard R. Egan Estate, *Pioneering the West* (Salt Lake City: Skelton Publishing Co., 1917), 227.

13. Layton Smith, interview with author, Henrieville, Utah, 1988.

14. Cass Mulford, interview with author, Torrey, Utah, 1968.

15. Earl Mulford, interview with author, Grover, Utah, 1968.

16. Wells Robbins, interview with author, Scipio, Utah, 1988.

17. J. P. Gonzales, interview with author, Monticello, Utah, 1990.

18. Barney McWilliams, interview with author, Grouse Creek, Utah, 1988.

19. National Live Stock Association, "The Salt Lake City Convention, January 15, 16, 17, and 18, 1901," brochure.

Additional Readings

Arrington, Leonard J., and Hope A. Hilton. *Setting the Record Straight: Profiles of William Adams Hickman.* Hickman Family Organization, 1980.

Austin, Thomas, and Robert S. McPherson. "Murder, Mayhem, and Mormons: The Evolution of Law Enforcement on the San Juan Frontier, 1880–1900."*Utah Historical Quarterly* 55 (Winter 1987): 36.

Bailey, Lynn Robison. *Indian Slave Trade in the Southwest.* Los Angeles: Westernlore Press, 1966.

Bancroft, Hubert Howe. *History of Utah.* Salt Lake City: Bookcraft, 1964.

Barnes, Lyle." 'Two-Bit Street,' 1879–1954." Master's Thesis, Utah State University, 1969.

Bolton, Herbert E. *Pageant in the Wilderness.* Salt Lake City: Utah State Historical Society, 1972.

Burton, Doris Karren. *Silver Stars and Jail Bars.* Salt Lake City: K/P Graphics, 1987.

Carter, Kate B. *Our Pioneer Heritage.* Vol. 9. Salt Lake City: Daughters of the Utah Pioneers Central Company, 1966.

Creer, Leland Hargrave. *The Founding of an Empire.* Salt Lake City: Bookcraft, 1947.

Culmsee, Carlton. *Utah's Black Hawk War.* Logan: Utah State University Press, 1973.

Dalton, Luella Adams. *History of the Iron County Mission.* Parowan, Utah: Daughters of the Utah Pioneers, n.d.

Daughters of the Utah Pioneers, Washington County Chapter. *Under Dixie Sun.* Panguitch, Utah: Garfield County News, 1950.

———, Weber County Chapter. *Beneath Ben Lomond's Peak.* Salt Lake City: Publishers Press, 1966.

Denver and Rio Grande Western Railway. *The Agricultural, Manufacturing, Mineral and Range Productions of Utah.* Circular no. 3, 1887.

Furniss, Norman F. *The Mormon Conflict.* Westport, Conn: Greenwood Press, 1940.

Gottfredson, Peter. *Indian Depredations in Utah.* Salt Lake City: Privately printed, 1969.

Long, E. B. *The Saints and the Union.* Urbana: University of Illinois Press, 1981.

Pettit, Jan. *Utes, the Mountain People.* Colorado Springs: Century One Press, 1982.

Sonne, Conway B. *World of Wakara.* San Antonio: The Naylor Co., 1962.

Taylor, Samuel W. *Rocky Mountain Empire.* New York: Macmillan Publishing Co., 1978.

West, Ray B., Jr. *Kingdom of the Saints.* New York: Viking Press, 1957.

Index

White Horse, Chief, 23
White Rocks, Utah, *180*
White Saddlery, 131
Whiting, John, *210*
Whitmore, Dr. James, 56
Whitmore James, Jr., and George, 42, 56–57
Whitmore, Roscoe, *58*
Whitmore Ranch, 173
Wilbur, Henry, 170
Wilcox, Ray (Budge), 86
Wild Bunch gang: East Tavaputs plateau, 86; ends of
    members' careers, 170–171; photographs of, *163, 164*; and
    Charles Siringo, 191; storytelling, 255. *See also* Cassidy,
    Butch
Wild West shows, 243–245, *244*, 247
William, Albert, 171
Williams, Deputy, 199
Williams, Harve, 215

Wilson, Charley, 144
Winters, 17, 19, 95
Witbeck, Otto, 225
Women, photographs of, *55, 80*, 104, 161, *255*
Wood family, 221
Wood Land and Livestock Company, 221
Woodruff, Utah, 97, *98*
Wyoming, 51, 165

Y
Yardley family, 260
Yates, Joseph, 63, 65
Young, Bill, 233
Young, Brigham: California cattle trade, 8, 9; colonization of
    Utah, 17; establishment of cattle industry in Utah, 5, 6;
    federal army, 19–20; and Bill Hickman, 137, 138, 139;
    horse herd on Antelope Island, 11; land distribution system,
    13, 15; and Porter Rockwell, 180